QuickBooks Online

A Wiley Brand

QuickBooks® Online

2024 Edition

by David H. Ringstrom, CPA

A Wiley Brand

QuickBooks® Online For Dummies®, 2024 Edition

Published by: **John Wiley & Sons, Inc.,** 111 River Street, Hoboken, NJ 07030-5774, www.wiley.com

Copyright © 2024 by John Wiley & Sons, Inc., Hoboken, New Jersey

Published simultaneously in Canada

For general information on our other products and services, please contact our Customer Care Department within the U.S. at 877-762-2974, outside the U.S. at 317-572-3993, or fax 317-572-4002. For technical support, please visit https://hub.wiley.com/community/support/dummies.

Wiley publishes in a variety of print and electronic formats and by print-on-demand. Some material included with standard print versions of this book may not be included in e-books or in print-on-demand. If this book refers to media such as a CD or DVD that is not included in the version you purchased, you may download this material at http://booksupport.wiley.com. For more information about Wiley products, visit www.wiley.com.

Library of Congress Control Number: 2023946608

ISBN: 978-1-394-20651-3 (pbk); 978-1-394-20652-0 (ebk); 978-1-394-20653-7 (ebk)

SKY10057093_100623

Contents at a Glance

Table of Contents

Introduction

Welcome to QuickBooks Online! If you're new to QuickBooks, my goal in this book is to help you get up and running quickly and then carry out tasks in the most efficient way possible. QuickBooks Online is known as *cloud-based accounting software*, whereas QuickBooks Desktop is typically installed locally on your computer. I only discuss QuickBooks Online in this book, so if you need help with QuickBooks Desktop, please refer to Stephen L. Nelson's *QuickBooks All-in-One For Dummies 2024* (John Wiley & Sons, Inc.).

QuickBooks Online has good intentions and is designed in a way that tries to take the pain out of accounting, but it sometimes falls short. I do my best to anticipate those areas for you and offer explanations, but if you have a question that this book doesn't answer, please feel free to email me at ask@davidringstrom.com.

Some of the tasks in QuickBooks are easy. For instance, you jump-start entering transactions in QuickBooks by emailing receipts to a unique address for your company. You can automate other tasks after you complete an initial setup process, such as downloading activity from your bank accounts and credit cards into your accounting records. Other tasks, such as entering journal entries, may appear to be difficult, particularly if you don't have much of an accounting background, but I guide you through just about everything you may want to do inside QuickBooks (and sometimes outside of QuickBooks with Microsoft Excel).

About This Book

In the past, QuickBooks Online was a fairly static platform, with new features being rolled out incrementally. Now, we seem to be in uncharted waters. As I wrote this book, I noticed that QuickBooks Online features would sometimes appear and then disappear, only to reappear again, all without notice. My editors and I have done our best to describe what has in some cases been a moving target.

Because updates occur so frequently in QuickBooks, by the time this book is published, some features and screens may have changed. (On second thought, make that *will* have changed.)

Then there's the matter of the six subscription levels:

- **Self-Employed** ($20/month, $240/year): This is best suited to users who are operating a side business. This book has some feature overlap, but I don't cover QuickBooks Online Self-Employed specifically.

- **Simple Start** ($30/month, $360/year): This most basic business version of QuickBooks has the lowest monthly cost, includes 57 reports, and allows one business and two accountant users.

- **Essentials** ($55/month, $660/year): This version is a step up in price and functionality. The biggest differences are the ability to enter bills to be paid later, time tracking, three business and two accountant users, and unlimited "reports only" users who can access up to 85 reports.

- **Plus** ($90/month, $1,080/year): This version represents another step up in price but also a much greater depth of functionality, including inventory, budgeting, project tracking, customizable access for up to five business and two accountant users, and unlimited "reports only" users who can access up to 124 reports.

- **Advanced** ($200/month, $2,400/year): This high-end version of QuickBooks offers built-in business analytics with Microsoft Excel, employee expense tracking, customizable user roles for up to 25 business users, unlimited "reports only" users, a custom report writer, workflow automation, and data restoration.

TIP

Opting for an annual subscription, instead of monthly, reduces your subscription fees by 10%.

- **Accountant** (free for members of the QuickBooks Pro Advisor program, which is also free): This version of QuickBooks offers one free Advanced subscription for accountants and bookkeepers to manage their own books. It also offers practice management features and allows seamless access to clients' QuickBooks companies.

As you can see, much of QuickBooks' best features are stratified into the higher price points. Accordingly, for this edition of the book I've gone with a "choose your adventure" approach for organizing the material. Every QuickBooks Online user will benefit from reading Part 1 of this book, which is where I cover all the core functionality that's available in QuickBooks versions from Simple Start through Advanced. Whether you keep reading is predicated upon your current subscription level or curiosity of what you would gain by opting for a higher subscription level.

Here's how the book is broken down:

>> Part 1, "Core Functionality," describes the core functionality available to all QuickBooks users.

>> Part 2, "QuickBooks Online Essentials Features," covers additional features that upgrading to an Essentials subscription adds, such as accounts payable functions, recurring transactions, user access, and additional reports.

>> Part 3, "QuickBooks Online Plus Features," describes capabilities that a Plus subscription adds, including inventory management, purchase orders, tracking profitability by project, and creating budgets.

>> Part 4, "QuickBooks Online Advanced Features," covers the additional features that an Advanced subscription provides, such as enhanced reporting features, including multi-company consolidations, analyzing your data in Excel with Spreadsheet Sync, customizing access by role, automating workflows, and backing up and restoring your company data.

>> Part 5, "QuickBooks Online Accountant Features," walks through accountant-specific features, such as practice management tools. It also shows how to perform advanced data analysis in Microsoft Excel.

>> Part 6, "Microsoft Excel Analysis," discusses ways that you can analyze your data in Microsoft Excel, including automating repetitive analysis with Power Query.

>> Part 7, "The Part of Tens," covers ten common journal entries and ten shortcuts for the Chrome browser to help you optimize your use of QuickBooks.

Before diving in, I have to get a few technical conventions out of the way:

>> Text that you're meant to type as it appears in the book is **bold**. The exception is when you're working through a list of steps. Because each step is bold, the text to type is *not* bold.

>> Web addresses and programming code appear in monofont. If you're reading a digital version of this book on a device connected to the internet, note that you can tap or click a web address to visit that website, like this: www.dummies.com.

>> Everyone can use QuickBooks Online in a web browser or a mobile app. Intuit recommends Google Chrome, Mozilla Firefox, or Safari version 12 or higher on your desktop computer. Mobile devices need to be running iOS 11.1 or higher or Android Nougat 7.1.1 or higher. Advanced and Accountant subscribers can download and install a desktop app that offers functionality unavailable within a web browser.

>> When I discuss a command to choose, I separate the elements of the sequence with a command arrow that looks like this: ⇨. For example, when you see Sales ⇨ Invoices, that command means that you should click Sales in the left bar and then click Invoices in the drop-down menu that appears.

Foolish Assumptions

I had to assume some things about you to write this book, so here are the educated guesses I made:

>> You know that you need to manage a set of accounting records for one or more businesses, and you might even have some sort of setup in place already. I *did not* assume that you know how to do all those things on a computer.

>> You may want to analyze some of your accounting data outside QuickBooks, which is why I include chapters on using Microsoft Excel. Some of that information translates to Google Sheets as well.

>> You have a personal computer running Windows 10 or 11 (I wrote this book in Windows 10) or a Mac running macOS 10.11 or later.

>> You have a copy of Microsoft Excel on your computer, or you plan to use Google Sheets at `https://sheets.google.com`.

Icons Used in This Book

Throughout the book, I use icons to draw your attention to various concepts that I want to make sure that you don't skip over in the main part of the text. Sometimes I share information to help you save time; in other cases, the goal is to keep your accounting records safe.

TIP

This icon points out time-saving tricks or quirks that you may encounter in QuickBooks.

REMEMBER

This icon points out tricky aspects of QuickBooks that you should keep in mind.

WARNING

This product can burn your eyes. Oh, sorry. Wrong type of warning! Your eyes are safe in this book. But do pay careful attention to warnings that you encounter so that you can avoid problems that could wreak havoc in your accounting records or more often simply cause you frustration.

TECHNICAL STUFF

At some points, I may include some geeky stuff about QuickBooks, your web browser, or your computer. You can safely skip over the technical stuff if that's not your cup of tea.

Beyond the Book

In addition to the book content, this product comes with a free, access-anywhere Cheat Sheet that lists keyboard shortcuts and toolbar buttons. The Cheat Sheet also covers how to use the multicurrency feature, convert a company from Quick-Books Desktop or Sage 50 to QuickBooks Online, and enter payroll history. To get this Cheat Sheet, go to www.dummies.com and search for **QuickBooks Online For Dummies Cheat Sheet**.

TIP

You can keep the learning going with the most up-to-date information and tutorials from School of Bookkeeping (https://schoolofbookkeeping.com/). The folks there (one of whom is the technical editor of this book) have broken down every version of QuickBooks Online, QuickBooks services (Payments and Payroll), and other tasks into bite-sized lessons that you can watch and get back to business. Use promo code QBO4DUMMIES to save 20 percent on any membership. If you're looking for video-based Excel training, please visit my site at www.professionalsexcel.com. The same QBO4DUMMIES promo code enables you to save 20 percent on any individual videos or subscriptions here as well.

Where to Go from Here

Part 1 and Parts 6 and 7 cover material that relates to all versions of QuickBooks Online. Continue on with Part 2 if you have an Essentials, Plus, or Advanced subscription to discover additional functionality available to you. Plus and Advanced subscribers will want to read Part 3 about even more features that are available, and Part 4 covers tasks and features that can only be completed in the Advanced version. Part 5 covers the Accountant version of QuickBooks, and Part 6 is aimed squarely at anyone who wants to do some number crunching in Excel. The book closes out with Part 7, where I break down common journal entry transactions and offer suggestions on ways to streamline repetitive Google Chrome tasks.

REMEMBER

It can be confusing any time a software platform uses the same term, such as *accountant*, in multiple contexts. For example, all QuickBooks companies offer an Accountant View, which reconfigures the sidebar menu at the left but doesn't add features to QuickBooks. This is separate from inviting your accountant or bookkeeper to oversee your books. This is also separate from the QuickBooks Online Accountant subscription that your accountant or bookkeeper probably uses to manage your books and their own.

1

Core Functionality

Chapter **1**

Getting Started with QuickBooks

Welcome to QuickBooks Online! In this book, you'll discover all the ins and outs of your accounting platform so that you can handle your clients' or your own accounting records (colloquially referred to as *books*) more effectively. I've organized this book by subscription level so you can easily determine what's possible in any version, from Simple Start, Essentials, and Plus through the Advanced subscription levels and even the Accountant version.

I start this chapter by going over some differences between QuickBooks Online and QuickBooks Desktop and then give you a sense of the annual costs to expect for QuickBooks Online. To wrap up, I discuss reviewing your chart of accounts to ensure that you can categorize your assets, liabilities, equity, revenue, and expenses correctly.

QuickBooks Online vs. QuickBooks Desktop

QuickBooks Online is a cloud-based accounting software for computers and mobile devices. The software and your data are housed securely in remote data centers and accessed over the internet. QuickBooks Desktop is a traditional accounting software installed locally, alongside your data, on your office computer. Both the online and desktop version are subscription based, but working in the cloud with QuickBooks Online enables you to work wherever you have internet access so that you can communicate easily with others and collaborate in real time. Your data is backed up automatically, which can help you avoid disasters such as fire or flood that can take out both your workspace and your locally housed accounting records. Intuit has embarked on a slow-motion discontinuation of QuickBooks Desktop, so eventually QuickBooks Online will be the only QuickBooks option.

REMEMBER

Some folks see the "anywhere, anytime" aspect of the cloud as a potential disadvantage because it makes information too readily available — and therefore a target for hackers. Rest assured that Intuit, the maker of QuickBooks, stores your data on servers using bank-level security that creates encrypted backups of your data automatically.

With QuickBooks Online, your accountant or bookkeeper also has access from anywhere. The Accountant version empowers accountants and bookkeepers to quickly toggle between multiple clients' accounting records and keep up with deadlines and tasks using a centralized communication hub. Conversely, QuickBooks Desktop requires you to send an electronic Accountant's Copy to your accountant and specify a dividing date, before which you can't make changes until your accountant returns the Accountant's Copy to you. QuickBooks Desktop also requires you to install periodic software updates, which are a thing of the past with QuickBooks Online.

Most modern computers should easily exceed the minimum requirements for QuickBooks Online, but you can get the nitty-gritty computer specification details here: https://intuit.me/3yEaSJL.

TIP

My technical editor extraordinaire, Dan DeLong, has created a free QuickBooks Chooser chatbot that can help you choose the right version of QuickBooks Online based on your specific business needs. Check it out at https://chat.schoolof bookkeeping.com/QBChooser.

Considering QuickBooks Pricing

You can cancel QuickBooks subscriptions at any time, although the service is billed in monthly or annual increments with no refunds or prorations. You can no longer create new transactions once your subscription expires, but you can view your accounting records and run reports for up to one year. As you will see in the next three sections, your "drive-out" price for using QuickBooks may mushroom far beyond the base subscription price. You've likely experienced how the base price of a car is far from what the bottom-line price ends up being. Similarly, depending upon your needs, you may end up paying more than you expected for QuickBooks Online. In Chapter 7, I discuss apps that you can install, which also often come with additional subscription fees.

REMEMBER

QuickBooks Online subscriptions and the various add-ons are priced on a per-company basis. If you maintain the books for two or more entities, you have to pay for two or more subscriptions plus fees for ancillary add-ons.

QuickBooks Online base pricing

As shown in Table 1-1, QuickBooks Online is available in six different versions and price points. The Self-Employed and Simple Start versions are best suited to fledging businesses, whereas QuickBooks Online Accountant is a free portal that accountants and bookkeepers can use to support their clients. You can get more details and start a QuickBooks Online subscription at `https://quickbooks.intuit.com/pricing/` or start using QuickBooks Online Accountant at `https://quickbooks.intuit.com/accountants/products-solutions/accounting/online`.

TABLE 1-1   **QuickBooks Online Subscription Pricing per Company**

Version	Monthly	Annually	Users
Self-Employed	$20	$240	1 billable user + 2 accountant users
Simple Start	$30	$360	1 billable user + 2 accountant users
Essentials	$60	$720	3 billable users + 2 accountant users + unlimited time tracking users
Plus	$90	$1,080	5 billable users + 2 accountant users + unlimited time tracking users + unlimited reports only users
Advanced	$200	$2,400	Up to 25 billable users + 3 accountant users + unlimited time tracking users + unlimited reports only users
Accountant	$0	$0	No limit

PROADVISOR DISCOUNT

Accounting professionals can arrange an ongoing 30 percent discount on QuickBooks Online (excluding QuickBooks Self-Employed), QuickBooks Payroll, and QuickBooks Time in exchange for being billed directly by Intuit. Accountants can pass all or part of the savings on to their clients if they want. Alternatively, accountants who prefer that their clients pay for QuickBooks directly can arrange a 30 percent discount for 12 months for charges billed directly to their clients. I discuss the ProAdvisor Discount in more detail in Chapter 17.

TIP

QuickBooks allows you to choose either a 50 percent discount for the first three months of your subscription or a free 30-day trial. You may also be offered a 70% discount for the first three months during the 30-day trial. Take the deal immediately if you plan to move forward with QuickBooks because it's unlikely to be offered again during your trial period.

REMEMBER

You must cancel your subscription if you opt for the discount and decide QuickBooks isn't right for you. Conversely, the 30-day trial simply expires, and no further action is required on your part.

REMEMBER

A QuickBooks company is a set of accounting records for a single business entity. Each QuickBooks company entails separate subscription fees, and you need to establish a QuickBooks company for each company you own or maintain accounting records for.

Payroll and time tracking pricing

You will incur additional subscription costs if you need to process payroll or enable employees to track their time. As shown in Table 1-2, QuickBooks offers three different payroll options. I've calculated the associated costs for a hypothetical team of five employees to give you a frame of reference. The Premium and Elite plans offer time tracking, which you can also purchase on an à la carte basis.

TABLE 1-2 **QuickBooks Payroll Subscription Pricing for Five Employees**

Version	Monthly	Annually
Core	$75 ($45/month + $6/employee × 5 employees)	$900
Premium	$120 ($80/month + $8/employee × 5 employees)	$1,440
Elite	$175 ($125/month + $10/employee × 5 employees)	$2,100

You can test-drive the QuickBooks payroll service for free for up to 30 days.

All QuickBooks Payroll plans include the following features:

>> Paying employees with printed checks or by direct deposit

>> Calculating tax payments automatically and paying them electronically

>> Processing federal and state quarterly and annual reports and preparing W-2 and 1099 forms

>> Processing payroll for employees who work in your company's state or another state

>> Keeping payroll tax tables up to date without having to install updates (as you do with the QuickBooks Desktop product)

>> Using the QuickBooks Payroll mobile app to pay employees, view past paychecks, file tax forms electronically, and pay taxes electronically

The Core tier offers next-day direct deposit, and the Premium tier enables same-day direct deposit and adds time tracking. The Elite tier also adds project tracking, tax penalty protection, and a personal human resources advisor. You can get more details and start a payroll subscription at `https://quickbooks.intuit.com/payroll/pricing/`, or you can choose Payroll from the left-hand menu within your QuickBooks company.

Make sure that you're ready to start processing payroll immediately before you embark on a QuickBooks Payroll subscription because you must connect your bank account and provide your tax identification numbers. If you want to try before you buy, use the online test drives I mention later in this chapter in the sections "QuickBooks Online Plus" and "QuickBooks Online Advanced."

Table 1-3 shows the additional annual cost of adding a standalone QuickBooks Time subscription if you want time and attendance tracking but not necessarily payroll processing. It's worth running the numbers for the various offerings because QuickBooks Core Payroll for five employees at $65 per month plus QuickBooks Premium Time at $60 per month is $125 per month versus paying $115 per month for QuickBooks Premium Payroll, which also offers time tracking. With that said, an Elite time subscription does include project tracking.

Although you can add time tracking on an á la carte basis, it typically makes more financial sense to use the time tracking bundled into the upgraded payroll service tiers. This also ensures that you avoid the complications that can arise if you start out with QuickBooks Time and then switch to a QuickBooks Payroll tier that offers time tracking.

TABLE 1-3

QuickBooks Time Subscription Pricing for Five Employees

Version	Monthly	Annually
Premium	$60 ($20/month + $8/employee × 5 employees)	$720
Elite	$90 ($40/month + $10/employee × 5 employees)	$1,080
ProAdvisor	Free for accounting professionals	$0

QuickBooks Payments

QuickBooks Payments enables you to accept electronic payments from customers and entails per-transaction fees instead of a monthly subscription. Table 1-4 shows the current rates as of this writing.

TABLE 1-4

QuickBooks Payments per Transaction Fees

Payment Type	Rate per Transaction
ACH Bank payments	1% (customer enters bank information online). Note: The maximum fee is $15 for customers who created accounts prior to September 5, 2023; otherwise, there is no maximum.
Swiped credit card	2.5%; you swipe the card via the available mobile reader.
Invoiced credit card	2.99%; your customer enters credit card online.
Keyed credit card	3.5%; you enter your customer's credit card information online.

TIP

QuickBooks Payments deposits money from qualifying credit or debit card transactions into your bank account the next business day. Your payments and deposit transactions are recorded in your books automatically, based on the funding date.

Comparing QuickBooks Features

As you can see, the ongoing expenses for QuickBooks can add up fast. You can upgrade or downgrade your subscription at any time, although downgrading can entail disabling inventory or removing users. Use the search term **downgrade** at `https://quickbooks.intuit.com/learn-support/en-us` for more details. Read on for information on the various tiers so that you can find the right fit for your needs.

QuickBooks Online Self-Employed

This version of QuickBooks is aimed at freelancers and self-employed people who file Schedule C of IRS Form 1040 (`www.irs.gov/forms-pubs/about-schedule-c-form-1040`). Unlike the higher-level offerings, QuickBooks Self-Employed allows you to mix business with pleasure, meaning that you can track personal and business expenses, as well as mileage. It's best suited to someone with a side hustle who wants to keep track of their business and simplify income tax filing.

REMEMBER

I don't discuss QuickBooks Online Self-Employed any further in this book, although some of the features may mirror what you see in the higher subscription levels.

QuickBooks Simple Start

A QuickBooks Simple Start subscription is great for a new business with basic bookkeeping needs. With Simple Start, you can

>> Track your income and expenses, which I cover in Chapters 2 and 3, respectively.

>> Download transactions from your bank and credit card accounts, as described in Chapter 5.

>> Create an unlimited number of customers. Chapter 2 shows how to get started.

>> Send estimates and invoices. You guessed it — this is in Chapter 2.

>> Print checks and record transactions to track expenses (see Chapter 3).

>> Track and pay sales taxes (Chapter 2).

>> Track mileage.

>> Categorize expenses by taking pictures of receipts, as I discuss in Chapter 7.

>> Pay contractors and send 1099 forms (see Chapter 4).

>> Connect one online sales channel, such as Amazon, eBay, or Shopify (see Chapter 7).

>> Import data from Microsoft Excel or QuickBooks Desktop.

>> Integrate with available apps in the QuickBooks Online App Center, as discussed in Chapter 7.

>> View and customize more than 50 reports. Chapter 6 shows how.

Although the Simple Start version supports accounts-receivable functions, you can't set up invoices to bill customers on a recurring basis or track unpaid bills. If you're on the fence between Self-Employed and Simple Start, you'll have more options in the future with Simple Start.

QuickBooks Online Essentials

Established businesses that don't have inventory may be able to use QuickBooks Essentials, which includes all the Simple Start functionality and allows you to do the following:

>> Set up invoices to bill automatically on a recurring schedule. I cover automation capabilities like this in Chapter 7.

>> Use accounts-payable functions, including scheduling payment of vendor bills and online bill payment (see Chapter 8).

>> Create and post recurring transactions.

>> Track time for unlimited users, as discussed in Chapter 9.

>> Connect three online sales channels, including Amazon, eBay, and Shopify (see Chapter 7).

>> Control the areas of QuickBooks your users can access (see Chapter 9).

>> View and customize up to 85 reports (see Chapter 6 for more on QuickBooks reports).

QuickBooks Online Plus

A Plus subscription goes beyond the Essentials level by adding the ability to do each of these tasks:

>> Create, send, and track purchase orders (see Chapter 10).

>> Track inventory using the first in, first out (FIFO) inventory valuation method. QuickBooks Online supports light inventory needs. If you sell finished goods, QuickBooks Online should be able to meet your needs. But if you need to assemble finished goods to sell, QuickBooks Online can't meet your needs on its own. You can look for an add-on app to supplement your inventory needs. I talk about add-on apps in Chapter 7.

>> Categorize income and expenses by using class tracking (see Chapter 11).

>> Track sales and profitability by business location. You can assign only one location to a transaction, but you can assign multiple classes to a transaction. I go deep on this in Chapter 11.

>> Give employees and subcontractors limited access to the QuickBooks company to enter time worked, which I discuss in Chapter 9.

>> Track billable hours by customer. QuickBooks Online supports light job-costing needs, but it doesn't allow you to cost labor automatically.

>> Track projects, as shown in Chapter 11.

>> Connect all online sales channels, currently Amazon, eBay, and Shopify, along with any future channels that get added (see Chapter 7).

>> Create budgets to estimate future income and expenses. You can create multiple budgets per year, location, class, or customer. All of the details are in Chapter 12.

>> View and customize 124 reports. I cover report basics in Chapter 6.

TIP You can test-drive the QuickBooks Online Plus sample company at `https://qbo.intuit.com/redir/testdrive`.

Usage limits for QuickBooks Simple Start, Essentials, and Plus

Simple Start, Essentials, and Plus subscriptions are subject to the limits shown in Table 1-5. Long-term users may be allowed higher limits but can't add any element that exceeds the use limit without upgrading to a higher-level plan or deactivating current elements. As detailed in the next section, you can work without limits in QuickBooks with an Advanced subscription.

TABLE 1-5

Usage Limits for Simple Start, Essentials, and Plus Subscriptions

QuickBooks Element	Use Limit
Annual transactions	350,000
Chart of accounts	250
Classes and locations	40 combined; further, you can't track your balance sheet by class.
Billed users	1 for Simple Start, 3 for Essentials, 5 for Plus
Unbilled users	2 Accountant users; unlimited time tracking for Essentials and Plus; unlimited reports-only users for Plus

QuickBooks Online Advanced

QuickBooks Online Advanced is the flagship subscription for users who have outgrown QuickBooks Online Plus. It allows you to

>> Have unlimited accounts, transactions, classes, time tracking users, and reports-only users.

>> Connect with a dedicated customer success manager to handle support questions. (Support calls go to the front of the line instead of waiting in a queue.) Customer success managers also provide information on online training and QuickBooks products; Advanced subscribers are entitled to five free on-demand training courses annually.

>> Establish custom permissions for your users, as discussed in Chapter 13.

>> Efficiently import invoice and sales receipt transactions into QuickBooks by way of a comma-separated-value (CSV) file. You can create such a file in Microsoft Excel or Google Sheets, as discussed in Chapter 12.

>> Use Spreadsheet Sync to create customized reports and edit existing records in Excel, and then post the changes back to QuickBooks. I get into the nitty-gritty of this in Chapter 16.

>> Create custom reports using the Custom Report Builder that I discuss in Chapter 14.

>> Enter, edit, or delete multiple transactions by way of the Batch Transactions feature, which I discuss in Chapter 15.

>> Enable workflows to trigger reminders for customers and team members, which is also covered in Chapter 15.

>> Use up to 48 custom fields.

>> Visualize your data in the Performance Center with customizable chart widgets, as shown in Chapter 7.

>> Employ premium app integration with services such as Bill.com, HubSpot, Salesforce, LeanLaw, and DocuSign. (Third-party subscription fees apply.)

>> Restore QuickBooks data to a particular date and time. You can also schedule automatic backups and reverse changes made to customers, vendors, and company settings, which I discuss in Chapter 13.

>> Export the lists and transactions for your entire company to comma-separated value (CSV) files by way of the Local Backup feature (see Chapter 13).

>> Set up workflow automation to generate payment and invoicing reminders and assign tasks to team members, as discussed in Chapter 15.

TIP

You can test-drive the QuickBooks Online Advanced sample company at `https://qbo.intuit.com/redir/testdrive_us_advanced`.

QuickBooks Online Accountant

The Accountant version is a free cloud-based portal that accounting professionals use to access clients' QuickBooks Online companies and communicate with clients. It includes one free QuickBooks Online Advanced subscription that accountants can use to keep track of their own books. Standard subscription fees apply for each additional QuickBooks company you create. I discuss QB Accountant in great detail in Chapters 17 to 19. You can create your QB Accountant account at `https://quickbooks.intuit.com/accountants/products-solutions/accounting/online`.

Tailoring Your QuickBooks Environment

Once you choose a subscription, a comprehensive wizard walks you through the set-up process. I don't regurgitate the steps here, but I do share some customizations you may want to make. For instance, the navigation menu along the left side of the screen is called the *sidebar menu*, which I sometimes refer to as the *sidebar*. I also explain customizing the chart of accounts, which you use to categorize every transaction you make, but let's first see how to prevent QuickBooks from logging you out of a work session prematurely.

Extending the default length of a QuickBooks session

By default, QuickBooks signs you out of your company after 60 minutes of inactivity. You can extend this to as much as three hours like so:

1. **Choose Settings ➪ Account & Settings ➪ Advanced.**

2. **Click the Edit icon in the Other Preferences section.**

3. **Make a choice from the Sign Me Out If Inactive For list.**

4. **Click Save and then Done.**

TIP

Advanced and Accountant users can use the QuickBooks Online desktop app, which I discuss in Chapter 13, in lieu of working in a browser window. The desktop app requires you to log in to your Intuit account only once every six months, unless you choose to manually log out of the app.

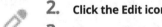

Customizing the sidebar menu

The sidebar menu is on the left side of your QuickBooks company and is the primary navigation aid for working with QuickBooks. You can customize this menu to hide commands you don't use and bookmark commands you do use. For instance, you're not going to need the Commerce choice on the menu if you don't sell products online. Here's how to customize the sidebar:

1. **Click the Edit icon next to the Menu or Bookmarks sections of the sidebar menu.**

   A Customize Your Menu dialog box appears with Menu and Bookmarks tabs.

2. **Optional: Toggle checkmarks on or off to enable or disable menu groupings or bookmarks by clicking on Menu or Bookmarks to switch between the lists.**

3. **Click Save to preserve your changes or Cancel if you change your mind.**

REMEMBER

Turning commands off doesn't remove any functionality from QuickBooks but instead moves those commands into a More section at the bottom of the Menu portion of the sidebar menu.

You can also use a second approach to add bookmarks:

1. **Click a grouping from the sidebar, such as Payroll, to reveal a submenu.**

2. **Hover your mouse over a command, such as Employees, and then click the Bookmark icon that appears at the right edge of the submenu.**

Touring the Chart of Accounts page

When you create a new company, QuickBooks starts you off with a chart of accounts that it thinks matches your industry. You can keep this list intact, edit it manually as I describe, or replace it with what you import from Excel, a CSV file, or Google Sheets, which I discuss in the later section titled "Importing a chart of accounts." Your chart of accounts is limited to 250 active accounts unless you have an Advanced subscription.

I encourage you to review the chart of accounts that QuickBooks establishes for your company. To do so, choose Settings ⇨ Chart of Accounts or Transactions ⇨ Chart of Accounts. The page shown in Figure 1-1 displays your chart of accounts and lets you carry out a variety of actions:

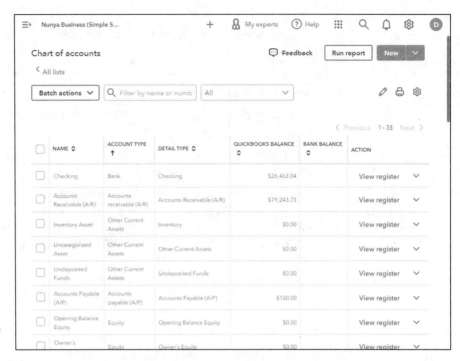

	NAME ↕	ACCOUNT TYPE ↑	DETAIL TYPE ↕	QUICKBOOKS BALANCE ↕	BANK BALANCE ↕	ACTION
☐	Checking	Bank	Checking	$26,463.04		View register ⌄
☐	Accounts Receivable (A/R)	Accounts receivable (A/R)	Accounts Receivable (A/R)	$79,243.73		View register ⌄
☐	Inventory Asset	Other Current Assets	Inventory	$0.00		View register ⌄
☐	Uncategorized Asset	Other Current Assets	Other Current Assets	$0.00		View register ⌄
☐	Undeposited Funds	Other Current Assets	Undeposited Funds	$0.00		View register ⌄
☐	Accounts Payable (A/P)	Accounts payable (A/P)	Accounts Payable (A/P)	$100.00		View register ⌄
☐	Opening Balance Equity	Equity	Opening Balance Equity	$0.00		View register ⌄
☐	Owner's	Equity	Owner's Equity	$0.00		View register ⌄

FIGURE 1-1:
The Chart of Accounts page.

>> Click the Run Report button to generate a report that lists your chart of accounts.

>> Click the New button to create a new account.

>> Choose New ⇨ Import to import a new chart of accounts, which I discuss later in more detail in the "Importing a chart of accounts" section.

>> Click the Edit icon below the New button to turn on the Batch Edit feature, which enables you to edit multiple account names at once.

>> Click the printer icon to print your chart of accounts.

You're better off clicking Run Report versus clicking Print because the Print command generates a rather unaesthetic-looking report.

WARNING

>> Click the Settings icon to control which columns appear on the page and whether inactive accounts are displayed.

>> Click the checkbox for one or more accounts, and then choose Batch Actions ⇨ Make Inactive to deactivate unnecessary accounts.

>> Click View Register adjacent to balance sheet accounts or Run Report adjacent to income and expense accounts to view a register or report showing all activity.

>> Click the arrow next to an account to reveal the following choices, depending on the account type:

- Connect Bank: Starts the process of syncing checking and credit card accounts with a financial institution.

- Edit: Allows you to change the account type, detail type, name, description, or subaccount status of an account.

- Make Inactive: Deactivates an account so that it can no longer be used for new transactions.

WARNING

QuickBooks zeros out accounts that you make inactive, so make sure that you move the account balances by way of a journal entry or other transaction. I discuss journal entries in Chapter 22. You can mark multiple accounts inactive by clicking the checkbox for one or more accounts and then choosing Batch Actions ⇨ Make Inactive.

- Run Report: Enables you to run a report showing the activity for a given account.

Adding new accounts to your chart of accounts

Here's how to add an account to your chart of accounts:

1. **Click the New button on the Chart of Accounts page to open the New Account task pane, shown in Figure 1-2.**

2. **Make a selection from the Account Type list.**

   This list contains the major categories that typically appear on the balance sheet and profit-and-loss reports for a business.

3. **Make a selection from the Detail Type list.**

   Depending upon the Account Type you chose, you may only have one choice here, or you may have many.

4. **Fill in the Name field to assign a name to your account.**

   Only enter words in this field. Later in the chapter, I show you how to enable account numbers for your chart of accounts. Don't be fooled by the relatively small size of the field; it accepts up to 100 characters.

FIGURE 1-2:
The dialog box
you use to create
an account.

5. **Optional: Enter a description for your account.**

   Enter up to 100 characters providing additional documentation as to the purpose of the account.

6. **Optional: Click Is Sub-account if you want to have this account roll up into a higher-level account on your reports.**

   You must specify a parent account for each sub-account that you create.

7. **Choose an option from the When Do You Want to Start Tracking Your Finances from This Account in QuickBooks? list.**

   Always defer to your accountant or bookkeeper if you're unclear how to answer a question like this. Options include Beginning of the Year, Beginning of This Month, Today, and Other, which allows you to specify any date that you want.

8. **Click Save and Close if you only need to create one account; otherwise, click the arrow and choose Save and New.**

   This is an example of a sticky preference in QuickBooks. When you alter the functionality of a button, it retains that functionality going forward until you make another choice from that button's drop-down menu.

A FEW NOTES ON PAYING OWNERS

Many small-business owners wonder about the accounts they should use to pay themselves. Owners and partners typically aren't considered to be employees and therefore aren't paid through payroll. To pay an owner or partner, use the Chart of Accounts page to set up a Draw account (Owner's Draw, Partner's Draw, or whatever is appropriate; if you have multiple partners, set up Draw accounts for each partner) and use it to pay owners. The Draw account is an equity account. Similarly, owners and partners sometimes put their own money into the business. To account for these contributions, set up equity accounts (again, one for each owner or partner) called Owner's Contribution, Partner's Contribution, or whatever is appropriate.

Note that you use the Draw account not only to pay the owner, but also to account for personal items an owner might buy with the business's money. You record the withdrawals by using the appropriate bank account and the appropriate Draw account. Note that these transactions don't show up on your profit-and-loss report because they're not business expenses. To find out the total amount paid to an owner, run a report for the Draw account.

At the end of your fiscal year, you need to enter a journal entry, dated the last day of your fiscal year that moves the dollar amounts from the appropriate Draw or Contribution account to Retained Earnings, which is another equity account. If I've just lost you, talk to your accountant about how to handle closing the year.

Adding account numbers

By default, QuickBooks doesn't use or display account numbers; however, you can enable this feature:

1. **Choose Settings ⇨ Account & Settings ⇨ Advanced.**

2. **Click the Edit icon in the Chart of Accounts section.**

3. **Toggle on the Enable Account Numbers option.**

4. **Click Show Account Numbers if you want to display the account numbers in QuickBooks.**

5. **Click Save and then click Done.**

You can enable or disable these settings as needed at any time. Use the Batch Edit method I discuss in the "Touring the Chart of Accounts page" section earlier in this chapter. After you add account numbers, you can sort the chart of accounts in account-number order by clicking the Number heading of the Chart of Accounts page.

Click Save periodically as you enter account numbers in case you get pulled away unexpectedly to prevent QuickBooks from signing you out and causing you to lose your work.

Importing a chart of accounts

QuickBooks automatically sets up the chart of accounts it thinks you'll need, but you can replace it by importing one that you've set up in Microsoft Excel, as a CSV file, or as a Google Sheet spreadsheet. The import file can include sub-accounts and parent accounts.

Use the convention *Account: Sub-account* when establishing sub-accounts, with *Account* representing the parent account.

Here's how to import a chart of accounts:

1. **Choose Settings ⇨ Chart of Accounts or Transactions ⇨ Chart of Accounts.**

2. **Choose New ⇨ Import to display the Import Accounts page.**

3. **Use the links to download a sample CSV or Excel file or to preview a sample Google Sheet.**

4. **After you set up your chart of accounts file, choose New ⇨ Import again on the Chart of Accounts page.**

5. **Click Browse or Connect, as appropriate, to select your import file.**

6. **Click Next to display the Map Data page.**

7. **Map the headings in your import file to the fields in QuickBooks by making selections from the drop-down lists in the Your Field column.**

8. **Click Next to display a preview of the accounts to be imported.**

9. **Click Import if everything looks to be in order.**

Reviewing company settings

Now that your chart of accounts is set up, it's worth your while to review the default settings for QuickBooks and make changes as appropriate. I discuss payroll settings in Chapter 4. Choose Settings ⇨ Account and Settings to display the Account and Setting page, and then select a category and make any changes needed. Some setting changes require you to click Save, and you need to click

Done to close the Account and Settings page. Here's a rundown of the settings you can change:

>> **Company:** You can edit your company name, address, and contact information, as well as your marketing preferences for Intuit. Click anywhere in the group where the setting appears to make updates, and then click the Save button before you move on to another group of settings.

>> **Billing & Subscription:** You can view the current status of your subscription and change your payment method. You can convert a QuickBooks or QuickBooks Payroll trial to a regular subscription, but doing so terminates the trial period. You can also scroll down to order checks and supplies. As of this writing, you can choose to opt for annual billing — instead of monthly — and reduce your QuickBooks subscription fees by roughly 10 percent.

REMEMBER

The Billing & Subscription section isn't shown if your QuickBooks company is being managed by an accountant who participates in the ProAdvisor Discount program, which I discuss in Chapter 17.

>> **Usage:** This section shows any usage limits based on your subscription. Click the link showing the count of users, accounts, and so on to display the corresponding page.

>> **Sales:** This section enables you to customize certain fields within your sales forms, including determining whether to show Product/Service or SKU fields. You can add a default charge to overdue invoices, utilize progress invoicing, customize default email messages, and include an aging table at the bottom of account statements.

>> **Expenses:** You can opt to display a table of expense and purchase forms so that you can itemize and categorize the products and services you buy. You can also choose to add a column for identifying the customer a purchase relates to, as well as a column where you can mark items and expenses as billable to your customers.

>> **Payments**: Use this section to establish a new QuickBooks Payments account here or connect an existing account so that you can accept credit cards payments or bank transfers from your customers. This feature also enables you to include a Pay Now button on invoices that you email to customers. This service entails per-transaction fees that I discuss in the "QuickBooks Payments and Commerce" section earlier in this chapter.

>> **Time:** Your options here vary, based upon your subscription level, but at a minimum, you can set the first day of the work week and determine if a service field should appear on timesheets, and if time should be billable.

>> **Advanced:** Here you'll mostly find nitty-gritty accounting settings that you'll probably want to hand off to your accountant. They include specifying the first month of your fiscal and tax years; choosing Cash or Accrual for your accounting method; picking a tax form; and, as mentioned earlier, determining if you want to use account numbers in your chart of accounts.

Customizing Invoices and Estimates

Intuit is developing "modern" versions of on-screen, print, and PDF versions of the invoices and estimates forms. As of this writing, if you have a Simple Start, Essentials, or Plus subscription, you'll likely still have the "classic" versions of these forms, whereas Advanced users will likely have the "modern" formats. The classic format actually offers more flexibility, such as the ability to add subtotals. In this section, I show you how to identify classic versus modern forms, and how to add automated subtotals to classic forms, which presently cannot be done with modern sales forms.

Redesigning classic sales forms

A Customize command appears at the bottom row of the screen of "classic" invoices and estimates. Use these steps to customize these forms:

1. **Choose + New ⇨ Invoice or +New ⇨ Estimate.**

   The corresponding form appears onscreen.

2. **Click Customize at the bottom of the screen.**

3. **Make a selection from the resulting menu:**

   - Switch forms by choosing Standard or one of your customized forms.

   - Choose New Style to create a new form.

   - Click Edit Current to modify the current form.

4. **Use the Design, Content, and Emails views to customize the look and feel of your sales forms.**

5. **Click Done to save your changes.**

Refining modern sales forms

Edit, Email View, PDF View, and Payor View tabs appear at the top of the screen. I'll walk you through the customization options in a moment, but first let me mention that you can click Old Layout to reactivate the "classic" style for invoices or estimates. An optional prompt asks you why you're making the switch, and then the classic format appears. You can return to the "modern" format at any time by clicking Try the New Invoices or Try the New Estimates at the top of any invoice or estimate page, respectively.

Now let's see how you can somewhat change a modern sales form:

1. **Choose + New ⇨ Invoice or + New ⇨ Estimate.**

    The corresponding form appears onscreen.

2. **Click Manage to display a design task pane.**

3. **Expand the Design section, choose Modern, and then click Make Default if necessary.**

    This one-time step is necessary if your "classic" sales forms have been carried forward into the modern interface.

4. **Expand the Customization section to toggle selected fields on or off, and manage custom fields if available.**

5. **Expand the Payment Details section to show or hide the invoice detail and enable or disable discounts and shipping fees.**

6. **Expand the Automation tab if you want to create a recurring invoice or establish invoice reminders.**

Simplifying your invoicing process

Invoicing your customers generally involves a lot of rote work. QuickBooks offers a couple of features that can speed things up for you:

» **Bundles:** In Chapter 9, I discuss how bundles allow you to add a collection of two or more items to an invoice by selecting a single item.

» **Pricing rules:** In Chapter 10, I discuss how Plus and Advanced users can enable *pricing rules* that automatically discount or increase the price of items for some or all customers, either permanently or for some period.

» **Automatic subtotals on classic sales forms:** Here, in Chapter 1, I discuss the difference between classic and modern sales forms. As of this writing, you can't add subtotals to modern sales forms but you can use these steps to add subtotals to the Classic layout invoices, estimates, and sales receipts:

1. **Choose Settings ⇨ Custom Form Styles.**

   The Custom Form Styles page displays any form styles you've set up.

2. **Select a form to customize, and then click Edit in the Action column.**

   The Customize Form Style page contains three buttons in the top-left corner: Design, Content, and Emails.

3. **Click Content.**

   The Content page appears, with all sections disabled.

4. **Click the Table section.**

   The Table section is where you see column titles such as Date, Product/Service, and Description.

5. **Scroll down the page, and click Show More Activity Options in the bottom-left corner.**

   Additional options for the Table section appear.

6. **Click the Group Activity By checkbox, and make a choice from the drop-down list.**

   You can group items by day, week, month, or type. For this example, choose type.

7. **Click Subtotal Groups.**

8. **Click Done in the bottom-right corner of the window to save the settings.**

   Although you can click Preview PDF, there's not much point in this context because QuickBooks doesn't show you the subtotals in use until you actually create an invoice.

You need to repeat the preceding steps to include subtotals for estimates and sales receipts to have a consistent look and feel across all the forms you use.

REMEMBER

Chapter **2**

Recording Sales and Accounts Receivable

The first three sections of this chapter cover groundwork that you'll need to complete before you can start recording sales transactions. I first show you how to create new customers in QuickBooks and then how to enable sales tax — you can skip this section if it doesn't apply. Make sure to read the section on creating products and services. I conclude the chapter with the nuts and bolts of recording your sales in QuickBooks.

Managing Customers

Customers are the lifeblood of any business, so you need to be intimately familiar with the ins-and-outs of managing your customer records. I'll start by going over how to add customers.

Creating customer records

You can't create a new customer-related transaction without first creating a customer record. Don't worry about having all your ducks in a row with regard to completeness. Customer Display Name is the only required field.

Follow these steps to create a customer:

1. **Display the Customer page by using one of these techniques:**

- + New ⇨ Add Customer

- Get Paid & Pay, Customers, or Customers & Leads ⇨ Customers ⇨ New Customer (or Add Customer Manually)

- Get Paid & Pay, Sales & Expenses, or Sales ⇨ Invoices, click Create Invoice, and then choose Add New from the Customer drop-down list

2. **Optional: Provide the contact name information for your customer.**

3. **Enter the company name in one of two ways:**

- Look up the customer name in the Company Name field to search the QuickBooks Business Network. If you find a match, click Save and Send to populate the Customer Display Name field and send a connection request to your customer. If your customer accepts your invitation, invoices that you send post directly to their books as accounts payable bills. You can click the Reset Link in the field if you change your mind or find that you chose the wrong customer.

- Complete the Customer Display Name field.

TIP

You are only required to complete the Customer Display Name field when creating a customer record, so you can save all other fields for later if you want.

4. **Optional: Complete the other aspects of the record.**

The Customer task pane includes the following sections:

- **Name and Contact:** The name and contact information for your customer.

- **Addresses:** The billing address and optional shipping address.

REMEMBER

Sales tax is assessed based on each customer's shipping address. In other words, sales tax will be calculated based upon the shipping address if you provide both a billing address and a shipping address. Otherwise, QuickBooks assumes the billing and shipping addresses are one and the same.

- **Notes and Attachments:** A free-form notes field allows you to enter up to 4,000 characters, and a separate Attachments field lets you attach files. These may include copies of contracts, approvals, or any files that you want, each up to 20MB in size, in any of the following formats: PDF, JPEG, PNG, DOC, XLSX, CSV, TIFF, GIF, and XML.

REMEMBER

You can add attachments to both customer records and transactions. Any documents that you've attached appear in sequential order within the Attachments dialog box. QuickBooks notifies you of file types that are unacceptable, such as compressed ZIP files and Excel Binary workbooks (XLSB files).

WARNING

Any files that you upload as attachments become a permanent part of your QuickBooks Online company and cannot be removed. You can unlink an attachment from a record by clicking the X to the right of the filename, but the document will still appear in the Attachments list for your company as a whole. Click Show Existing beneath any Attachments field to see all attachments, and choose Unlinked to view attachments that aren't tied to a specific transaction or record.

- **Payments:** A section related to customers that allows you to specify the primary payment method, customer terms, and sales form delivery options and choose one of six languages to use when sending invoices.

- **Additional Info:** This section allows you to specify a sales tax exemption and set an opening balance if needed.

5. **Click the Save button to close the Customer page and then display the Customers list or the corresponding transaction page that you started from.**

Accessing and editing customer records

The Customers page is sorted alphabetically by contact name, but you can also sort by the Company Name or Open Balance fields. Click anywhere in a customer's row except the Action column to display their customer record. If you have many customers, you can enter as little as a single character in the Search field to display a list of matching records, but you'll likely need to enter additional characters to winnow the list down. Choose any customer from the resulting list to display the corresponding record.

As shown in Figure 2-1, a customer page appears. It may have multiple tabs:

>> **Transaction List:** A list of all transactions associated with this customer.

>> **Statements:** A list of any statements that you've generated for this customer.

>> **Customer Details:** A summary of the customer record, including an Attachments section that you can use to add attachments in the fashion that I described in the "Creating customer records" section.

>> **Late Fees:** A list of any late fees assessed to the customer.

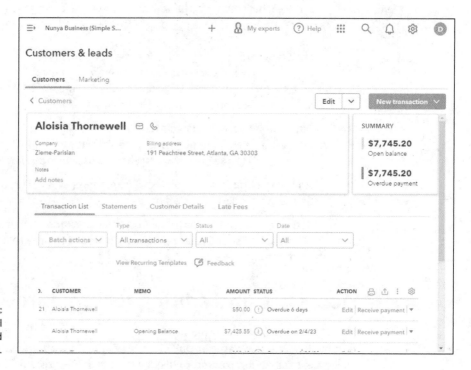

FIGURE 2-1:
A typical customer record page.

At the top of the customer record are the Edit and New Transaction buttons. The Edit button enables you to carry out any of three actions:

>> Click Edit to return to the Customer task pane, which I discuss in the "Creating customer records" section of this chapter.

>> Click Edit⇨Make Inactive to mark a customer as inactive.

REMEMBER

You can't delete customers from QuickBooks Online, but you can mark them as inactive as long as their balance is zero.

>> Click Edit➪Merge Contacts to combine transactions from two different customer records.

All customer-specific detail from the first customer, such as their address and phone numbers, is discarded.

The New Transactions button enables you to create a variety of customer-related transactions as well as statements. I discuss each transaction type later in this chapter.

Switching from record to record

When you finish working with one record, you can easily switch to another in that list by using the list's Split View pane shown in Figure 2-1. You can click the Split View icon, which looks like an arrow pointing to the right toward three stripes, to display a pane that shows the records stored in the list. The Split View icon appears only when you're displaying a customer record; the icon vanishes when you're viewing the customer list. To close Split View, click the Close Split View button, which is an arrow pointing left toward three stripes.

While working in the Split View pane, you can scroll down to find a record, or you can type a few letters of the person's or company's name in the Search box at the top of the list to find that record. You can use the Sort By drop-down list to sort the list by name or by open balance. Click a record to switch to that page.

To add a new record to the list, click the plus (+) symbol at the top of the list in the Split View pane. To return to the Customers list page, click Customers at the top of the Split View list.

Batching activities for customers

A hidden Batch Actions button appears on the Customers page when you click the checkboxes for one or more customers. You can also click the checkbox to the left of the Name caption at the top of the customer list to select all customers at once. The Batch Actions menu offers three options:

>> **Create Statements:** Use this command to generate the following types of statements:

- **Balance Forward:** This type of statement shows an open balance for the start date of your choice and reflects activity through the end date that you specify.

- **Open Item:** Use this statement option to list only unpaid invoices and unapplied credits for a time period of your choice.

- **Transaction Statement:** This statement reflects all transactions that occurred during a set time period.

» **Email:** This command creates a blank message in your email software or platform and lists the customer(s) that you choose in the BCC field.

» **Make Inactive:** Choose this option to mark one or more customers that don't have an open balance as inactive.

Customizing customer list columns

You can control the appearance of your customer list by hiding or displaying columns and including or hiding inactive customers:

1. Click the Settings button above the Action column.

2. Toggle checkboxes as needed to display or hide columns in the list and control how many records are shown per page.

3. Click the Settings button again to close the menu.

To adjust the width of any column, hover over the right edge of a column heading, and drag the double-headed arrow to the left or right. When you start to drag, the mouse pointer changes to a pointer, and a vertical bar appears to guide you in resizing the column. Release the mouse button when you're satisfied with the column width.

QuickBooks remembers column width adjustments that you make on pages such as Customers and account registers even after you sign out.

TIP

Setting Up Sales Tax

Sales tax calculations in new QuickBooks companies are automated. Once you walk through a short wizard, QuickBooks calculates sales tax automatically on the fly based on your customer's address. Conversely, existing QuickBooks companies, or those converted from QuickBooks Desktop, may still be using the old system, which required manually establishing sales tax rates, assigning the corresponding rates to each customer. Here, I show you how you can switch to the Automated Sales Tax feature if you're currently using the manual system. In addition, I discuss how the Economic Nexus feature can help you identify when you might not be collecting sales tax but are legally required to. Taxes come in all sorts of shapes and sizes, so I show how to create custom sales tax rates when needed, such as for tariffs or excise taxes. Government agencies will look to you for any taxes that you fail to collect, so review your sales tax settings. After that, you'll see how to report and pay sales taxes to the corresponding taxing authorities.

REMEMBER

QuickBooks can calculate your sales tax liability and walk you through recording the payment, but it doesn't file your sales tax return for you. You or your accountant must file your return by mailing in a paper copy or by filling out the return online by way of the taxing authority's website.

Understanding sales tax liability

Depending on your volume of taxable transactions, you're required to remit sales tax to your taxing authority monthly, quarterly, or annually. When you enable the Sales Tax feature, you're asked to specify the method for QuickBooks to calculate your sales tax liability for each period:

>> **Accrual:** QuickBooks considers sales tax due in the period that you create the invoice, regardless of whether your customer has paid the invoice. If you later write off the invoice, you get a credit for the sales taxes you previously paid.

>> **Cash:** QuickBooks considers sales tax due in the period that your customer pays the invoice. Tracking this liability is easiest if your customers pay their invoices in full. Partial payments, non-taxable items, and discounts or credits that you apply can make it harder to follow how sales tax has been calculated.

REMEMBER

You must provide accurate mailing addresses for your company and your customers once you enable the Sales Tax feature. QuickBooks verifies the addresses in real time and rejects illegitimate addresses. Your home state taxing authority is determined based on your physical address, whereas sales taxes are computed automatically based on your customers' shipping addresses, if you provide one; otherwise, the billing address is treated as the shipping address.

Enabling the Automated Sales Tax feature

You're prompted to set up sales tax the first time you click the Taxes command in the left menu in a recently created QuickBooks company:

1. **Choose Taxes ⇨ Sales Tax and then click the Use Automated Sales Tax button.**

The wizard asks you to verify or enter your company's physical address, after which you click Next.

TIP

As is the case throughout QuickBooks, the State drop-down list is a little tricky. You can type the two-letter abbreviation for your state, but you then have to choose it from the list with your mouse. If I had my way, you'd be able to type in an abbreviation and press Enter.

2. **The next screen asks if you need to collect tax outside of your state.**

   If you choose No, you can click Next to advance to the next screen. If you click Yes, you're prompted to specify the additional tax agencies. If you're not sure, check out the section titled "Exploring the Economic Nexus feature" later in this chapter.

WARNING

You can't edit or delete tax agencies that you set up in your company.

3. **Click Next once you've answered the Yes or No question to display an Automated Sales Tax Is All Set Up page.**

   You can either click Create Invoice or close the page, but — spoiler alert — sales tax isn't completely set up at this point. You have one more screen at a minimum, and you may need to mark certain customers as tax-exempt.

4. **When the How Often Do You File Sales Tax window appears, specify your filing frequency for each agency and then click Save.**

   This step marks the true end of the sales tax wizard, so your next step is to indicate any tax-exempt customers.

QuickBooks assumes that all customers are subject to sales tax, so you need to edit any tax-exempt customers (such as government agencies, schools, and charities) by following these steps:

1. **Choose Get Paid and Pay, Customers, or Customers & Leads ⇨ Customers.**

2. **Click the name of a tax-exempt customer and then click Edit on the customer record page that appears.**

3. **Scroll down to the Additional Info section and click This Customer Is Tax Exempt, as shown in Figure 2-2.**

4. **Specify a choice from the Reason for Exemption, which is a required field.**

5. **Optional: Enter up to 16 characters in the Exemption Details field.**

   You can record a customer's exemption certificate ID in this field, or optionally upload a copy of the exemption certificate in the Notes and Attachments section.

FIGURE 2-2:
Marking a customer as tax exempt.

Figure content:

Customer ✕

Additional info ⌃

Taxes

☑ This customer is tax exempt

Reason for exemption *

Charitable organization ⌄

Exemption details

12-1234567

Learn more

Select tax rate

Based on location ⌄

Opening balance ⑦

Opening balance

As of

09/02/2023 📅

Privacy

Save

Converting sales tax from QuickBooks Desktop

Setting up sales tax is a little different if you've imported your books from Quick-Books Desktop:

1. **Choose Taxes and then click the Get Started button.**

   This screen gives you the option to Do It Later, but seize the moment and click Get Started.

2. **Confirm your business address on the first screen of the wizard and then click Next.**

3. **A Bulk Matching screen asks you to link your tax rates from QuickBooks Desktop to the tax agencies that QuickBooks Online recognizes.**

   Click the checkbox to the left of the Tax Rate Name column heading if all your tax rates relate to a single tax agency. You can make a choice from the Official Agency drop-down list, and then click Apply.

4. **Click Next to display a Review Your Rates page.**

   Click Change next to any tax rates you want to modify.

5. **Click Save to finalize your changes.**

6. **Click Continue when prompted.**

   A two-screen help wizard appears to give you background about the Sales Tax Center. You can click through this wizard or close it without reviewing it.

7. **Specify your filing frequency for each agency when the How Often Do You File Sales Tax window appears, and then click Save.**

   You can continue forward with your custom sales tax rates from QuickBooks Desktop, or you can enable automated sales tax.

Switching from manual to automated sales tax

You can easily switch to the Automated Sales Tax feature, whether you've just converted from QuickBooks Desktop or you've been continuing with the traditional manual sales tax method as a long-term QuickBooks Online user:

1. **Choose Taxes and then click the Sales Tax Settings button to display the Edit Settings page.**

2. **Click Turn Off Sales Tax, and then click Yes when prompted to confirm.**

   In effect, this puts all your sales tax in a deep freeze, meaning the sales tax fields and settings vanish from QuickBooks, but you're just a few clicks away from restoring them again.

3. **Carry out the techniques listed in the "Enabling the Automated Sales Tax feature" section earlier in this chapter.**

REMEMBER

   You can control whether QuickBooks automatically calculates sales tax for your customers or uses a custom tax rate that you establish. Click once on any customer in your customer list, and then click Edit. Scroll down to the Additional Info section and choose a custom tax rate from the Select Tax Rate field. Alternatively, choose Based On Location to instruct QuickBooks to automatically calculate sales tax.

Exploring the Economic Nexus feature

As your business grows, you may draw in customers from other states and start wondering whether you're subject to sales or use tax in those states. The Economic Nexus feature removes all doubt by analyzing your sales for a time period of your choosing from January 2022 onward. You can run a report that informs you where you should be collecting and paying sales tax:

1. **Choose Taxes ⇨ Sales Tax.**

2. **Click the Economic Nexus button.**

3. **Review your activity by state.**

   States where you have a tax liability are marked with a green checkmark.

Custom sales tax rates

You can establish custom tax rates if you have a tariff, excise tax, or other amount that you must collect on behalf of a governmental agency that QuickBooks doesn't automatically compute. Or you may be a free spirit who prefers to handle sales tax calculations on your own. Either way, just follow these steps:

1. **Choose Taxes ⇨ Sales Tax.**

2. **Click the Sales Tax Settings button to display the Edit Settings page.**

   This page enables you to add agencies.

3. **Optional: Click Add Agency if you want to add a new tax agency.**

   A task pane prompts you to select an agency, specify your filing frequency, indicate your start date for collecting sales tax, and specify accrual or cash for your reporting method.

TIP

   Your sales tax reporting method can be the same as the reporting basis for your books, or you can make it different.

4. **Click Save to close the task pane.**

   Your new agency appears in the Tax Agencies list.

5. **Optional: Click Add Rate to display the Add a Custom Sales Tax Rate task pane.**

   Choose Single if you have a single tax rate paid to a single agency or Combined if you have multiple tax rates that are paid to one or more agencies.

6. **Click Save to close the task pane.**

   The next step is to apply the custom rate to your customers as needed.

7. **Choose Customers & Leads ⇨ Customers or Sales ⇨ Customers.**

8. **Select a taxable customer from your customer list and then click Edit within their record.**

9. **Scroll down to the Additional Info section and choose the custom tax rate from the Select Tax Rate drop-down menu.**

10. **Click Save to close the task pane.**

    Repeat Steps 8 to 10 as needed to apply your custom tax rates to your customers.

Auditing your customers' sales tax settings

As I discuss earlier in this chapter, the Company Name and Customer Display Name fields are the only required fields when you create a new customer. Filling in the Company Name field isn't an issue because that feature fills in the address fields automatically. However, you can't charge sales tax to a customer if you've only completed their Customer Display Name field. Further, you may also want to review the tax rates assigned to each customer. Here's how to audit your sales tax settings by customer:

1. **Choose Taxes⇨Sales Tax.**

2. **Choose Reports⇨Taxable Customer Report.**

3. A modified version of the Customer Contact List report includes the following columns:

   - **Customer:** As you might expect, this field displays the customer name.

   - **Billing Address:** If this field is blank and sales tax is based on the billing address, you need to fill in this information.

   - **Shipping Address:** Sales tax in QuickBooks is based on the shipping address, but it defaults to the billing address if no shipping address has been provided.

   - **Taxable:** Yes appears in this column if the customer is subject to sales tax. No indication appears if you marked a customer as exempt or the customer is located out of state or out of the country.

   - **Tax Rate:** This column shows the tax rate applicable to the customer, even if they've been marked as exempt.

   Click any customer name or address to drill down into their customer record to make changes or to carry out a more detailed review.

TIP

4. **Optional: Click the Export button and choose Export to Excel if you want to view the report in Excel.**

   In Chapter 20, I discuss how to use the Filter feature in Excel, which can make it easy to view all customers who have the same tax rate or to display customers where the billing or shipping addresses are blank.

Paying and filing sales taxes

Either you or your accountant can handle the sales tax filing process in this fashion:

1. **Choose Taxes⇨Sales Tax.**

2. **Scroll down to where you see all sales tax returns that are due and any that are overdue.**

3. **Click View Tax Return for the return you want to file.**

4. **Optional: Click Add an Adjustment on the File Your Taxes Now page if necessary to display the Add an Adjustment task pane.**

   Provide a reason for the adjustment and the adjustment date, along with an account and an amount for the adjustment. Click Add to post the adjustment, or click the X at the top-right corner to close the task pane.

5. **Use the information onscreen to complete a paper return or electronic return by way of the taxing authority's website.**

6. **You can also click the report link on the next page of the sales tax wizard to get a report that you can use to file the sales tax return later.**

7. **Click Record Payment to display the Record Payment page.**

8. **Enter a payment date, select a bank account, optionally enter a memo, and optionally click Print Check.**

WARNING

   You can override the tax amount on the Record Payment page, but doing so creates a discrepancy in your accounting records. The Add an Adjustment command discussed in Step 4 is the safest approach for altering your sales tax liability.

9. **Click Record Payment and, if needed, print the check that was generated.**

Working with Products and Services

QuickBooks expects you to create items for each product or service that you offer. If you leave the Product/Service field blank on a sales transaction form, Quick-Books fills the field with a default item named Service. You can create the following items in any QuickBooks company:

>> **Non-inventory:** These include items that you don't physically own, such as drop-ship items, or consumable items that are of immaterial value, such as nuts and bolts, where it's not feasible to charge for each nut or bolt.

TIP

>> **Services:** These items can streamline the invoicing process by giving you a way to standardize descriptions and pricing.

In Chapter 10, I discuss how users with Plus or Advanced subscriptions can track physical inventory items in QuickBooks.

Creating non-inventory and services items

Here's how to create a new item:

1. **Choose Settings⇨Products and Services to display the Products and Services page.**

   Alternatively, choose Get Paid and Pay, Sales & Expenses, or Sales⇨Products and Services.

2. **Click New to display the Product/Service Information task pane shown in Figure 2-3.**

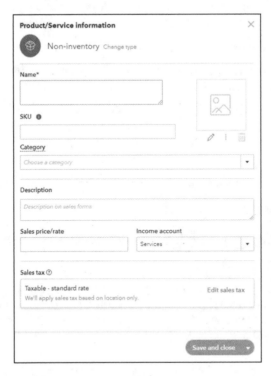

FIGURE 2-3:
A blank Product/
Service
Information
task pane.

3. **Choose Non-Inventory or Service.**

4. **Supply a name for the item.**

   This is the only required field for non-inventory and service items.

5. **Optional: Enter a SKU.**

   SKU is short for *stock-keeping unit.* It's another way of referring to a part number or other identifier for your products and services.

6. **Optional: Upload a picture of the item by clicking the Upload button, which looks like a pencil, and navigating to the location where you stored the picture.**

   Use the trash can icon adjacent to the pencil icon if you want to remove a picture from an item.

7. **Optional: Assign the item to a category.**

   Assigning items to categories enables you to group related items. You can add a category from this field, but you can't add a subcategory. See the "Managing categories" section later in this chapter for how to create a subcategory.

8. **Fill in the Description field for how the item should be described on sales forms.**

9. **Fill in the Sales Price/Rate field.**

   This is the amount you want to choose for a non-inventory item or the rate that you want to charge for a service.

10. **Specify an income account.**

    The Income Account field is prefilled, but you can choose or add a different account if you want.

11. **Optional: Click Edit Sales Tax to verify or change the sales tax settings.**

    QuickBooks asks you to specify the type of product or service so that sales tax can be calculated correctly. If your item is nontaxable, scroll down and choose Non-Taxable, and then click Done.

12. **Click Save and Close.**

    The Products and Services list appears, displaying your new item.

TAKING ADVANTAGE OF SKUs

You can control whether SKU information appears in the Products and Services list and on transaction forms from the Account and Settings task pane. Choose Settings⇨ Account and Settings⇨Sales. In the Products and Services section, toggle the Show SKU option, click Save, and then click Done. If you like, you can add the SKU to custom invoice forms, which I discuss in Chapter 1.

At any point, you can click Edit in the Action column of the Products and Services page to edit an existing inventory item. The arrow in the Action column displays a menu with up to six choices, depending on the item type:

>> **Make Inactive:** Choose this command to make an item inactive. To view items that you've marked inactive, click the funnel icon just above your list of products and services, change the Status to Inactive, and then click Apply. The Action contains a link that enables you to make an item active again.

WARNING

QuickBooks enables you to make items inactive even if the quantity on hand isn't zero. The Quantity On Hand field is automatically adjusted to zero when you make such items inactive. Making an item active again doesn't restore any quantity on hand that was present when you marked the item inactive.

>> **Run Report:** Choose this command to run a Quick Report for the past 90 days of transactions for this item.

>> **Duplicate:** Choose this command to display the Product/Service Information task pane that you used earlier in the chapter to create a new item. In this case, some fields are prefilled to ease the process of setting up similar items.

You use the Products and Services list pretty much the same way you use the Customer and Vendor lists. For example, you can search for an item by its name, SKU, or sales description. You can identify the columns you can use to sort the list by sliding your mouse over the column heading; if the mouse pointer changes to a hand, you can click that column to sort the list using the information in that column.

Managing categories

Categories can help you organize what you sell and group related items on your inventory and sales reports. Categories don't affect your accounting or your financial reports, and you can't assign categories to transactions. That's what classes and locations are for; I discuss them in Chapter 11. The Category field in the

Product/Service Information task pane that you use to create an item enables you to create new categories on the fly, or you can use the Product Categories page:

1. **Click Settings ⇨ All Lists to display the All Lists page.**

2. **Choose More ⇨ Product Categories.**

3. **Click New Category to display the Category Information task pane.**

4. **Enter a category name, optionally choose Is a Sub-Category, and then select a parent category.**

REMEMBER

You can't use existing item names as a category name. For instance, if you have a product called Fruit Basket, you can't use the words *Fruit Basket* as a category name, but you can be clever and use the plural *Fruit Baskets*.

5. **Click Save to create your new category, or click the Close button at the top right to cancel this action.**

TIP

You can create subcategories up to four levels deep, such as Clothing ⇨ Shoes ⇨ Women's Shoes ⇨ Sneakers. You can't create a subcategory for Sneakers because it's four levels down, but you can create another subcategory for Women's Shoes, which is three levels down, called *Dress Shoes*.

6. **Click Edit from the Action column of the Product Categories page if you want to modify or delete a category name.**

The resulting Category Information task pane includes a Remove button that you can use to delete the category. The Remove command also appears on the Action drop-down menu for each category. If you remove a subcategory, any items assigned move one level up. Any items assigned to a top-level category that you remove become uncategorized.

WARNING

Categories are an exception to the normal QuickBooks convention of keeping deleted items in an inactive state. When you remove a category, you physically remove it with no ability to undo your change other than to re-create the category and associate it with your items as needed.

7. **Optional: Choose two or more items from the Products and Services list, and then use the Assign Category drop-down menu that appears to update the category of the selected items.**

You can also click an individual item and then choose Edit on the page that appears to change the category for that single item.

Batching actions for products and services

A hidden Batch Actions button appears on the Projects and Services page when you click the checkboxes for one or more items. You can also click the checkbox to the left of the Name caption at the top of the products and services list to select all items at once. The Batch Actions menu offers three options:

>> **Make Inactive:** Choose this option to mark one or more items as inactive.

>> **Make Non-Inventory:** Use this command to convert service items to non-inventory items.

>> **Make Service:** Use this command to convert non-inventory items to service items.

Creating Sales Transactions

And now, the moment you've been waiting for: how do I create a dang invoice in this software? If you jumped to this page from the index, flip back a few pages, where I discuss how to set up customers, enable sales tax, and create non-inventory and service items. Customers and items are critical to the invoicing process, and for many users sales tax is critical as well.

WARNING

If your company is subject to sales tax, make sure to carry out the steps listed in the "Setting Up Sales Tax" section so that you don't inadvertently create transactions without sales tax. You'll be responsible for any sales tax that you don't collect should the tax representatives decide they want a look at your books.

Creating invoices

Invoices are written requests for payment for any goods or services that you've provided to your customers. An effective invoice makes it clear what value was provided. If you try to save a minute up front by creating a summary invoice with little detail, it could cost you time and frustration later in the form of delayed payment until you provide more detail about what the invoice covers.

Follow these steps to create an invoice:

1. **Choose + New ⇨ Invoice from the left menu bar.**

A new invoice window opens.

2. **Choose a customer from the Add Customer list.**

The customer's mailing address, payment terms, invoice date, and due date appear.

TIP

Any pending estimates or billable time entries appear in a Suggested Transactions pane on the right side of the screen. I talk about estimates in the "Generating Estimates" section later in this chapter and discuss time entries in Chapter 9.

3. **Confirm the Invoice Number, Terms, Invoice Date, and Due Date.**

4. **Optional: Enter one or more tags.**

I discuss the Tags feature in Chapter 6.

5. **Enter products and services.**

QuickBooks Online requires you to provide an item name in the Product/Service field for each row of your invoice. If you try skipping the Product/Service field, a generic item such as Services is entered for you.

(a) **Click the Product/Service column and select an item for the invoice you're creating.**

A list of matching items appears as you type a few characters in this field.

TIP

If you type an item name that doesn't exist, you can click Add New at the top of the list to create the new item. See the "Working with Products and Services" section earlier in this chapter if you're not clear on the process of adding items for products and services.

(b) **Optional: Edit the Description column for the selected item.**

(c) **Fill in the Qty and Rate columns to provide the quantity and price of the goods or services provided.** If you fill in these two columns, the Amount column calculates automatically. Or fill in Quantity and Amount, and the Rate column auto-populates.

(d) **Optional: Override the Tax setting if needed.** Click the three-dot menu to the right of the Tax checkbox to reveal the following choices:

- Edit Saved Item: This option displays a task pane from which you can modify the product or service.

- Edit Sales Tax: This option displays a task pane from which you can modify the sales tax settings for an item.

(e) Repeat Steps (a) to (c) as needed to add more items to the invoice.

Click Add Product or Service as needed to add additional rows to the invoice.

TIP

You can use the six-dot buttons to the left of each product/service item to change the order that items appear on your invoice. You can also select any row within the invoice and then click Add Subtotal to add a subtotal to your invoice.

6. Optional: Specify a discount amount/percentage or shipping amount.

The Discount field is hidden by default. To enable this field:

(a) Click the Manage button.

TIP

If you don't have a Manage button on your invoice, click Settings in the top-right corner of the invoice screen, and click the Total Discount checkbox on the panel that appears.

(b) Expand the Payment Options section of the task pane.

(c) Optional: Toggle Discount on and optionally click Apply Discount After Sales Tax.

(d) Optional: Toggle the Shipping Fee field on.

TIP

If you enable both sales tax and discounts, you can use the switch that appears to the left of these fields to control whether discounts are pretax or after-tax. Position the discount above sales tax for pretax or below sales tax for an after-tax discount.

7. Optional: Enter an invoice or statement message.

The bottom portion of the invoice screen allows you to include messages for your customer by typing an invoice or statement message. A statement message is the description for an invoice when you send customer statements.

ENABLING CUSTOMER DEPOSITS AND TIPS

You can enable a Deposit field in the Totals section of your invoice to record a downpayment that a customer has made on the goods or services that you're offering, as well as a Tips field if your customers sometimes offer gratuities. To do so, choose Settings⇨ Account and Settings⇨Sales. Click the pencil icon for the Sales Form Content section, toggle Deposit and/or Accept Tips on, click Save, and then click Done. You can now fill out these fields when needed during your invoicing process.

8. **Optional: Attach an electronic document to the invoice by clicking the Attachments field. You can then navigate to the document or drag the document into the Attachments field.**

Supporting documents must be no more than 20MB in size and one of these file types: PDF, JPEG, PNG, DOC, XLSX, CSV, TIFF, GIF, or XML. This means you can include pictures of your work, Aunt Mabel's pie recipe, a shipping confirmation, or anything else you want to include.

9. **At the bottom of the window, you can choose any of the following options:**

- Cancel to discard the invoice and close the window

- Print or Preview to choose Print Later, see a print preview of the invoice, generate a PDF version of the invoice from the Print or Preview screen, or print a packing slip

TIP

Packing slips are basically invoices that don't show prices — kind of like menus in certain fancy restaurants.

- Make Recurring to schedule the transaction as a recurring invoice

- Customize to choose or create a customized invoice form

- Save to assign an invoice number and save the transaction

- Save and New to create a new invoice

- Save and Send to assign an invoice number, save the invoice, edit the default email message, preview the invoice, and then send a copy to the customer

TIP

The email time- and date-stamp information appears in the header of invoices you send. Invoice emails are mobile-friendly and include invoice details so that customers see everything at a glance.

- Save and Share Link to copy a unique URL for the invoice for inclusion in an email you want send outside of QuickBooks

TIP

Choose between Save and New, Save and Send, and Save and Share Link by clicking the arrow on the button. The option you choose becomes the default behavior for invoices until you make a different selection in the future.

Recording invoice payments

Perhaps a customer pays you by check or sends you money through PayPal or Venmo. In such cases, there's a two-step process: 1) record the customer payments, and 2) record the bank deposit.

You can initiate receiving an invoice payment in a few ways:

>> On the Customer page, click Receive Payment if it appears in the Action column.

>> On a customer's page, choose New Transaction⇨Payment.

>> Choose + New⇨Receive Payment.

The first method in the preceding list displays the Receive Payment window, prefilled with the information for the invoice you selected as well as a default payment amount. The second and third methods display an unfilled Receive Payment window. Any unpaid invoices appear in the Outstanding Transactions section once you select a customer.

And now — the moment you've been waiting for — instructions for how to post a customer payment:

1. **Choose a customer if necessary.**

2. **Confirm the payment date.**

   Make sure the payment date matches the date you're depositing the funds to make reconciling your bank account easier.

3. **Optional: Choose a payment method.**

Default methods include cash, check, and credit card, but you can add others as needed. I discuss how to maintain other lists such as this in Chapter 1.

4. **Optional: Enter a reference number.**

This is the check number if your customer paid by check. You can leave the Reference field blank for cash or electronic deposits or repurpose it as a note field.

5. **Specify the account in which you want to deposit the payment.**

If you're posting a single check or payment for which no fees are deducted, you can choose your bank account from the drop-down list. If you're depositing two or more checks in your bank on the same day or making an electronic payment that incurs a processing fee, choose Payments to Deposit (Undeposited Funds).

6. **Select the invoice(s) being paid by clicking the checkbox for individual invoices or the checkbox at the top of the column to select all invoices.**

If your customer makes a partial payment, you can adjust the Payment field as needed for each invoice.

REMEMBER

You can't record payment-processing fees, such as those assessed by Stripe or PayPal, on the Receive Payment screen if your customer has paid you electronically. You can enter those fees on the Bank Deposit screen, which I discuss in the upcoming section titled "Recording bank deposits."

7. **Click Save and Close or click Save and New.**

The Save button is a sticky preference, meaning that you can click it and change the default behavior for future transactions.

Recording bank deposits

It's important to remember to post your bank deposits in QuickBooks so that the money doesn't end up in purgatory within your Payments to Deposit (Undeposited Funds) account. This account should always have a zero balance after you've recorded any current bank deposits. Here's how to post a bank deposit:

1. **Record one or more customer payments as described in the section "Recording invoice payments" earlier in this chapter.**

Make sure to apply the payment to your Payments to Deposit (Undeposited Funds) account.

PAYMENTS TO DEPOSIT/UNDEPOSITED FUNDS

Older QuickBooks companies may still have an Undeposited Funds account, which might sound like an oxymoron. You're going to deposit those funds pronto, of course! Thus, QuickBooks now refers to this as the Payments to Deposit account. If your bank deposits are always composed of a single check or ACH payment that doesn't incur a processing fee, you can skip this section. But if you make bank deposits composed of two or more checks, or if you receive electronic payments from which processing fees have been deducted, utilizing the Payments to Deposit account makes reconciling your bank account much easier.

The goal of the Payments to Deposit account is to enable QuickBooks to mirror what posts to your bank statement. If you deposit five checks on a single deposit ticket, your bank posts one lump sum to your account. You ideally want your bank account in QuickBooks to reflect that lump sum as well, as opposed to five individual deposits, which is what the Payments to Deposit account accomplishes. Think of this account as a holding area where you can accumulate customer payments and then batch them into amounts that match what the bank posts to your account. Then your bank-reconciliation process sails along because you're not trying to play Tetris by figuring out which combination of individual payments aligns with the amount that the bank posted.

2. **Select the payment(s) you want to deposit.**

   Click the checkbox next to each payment that you're including in this deposit.

3. **Optional: Enter a payment processing fee or bank charge:**

   (a) Choose a vendor name in the Received From field of the Add Funds to This Deposit section, such as Stripe or PayPal. If the name of the payment platform doesn't exist, type it in the Received From field and then click Add New. Change the type to Vendor and then click Save.

   (b) Choose an account, such as Bank Charges and Fees, or see Chapter 1 to add a new account to your chart of accounts, such as Payment Processing Fees.

   (c) Enter a description, such as Payment Processing Fee.

   (d) Optional: Choose the same payment method that you indicated when applying the payment, as shown in the Payment Method column of the Select the Payments Included in This Deposit section.

   (e) Enter a negative amount in the Amount field. QuickBooks displays a `This value is out of range` warning when you type the minus sign. You can ignore that. Simply enter the amount as usual, albeit with a minus sign in front.

WARNING

Make sure to enter a negative amount in the Add Funds to This Deposit section; otherwise, you overstate your deposit by *adding* the transaction fees to the deposit amount instead of *deducting* the fees.

4. **Confirm that the deposit total matches the net amount that posts to your bank account.**

If I deposit $12,075 and post –$350.18 in the Add Funds to this Account section, the net deposit is $11,724.82. Conversely, if you're simply depositing paper checks that you take to your bank, you likely don't need to enter anything in the Add Funds to This Deposit section, so the Total should match the sum of the checks that you're about to deposit.

5. **Click Save and Close or click Save and New.**

Click the arrow on the Save button to toggle between those two settings. Your choice then becomes the default for future transactions.

Entering a sales receipt

Sometimes you may get paid right when you provide goods or render services. Rather than entering an invoice and then immediately receiving a payment against it, you can create a sales receipt instead. You can also print a packing list based on the sales receipt. This approach also works well when you receive payments that you didn't invoice in advance via an electronic payment platform such as Stripe or PayPal.

To create a sales receipt, choose + New ⇨ Sales Receipt, or choose New Transaction ⇨ Sales Receipt on the Sales Transactions page. The sales receipt form is similar to the invoice form, but in this case, your saved transaction is recorded to your bank account or the Payments to Deposit account, instead of your Accounts Receivable account. Fill out the form in much the same way that you do an invoice: provide the payment-specific details, such as payment method and reference number, and select the account where the funds should go. See the sidebar "Payments to Deposit/Undeposited Funds" earlier in this chapter for information on selecting an account from the Deposit To list.

TIP

You can add a row for electronic payment transaction fees, such as those assessed by Stripe or PayPal. In this case, you need to create a Service or Non-Inventory item labeled Payment Processing Fee or something along those lines. Choose the Payment Processing Fee item and record a negative amount. QuickBooks displays a This value is out of range warning when you type the minus sign, but you can safely disregard the prompt. The net amount of the sales receipt should match the net deposit that posts to your bank account.

HANDLING OVERPAYMENTS

From time to time, a customer might pay you more than you're expecting. You can choose to give your customer credit for this overpayment or keep the excess as a gratuity. Either way, you must first instruct QuickBooks to apply credits automatically. Choose Settings ⇨ Account and Settings, and then click Advanced on the left side of the Account and Settings task pane. In the Automation section, toggle on Automatically Apply Credits, and then click Save. Going forward, QuickBooks creates credit transactions for overpayments automatically.

You receive a payment as described earlier in this chapter but include the overpayment when you fill in the Amount Received field. You can choose from three scenarios:

- **Apply the overpayment to an existing invoice.** Select the invoice(s) you want to apply the payment against in the Outstanding Transactions section of the Receive Payment window. Most likely, this option results in partial payment for at least one invoice and possibly payment in full for other invoices.

- **Apply the overpayment to a new invoice.** Choose an invoice to apply the overpayment to in the Outstanding Transactions section of the Receive Payment window. If the invoice is $100, but you received $120, show the amount paid as $120. QuickBooks creates a credit transaction for $20 when you click Save and Close. This credit is applied automatically to the next invoice you create for this customer.

- **Keep the overpayment as income.** Add a Gratuity income account to your chart of accounts and a Gratuity service item assigned to the Gratuity income account. Create a new invoice for the customer by using the Gratuity item and the overpayment amount. QuickBooks automatically marks the invoice paid because it uses the overpayment credit that it created from the overpaid invoice.

Generating credit memos and refund receipts

Occasionally, you need to return money you've received from a customer. It's a bummer, but it happens. You have two options for returning money to customers: issue a credit memo that the customer can apply against a future invoice, or issue a refund receipt when you need to return the funds immediately.

WARNING

I want to make a distinction between recording overpayments and posting credit memos. The "Handling Overpayments" sidebar earlier in this chapter provides the steps for posting an overpayment. Credit memos and refund receipts should never be used to record overpayments because doing so can result in confusion.

Credit memos allow you to reduce the outstanding or future balance for your customer when warranted. You enter a Credit Memo transaction pretty much the same way that you enter an invoice. To display the Credit Memo window, choose + New ⇨ Credit Memo, or on the Sales Transactions page, you can click the New Transaction button and choose Credit Memo.

REMEMBER

Enter credit memo amounts as a positive number. It can get confusing because you're trying to offset an invoice, so you might think that the credit memo needs to reflect a negative amount, but you want both transactions to reflect positive amounts, and then you can match them against each other.

Select the customer, fill in the products or services for which you're issuing a credit memo, or create a non-inventory item with a name such as Good Will Discount, fill in the bottom of the Credit Memo window with appropriate information, and save the transaction. This transaction window is like the Invoice transaction window; for details, refer to the section "Creating invoices" earlier in this chapter.

You can enter a credit memo for a customer even if that customer currently has no outstanding invoices. When you enter the customer's next invoice, the credit memo is applied to the invoice automatically unless you've disabled that option. Conversely, credit memos are applied automatically to outstanding invoices. If you view the Sales Transactions list for that invoice, you notice that its status is partially paid.

TIP

By default, credit memos are applied automatically to outstanding or future invoices. If you want to change that behavior, choose Settings ⇨ Account and Settings ⇨ Advanced ⇨ Automation, toggle off the Automatically Apply Credits option, click Save, and then click Close.

If you click the invoice to view it, you see a link just below the outstanding balance indicating that a payment was made (and the amount of the payment). And if you scroll to the bottom of the invoice, you see the credit amount on the Amount Received line at the bottom of the invoice.

Conversely, you'll need to create a Refund Receipt transaction if it's necessary to return money to a customer immediately. To do so, you'll issue a refund check to a customer, which deducts the amount of the refund from a bank account and reduces an income account.

TIP

To account for refunds that you issue when a customer doesn't return an item, first set up an account called something like Returns and Allowances. Assign this account to the Category Type of Income and a Detail Type of Discounts/Refunds Given. If you need the particulars, I discuss adding accounts to your chart of accounts in Chapter 1. Next, set up a service item on the Products and Services list and call it something like Customer Refunds or even Returns & Allowances. *Don't* select Is Taxable for the service. Assign the service to the Returns & Allowances account, and don't assign a default Price/Rate. See the "Working with Products and Services" section earlier in this chapter for details.

Filling in the Refund Receipt window is similar to filling in the Sales Receipt window. If you need more details than I supply here, refer to the section "Entering a sales receipt" earlier in this chapter. Follow these steps to display and fill in the Refund Receipt window:

1. **Choose + New ⇨ Refund Receipt.**

2. **Select a customer to fill in related information.**

3. **Select a payment method and make a choice from the Refund From drop-down list.**

   If you select a bank account, the current balance and the next check number associated with the account appear.

4. **Optional: Click the Print Later checkbox.**

   The Print Later checkbox doesn't appear onscreen until you make a choice from the Refund From drop-down list.

5. **If your customer is returning items, select the item that the customer is returning in exchange for the refund in the Product/Service column; otherwise, create or choose a non-inventory item with a name along the lines of Good Will Discount.**

   In this example, the customer isn't returning items, so I selected the Refunds & Allowances item.

6. **Optional: Scroll down to the bottom of the window and fill in the information (the same as the information at the bottom of an invoice).**

7. **Click either Print or Preview at the bottom of the screen, and then choose Print Check if you want to print a check, or make a choice from the Save button.**

   The transaction is saved when you print the check, or you can simply save the transaction if you want to print it later. The Save button allows you to choose between Save and New, Save and Send, or Save and Close. The Print or Preview button also allows you to simply print the check.

REMEMBER

If you're using QuickBooks Payments, you can only refund credit card charges processed through your payment account. You can't refund ACH payments electronically. You have to kick it old school and print a paper check or facilitate an electronic transaction outside of QuickBooks.

Batching activities for sales forms

Sometimes you may choose to print a sales document later. In other cases, one or more customers might ask for copies of all their invoices or other forms from a specific period of time. You can handle both of these situations if you access the All Sales page that I mention in the earlier "Accessing Recent Transactions" sidebar.

1. **Choose Sales⇨All Sales.**

A listing of all sales transactions appears.

2. **Use the Type, Date, and Customer fields to select the transactions.**

You can display a list of all transaction types at once, or you can choose a single transaction type. However, you can't choose, let's say, Invoices and Sales Receipts at the same time. Similarly, you can view a list for all customers, or a single customer. You can't display transactions for two or more customers at once.

3. **Within the transaction list, click the checkbox adjacent to each transaction of interest, or click the Select All checkbox to the left of the Date heading.**

4. **Click the Batch Actions button and then make a selection:**

- **Convert to Invoice:** Use this command to convert one or more estimates to invoices.

- **Send:** Use this option to send the sales form(s) to the corresponding customer(s).

- **Send Reminder:** Use this command to email a reminder, such as an invoice that remains unpaid.

- **Print:** Use this option to print a batch of sales forms in one fell swoop.

- **Print Packing Slip:** Use this option to generate packing slips for one or more invoices or sales receipts.

- **Delete:** Use this option with care. It physically deletes the selected transactions from your books, which you can't undo.

Writing Off Bad Debt

An unfortunate reality is that at some point you may not get paid for products delivered or services rendered. It's a frustrating aspect of being a business owner or manager, but it's part of the hard-fought knowledge that one accumulates over time. Some setup is required before you can write off an invoice, but once you accomplish those two one-time tasks, going forward, writing off bad debt is as simple as creating a credit memo that you then apply as a payment against the defunct invoices.

Setting up a bad debt account and item

You must create a Bad Debt account, and then a Bad Debt item, before you can create a transaction to write off an unpaid invoice. First I'll go over how to add a Bad Debt account to your chart of accounts:

1. **Choose Settings⇨ Chart of Accounts to display your chart of accounts.**

2. **Click New in the upper-right corner.**

3. **Enter a name such as** Bad Debt **in the Category Name field.**

4. **Click Select Category, choose Expenses, and then click Next.**

5. **Choose Uncategorized Expenses, and then click Select.**

6. **Optional: Complete the Description field if you want.**

7. **Click Save to create your new account.**

Now I'll go over how to create a Bad Debt item:

1. **Choose Settings⇨ Products and Services to display your item list.**

2. **Click New in the upper-right corner, and then choose Non-Inventory.**

3. **Assign a name, such as** Bad Debt**.**

4. **Optional: Assign the Bad Debt item to a category.**

   I skipped over the SKU field in this context because a stock-keeping unit isn't typically assigned to an administrative item like Bad Debt.

5. **Optional: Enter a description, such as $*#@_% (which stands in for curse words in comic strips), or be more reserved and enter** Bad Debt Write-Off**.**

6. **Choose Bad Debt from the Income Account list.**

   Make sure that you've already added Bad Debt to your chart of accounts; otherwise, you can't choose it here.

7. **Click Save and Close.**

Creating bad debt write-off transactions

Once you've created the Bad Debt account on your chart of accounts and created a Bad Debt non-inventory item, you're ready to grit your teeth and start writing off some uncollectible invoices.

1. **Choose New ⇨ Credit Memo.**

2. **Select your nemesis, er, I mean customer.**

3. **Choose Bad Debt in the first line of the Products/Services section.**

4. **Enter the amount that you're writing off in the Amount column.**

   In the particularly unfortunate event that you're writing off two or more invoices, the amount you enter here can be the sum of all invoices that you're writing off.

5. **Optional: Enter something along the lines of Write Off Bad Debt in the Message Displayed on Statement field.**

6. **Click Save and Close, or click Save and New if you have other non-paying customers to dispatch as well.**

7. **Choose New ⇨ Receive Payment.**

8. **Choose your customer.**

9. **Select one or more invoices from the Outstanding Transactions section.**

10. **Select the credit memo you created from the Credits section.**

11. **Click Save and Close.**

REMEMBER

A bit of cold comfort: if you file your taxes on the accrual basis, you'll most likely get a deduction for the bad debt. There's no deduction if you file your taxes using a cash-basis because you don't count invoices as taxable income until you receive payment.

Generating Estimates

You can use estimates, also known as quotes or bids, to prepare documents that forecast what you'll charge a client to complete a project. Estimates are nonposting transactions that don't affect your general ledger or financial statements but do enable you to track proposals you make to customers. As I discuss in Chapter 10, you can convert an estimate to a purchase order to facilitate ordering the items needed to complete the job. In this chapter, I show you that you can also convert an estimate to an invoice when it's time to bill your customer, which eliminates redundant typing.

You can only convert estimates with a Pending or Accepted status to purchase orders or invoices. Converting an estimate to an invoice sets its status to Closed, so convert estimates to purchase orders first if you need both.

Preparing an estimate

Creating an estimate is identical to creating an invoice. You can start the process in a couple of ways:

>> Choose + New ⇨ Estimate.

>> Choose Get Paid & Pay, Sales & Expenses, or Sales ⇨ Estimates.

From there the steps are the same as for creating an invoice, so refer to the "Creating invoices" section earlier in this chapter if you're unclear about the process.

Estimates don't affect your financial reports. If you enter an estimate for $10,000, you won't see that $10,000 in your Profit & Loss report until you convert the estimate to an invoice because estimates are nonposting transactions.

Invoices have a status of Unpaid or Paid, whereas estimates have a status of Pending, Accepted, Closed, or Rejected. An estimate's status remains Pending if the estimate is open and hasn't expired, been marked as Accepted or Rejected, or been converted to an invoice. The status drop-down menu appears just below the customer's name. You can change the status of an estimate from Pending to any of the following:

>> Accepted, meaning that the estimate is approved

>> Closed, indicating that the job is complete

>> Rejected, recording the fact that your customer declined your offer

You can open existing invoices in several ways. For instance, you can click the clock icon at the top-left corner of the Estimate screen to view recent transactions, choose the estimate from a customer's Sales Transactions list, or use the Search command on the QuickBooks dashboard.

Sales taxes, discounts, and shipping fees only appear on your estimates if you've enabled these fields for your invoices. See the "Creating invoices" and "Setting Up Sales Tax" sections that appear earlier in this chapter.

At the bottom of the Estimate page, you can do the following:

>> Click Cancel to discard the estimate before you've saved it or to cancel any changes after you've saved it and close the Estimate window.

>> Click Print or Preview to print the document now or mark it to print later.

>> Click Make Recurring to schedule the transaction as a recurring estimate.

>> Click Customize to choose or create a customized estimate form.

>> Click More to copy or delete the estimate or to view its audit trail. This button appears only after you've saved the estimate.

>> Click Save to assign a number to the estimate and save the transaction.

>> Click Save and Send to assign a number to the estimate, save it, and email a copy to the customer. After you send your estimate, the email time- and date-stamp information appears in the header.

TIP

QuickBooks offers an Estimates by Customer report that you can filter by status to generate a list of estimates.

Converting an estimate to an invoice

You've finished the project and delivered the goods, so it's time to send your customer an invoice. You're most of the way there; you simply need to convert the estimate to an invoice. You can adjust the invoice by adding or removing lines as needed. You have several ways to create an invoice from an estimate.

REMEMBER

Converting an estimate to an invoice changes the status to Closed, which means you can no longer convert the estimate to a purchase order. If you need to generate a purchase order from an estimate, make sure to do that *before* you create the invoice.

Use one of these options to create an invoice from an estimate:

>> Open the Invoice window and select a customer with the open estimate. You see a list of available documents you can link to the invoice, including any estimates. Click the Add button below an estimate to add the line items to your invoice.

>> Filter a customer's Sales Transactions page to display only open estimates and click the Create Invoice link in the Action column next to the estimate you want to convert. This action creates a new invoice based on the estimate.

>> On a customer's Sales Transactions page, open the estimate, and click the Create Invoice button. This button is available when the estimate status is Pending or Accepted. You can't create invoices from Closed or Rejected estimates.

No matter which routes you take, creating an invoice from an estimate changes the status of the estimate to Closed, even if you don't invoice the customer for all lines on the estimate. You can change an estimate's status from Closed to Pending or Accepted (or even Rejected), but doing so makes *all* lines on the estimate available for invoicing, which means that you could accidentally invoice your customer twice for the same items. If you need to create a partial invoice, it's best to first make a copy of the invoice that includes only the pending items and then close the original estimate.

If you frequently need to send an invoice for only a portion of an estimate, progress billing may be a better fit for you. Read more in the section "Creating a progress invoice for an estimate" later in this chapter.

Copying an existing estimate

Copying an estimate enables you to make an exact duplicate, which is helpful if you want to send a partial invoice or another customer wants the same set of items. Open an existing estimate from a customer's Sales Transactions list or choose New⇨Estimates and click the Recent Transactions icon to the left of the estimate number.

Click the More button at the bottom of the screen and choose Copy from the pop-up menu. A copy of the estimate appears, along with a message explaining that you're viewing a copy of an estimate. You might change the customer, for example, or add, delete, or modify the pricing. Click Save or Save and Send in the bottom-right corner of the window, as appropriate.

Creating a progress invoice for an estimate

Suppose that your business requires your work for a customer to stretch out over a lengthy period — say, six months, a year, or longer. If you must wait until you complete the work to collect any money, you'll have a tough time staying in business because you might not have enough money to pay your bills. Accordingly, you'll work out arrangements with your customers so that you're paid at various intervals, often known as *progress invoicing*.

Progress invoicing often goes hand in hand with project work, which I discuss in Chapter 11. You don't have to use the Projects feature to generate progress invoices, but if you plan to use projects, make sure to set up the project before you create an estimate.

Progress invoicing lets you send invoices to your customers at periodic milestones that you and your customer agree on. In short, you can create as many invoices as you need for a given estimate until the work is completed in full or all goods have been provided. Here's how to enable the Progress Invoicing feature:

1. **Choose Settings ⇨ Account and Settings ⇨ Sales.**

2. **Click the pencil icon for the Progress Invoicing section.**

3. **Click Update to confirm that you're cool with updating your invoice template to accommodate progress invoicing.**

4. **Click Save, and then click Done.**

Next, create an estimate in the usual fashion, as described earlier in this chapter. When you're ready to invoice a portion of the estimate, create an invoice as described in the "Converting an estimate to an invoice" section to display the window shown in Figure 2-4.

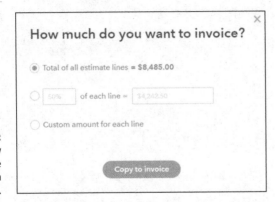

FIGURE 2-4:
Use this window to establish the amount of a progress invoice.

Based on the choice you make in this window; an invoice is created with the appropriate values filled. If you opt to create an invoice with custom amounts for each line, an invoice is created with no amounts filled in so that you can supply them. You create additional progress invoices for the estimate as appropriate until the estimate is closed out.

Chapter **3**

Posting Expenses, Checks, and Credit Card Charges

t's always more fun to record money coming in than going out. Alas, incurring expenses is part of life, and that's what this chapter is about. Notice that I didn't say paying bills because you need an Essentials subscription or higher to record those types of transactions, which I discuss in Chapter 8. This chapter explores the other transactions you use in QuickBooks to record money going out the door.

Working with Vendors

John Donne is famous for saying "No man is an island," but no business can be completely self-sufficient either. For instance, you're going to incur charges for using QuickBooks Online, and for internet access to use the software, and electricity to use your computer, and on and on. You need to set up each purveyor of the goods and services that you use as a vendor. An exception are folks who are quasi-employees. You can set them up as a vendor or, as I discuss in Chapter 4, as a contractor.

Creating vendor records

You can't pay anyone or record an expense without first creating a vendor record. Well, if you're super stubborn you can use journal entries, which I discuss in Chapter 22, but that's a brute force approach. Ostensibly, there's only one required field, Vendor Display Name, but if you plan on printing and mailing checks or using an online bill payment service, you also should fill in the vendor address at a minimum. Follow these steps to create a vendor:

1. **Display the Vendor page by using one of these techniques:**

   - Select + New ⇨ Add Vendor.

   - Select Get Paid & Pay, Sales & Expenses, or Expenses ⇨ Vendors ⇨ New Vendor.

   - Select Get Paid & Pay, Sales & Expenses, or Expenses ⇨ Expenses ⇨ New Transaction ⇨ Check or Expense, and then choose Add New from the Vendor drop-down list.

2. **Enter the company name in one of two ways:**

   - Look up the vendor name in the Company Name field to search the QuickBooks Business Network. If you find a match, click Save and Send to send a connection request to your vendor. If your vendor accepts your invitation, invoices that they send post directly to your books as accounts payable bills. You can click the Reset Link in the field if you change your mind or find that you chose the wrong vendor.

   - Complete the Vendor Display Name field.

     The Company Name or Vendor Display Name fields are the only required fields when creating a new vendor record.

3. **Optional: Provide the contact name information for your vendor.**

4. **Optional: Complete the other aspects of the record.**

   The Vendor task pane includes the following sections.

   - **Name and Contact:** The name and contact information for your vendor.

   - **Address:** The mailing address for the vendor.

   - **Notes and Attachments:** A free-form notes field allows you to enter up to 4,000 characters, whereas a separate Attachments field lets you attach files. These may include the following file types, as long as they're each 20MB or smaller: PDF, JPEG, PNG, DOC, XLSX, CSV, TIFF, GIF, and XML.

You can add attachments to vendor transactions. Any documents that you've attached appear in sequential order within the Attachments dialog box. QuickBooks notifies you of file types that are unacceptable, such as compressed ZIP files and Excel binary workbooks (XLSB files).

Any attachments that you add become permanent additions to your books that you can attach to other records or transactions but can't physically remove. When you click the X to the right of the filename, the attachment becomes unlinked. Click Show Existing beneath any Attachments field to see all attachments, and choose Unlinked to view attachments that aren't tied to a specific transaction or record.

- **Additional Info:** This section has three important subsections:

  - **Taxes:** Use the Business ID No./Social Security No. field to enter the Federal Employer ID for vendors that are incorporated or the Social Security Number for individuals. Click the Track Payments for 1099 checkbox for vendors that you need to submit Form 1099. I discuss generating 1099s in Chapter 4.

  - **Payments:** Enter the default payment terms for this vendor, such as Net 30 Days. Use the optional Account No. to enter your account number on file with the vendor, if applicable.

  - **Accounting:** Choose an account from your chart of accounts here, which QuickBooks maddeningly refers to as a category. This ensures that charges you incur for this vendor are always posted to the correct place on your financial statements.

- **Opening Balance:** Optionally, enter the opening balance for this vendor, meaning the sum of any unpaid bills, and the as of date.

5. **Click the Save button to close the Customer page and then display the Customers list or the corresponding transaction page you started from.**

Accessing and editing vendor records

The Vendors page is sorted alphabetically by contact name, but you can also sort by the Company Name or Open Balance fields. Click anywhere in a vendor's row except the Action column to display their vendor record. If you have numerous vendors, you can enter as little as a single character in the Search field to display a list of matching records, but you'll likely need to enter additional characters to winnow the list down. Choose any vendor from the resulting list to display the corresponding record.

As shown in Figure 3-1, a vendor page that has only two tabs appears:

>> **Transaction List:** A list of all transactions associated with this vendor.

>> **Vendor Details:** A summary of the vendor record, including an Attachments section that you can use to add attachments in the fashion that I describe in the "Creating vendor records" section earlier in this chapter.

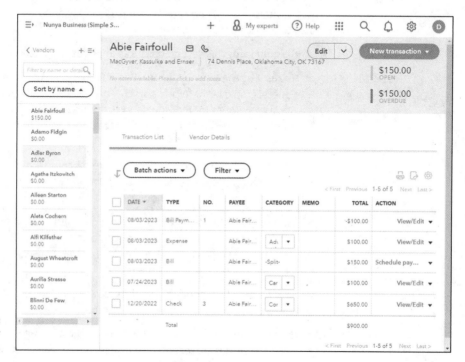

FIGURE 3-1:
A typical vendor
record page.

At the top of the vendor page are Edit and New Transaction buttons. The Edit button enables you to carry out any of three actions:

>> Click Edit to return to the Vendor task pane that I discuss in the "Creating vendor records" section earlier in this chapter.

>> Click Edit ⇨ Make Inactive to mark a vendor as inactive.

REMEMBER

You can't delete vendors in QuickBooks Online, but you can mark them as inactive as long as their balance is zero.

>> Click Edit ⇨ Merge Contacts to combine transactions from two vendor records.

All vendor-specific detail, such as address and phone numbers, from the first vendor in the list are discarded.

The New Transactions button enables you to create a variety of vendor-related transactions as well as statements. I discuss each transaction type later in this chapter.

Switching from record to record

When you finish working with one record, you can easily switch to another in that list by using the list's Split View pane shown in Figure 3-1. You can click the Split View icon, which looks like an arrow pointing to the right toward three stripes, to display a pane that shows the records stored in the list. The Split View icon appears only when you're displaying a vendor record; the icon vanishes when you're viewing the customer list.

To close Split View, click the Close Split View button, which is an arrow pointing left toward three stripes. A New Vendor icon, in the form of a + sign, appears to the left of the Close Split View button.

While working in the Split View pane, you can scroll down to find a record, or you can type a few letters of the person's or company's name in the Search box at the top of the list to find that record. You can use the Sort By drop-down list to sort the list by name or by open balance. Click a record to switch to that page.

To add a new record to the list, click the plus (+) symbol at the top of the list in the Split View pane. To return to the Vendors list page, click Vendors at the top of the Split View list.

Batching activities for vendors

The Batch Actions button enables you to carry out two different activities. This button appears on the Vendors page when you click the checkboxes for one or more vendors. You can also click the checkbox to the left of the Name caption at the top of the vendor list to select all vendors at once. The Batch Actions menu offers two options:

>> **Email:** This command creates a blank message in your email software or platform and lists the email addresses for the vendor(s) that you selected in the BCC field.

>> **Make Inactive:** Choose this option to mark as inactive one or more vendors that don't have an open balance.

The vendor page shown in Figure 3-1 also offers a Batch Actions menu with two options:

>> **Print Transactions:** This command enables you to print one or more transactions at once.

>> **Categorize Selected:** This command displays the Categorized Selected dialog box that allows you to reassign the category (er, account, on your chart of accounts) for one or more transactions.

REMEMBER

You can only use the Categorize Selected command for transactions that have a single line item in the Category Details section. Any transaction with two or more line items is considered a split transaction, which means you need to click the transaction itself and correct the categories one transaction at a time. Furthermore, you cannot use this feature with transactions that have one or more rows populated in the Item Details section.

Customizing vendor list columns

You can control the appearance of your vendor list by hiding or displaying columns and including or hiding inactive customers:

1. Click the Settings button above the Action column.

2. Toggle checkboxes as needed to display or hide columns in the list and control how many records are shown per page.

3. Click the Settings button again to close the menu.

To adjust the width of any column, hover over the right edge of a column heading and drag the double-headed arrow to the left or right. When you start to drag, the cursor changes to a pointer, and a vertical bar appears to guide you in resizing the column. Release the mouse button when you're satisfied with the column width.

TIP

QuickBooks remembers column width adjustments that you make on pages such as Customers and account registers even after you sign out.

Creating Payment Transactions

First, I want to make sure that you're aware of the various payment method options you have for recording costs that you incur because it isn't always readily apparent from the QuickBooks Online user interface.

>> **Checks:** QuickBooks enables you to fill out a check form onscreen and then print the check immediately or batch it for later.

>> **Expenses:** These include direct debits to your bank account, such as ACH (Automated Clearing House) transfers, wires, online bill payments, as well as credit and debit card transactions.

>> **Credit card credit:** QuickBooks doesn't offer a dedicated credit card expense transaction, but it does provide a way for you to record credits that post to your credit card.

>> **Pay down card credit:** You use this transaction type to pay your credit card account balance in full or in part.

Writing checks

Check transactions enable you to print a physical check to cover an expense that hasn't been paid yet, such as when the window washer is tapping their toes by your desk, or to record a handwritten check. You also have the option to click Print Later to queue up one or more checks to print later as a batch. If you're thinking, "What is this check thing he is speaking of?" feel free to skip on to the "Recording an expense or credit card charge" section that follows.

REMEMBER

In this context, I'm assuming that you haven't entered a bill and just want to write a check to pay for an expense. I discuss entering and paying bills in Chapter 8.

Here's how to write a check in QuickBooks:

1. **Choose + New ⇨ Check.**

   Alternatively, choose Expenses ⇨ Expenses from the left menu bar, click New Transaction, and then choose Check. Either way, the Check page appears.

WARNING

   Address changes that you made on the Check page in QuickBooks aren't saved back to the vendor record. If a vendor's address is missing or has changed, it's best to choose Pay & Get Paid, Sales & Expenses, or Expenses ⇨ Vendors, select the vendor, and edit their address. This can save you untold time in the future, from not having to enter the address again, to having checks sent to the wrong address or lost in the postal system from not having an address.

You also can't generate 1099 forms for vendors that have incomplete addresses.

2. **Select a vendor or contractor from the Payee field or choose Add New from the drop-down list to add a new vendor.**

   The vendor's or contractor's mailing address information appears if you choose an existing record; otherwise, a Vendor task pane appears. Fill in at least the Vendor Display Name and then click Save to create a new payee.

3. **Choose a Payment Account.**

   This is always a bank account.

4. **Enter the Payment Date.**

   Use the date that the check was or is being written.

5. **Enter the check number.**

   Make sure you use the actual check number printed on the check to make reconciling your bank account easier.

6. **Optional: Click Print Later.**

   Use this option when you want to enter one or more check transactions and then send the checks to the printer all at once, such as if you have a printer that uses MICR ink to generate checks on blank check stock.

7. **Optional: Fill in the Permit No. field.**

   This is a random field that QuickBooks has chosen to include on the check form. (This is the best explanation I can offer.)

8. **Optional: Enter one or more tags.**

   I discuss tags in Chapter 6.

9. **You see Category Details and Item Details sections if you have a Plus or Advanced subscription and have enabled the Inventory feature; otherwise, you only see a section where you can categorize your expenses.**

   The Category Details and Item Details sections have some differences:

   - **Category Details:** This section enables you to document any sort of general expense for your business that isn't related to purchasing an inventory item you plan to resell later. The Category Details section has three fields:

     - **Category:** In this context, *category* really means choosing an account from your chart of accounts, which Intuit has conflated with tax category, meaning the line on your tax return where the expense will appear. It's an attempt to make the software simpler to use, but in my mind, it folds back on itself and makes things more complex, particularly if you have accounting experience.

- **Description:** You can use up to 4,000 characters to describe what you exchanged for the money that you're about to send out the door.

- **Amount:** Enter the amount of money soon to leave your hands.

REMEMBER

Plus and Advanced users may also see Customer and Class columns in the Category Details section. You can enter a customer's name if the charge being recorded is reimbursable, and you can use the Class field to associate the expense with a particular class, which I discuss in more detail in Chapter 11.

- **Item Details:** This section is similar to the Category Details section, but it is used to record the purchase of inventory items, so it has some distinct differences:

  - **Product/Service:** Select the name of the product or service that you've procured, or click Add Item to add a new inventory item, product, or service. I discuss non-inventory and service items in Chapter 2, and I discuss inventory items in Chapter 10.

  - **Description:** The description should prefill based on the item that you chose. If it doesn't, it's a good idea to edit the corresponding item to provide the description to save yourself time in the future and improve the integrity of your books.

  - **Qty:** The quantity of items or services you purchased.

  - **Rate:** The per-unit price of the items or services you purchased.

  - **Amount:** The total cost of the goods or services you purchased.

WARNING

Most accounting platforms calculate the third field if you fill in any two fields in the quantity, rate, amount section. QuickBooks, on the other hand, multiplies the quantity by the rate to compute the amount but doesn't, say, calculate the quantity if you only fill in the rate and amount fields.

10. **Optional: Click Add Lines as needed to add lines to either section.**

Be mindful of the Clear All Lines buttons because they don't ask you if you're sure.

11. **Optional: Provide a memo.**

This can be any sort of note that you want to enter related to the transaction.

12. **Optional: Add one or more attachments.**

You can upload any of the following document types: CSV, DOC, GIF, JPEG, PDF, PNG, TIFF, XLSX, and XML. Each file is limited to 20MB.

13. **At the bottom of the page, you can choose any of the following commands:**

- **Cancel:** Discards the transaction and closes the Check window if you indicate yes, you would like to leave without saving.

- **Print Check:** Saves the transaction and displays a print preview screen for the check.

- **Order Checks:** Displays a page from which you can order QuickBooks-compatible checks from Intuit.

- **Make Recurring:** Sets up a recurring check on a schedule that you choose. An example of this is a rent payment. I discuss creating recurring transactions in Chapter 7.

- **More:** When you're initially writing a check, this menu contains a single Void command. Here's a list of all the commands that are available for saved transactions:

  - **Copy:** Creates a duplicate copy of the transaction that you then edit as needed.

  - **Void:** Marks a check as voided but keeps it in your accounting records. Reasons for voiding checks are legion, but some examples include being jammed in the printer, lost in the mail, and eaten by a dog. The list goes on and on.

  - **Delete:** Removes a check completely from your accounting records.

WARNING

    Think at least three times before you use the Delete command because deleting a check that has been marked as reconciled in your bank reconciliation is a surefire way to give whoever reconciles your bank statement a massive headache.

  - **Transaction Journal:** Displays a Transaction Drilldown Journal report that warms the cockles of any accountant's heart. The report breaks down the transaction into the nitty-gritty details of debits and credits.

  - **Audit History:** Displays a Transaction History report that reflects when the transaction was first entered and any subsequent edits.

- **Save and Close or Save and New:** Saves the transaction and closes the Expense window or makes way for a new transaction. This button is a sticky preference. Whichever choice you make by way of the drop-down arrow on the button becomes the default for that transaction page until you select something different down the line.

Recording an expense or credit card charge

Expense transactions are for when the money has already been spent, or, as they say, "the horse has already left the barn." You typically use expenses to record automatic withdrawals from your bank account, credit and debit card transactions, fees that your bank has debited directly to your account, outgoing ACH transactions, and so on.

Here's how to enter an expense:

1. **Choose + New ⇨ Expense.**

   Alternatively, choose Expenses ⇨ Expenses from the left menu bar, click New Transaction, and then choose Expense. Either way, the Expense page appears.

2. **Select a vendor or contractor from the Payee field or choose Add New from the drop-down list to add a new vendor.**

   The vendor's or contractor's mailing address information appears if you choose an existing record; otherwise, a Vendor task pane appears. Fill in at least the Vendor Display Name and then click Save to create a new payee.

   REMEMBER

   It's a best practice to record vendor addresses in your accounting software, but sometimes you can let that slide. First, you aren't required to send 1099 forms to vendors for expenses that you pay with a credit card because the credit card company handles the income reporting. You also don't necessarily need to fill in the address of your utility company if you pay via bank transfer because you don't have to send that company a 1099 form either.

3. **Choose a payment account.**

   You can post expenses to bank or credit card accounts.

4. **Enter the payment date.**

   Use the date that the check was or is being written.

5. **Optional: Choose a payment method.**

   The default payment methods include cash, check, and credit card, but you can also choose Add New to add a new method. I discuss maintaining the payment method list in Chapter 1.

6. **Optional: Enter a reference number.**

   You can enter up to 20 characters in the Ref. No. field, such as an invoice number or other short memo.

7. **Optional: Enter a permit number.**

   Permit No. is a random field that Intuit felt necessary to add to certain pages. I wish I had a better explanation for it.

8. **Optional: Enter one or more tags.**

   I discuss tags in Chapter 6.

9. **You will see Category Details and Item Details sections if you have a Plus or Advanced subscription and have enabled the Inventory feature; otherwise, you only see a section where you can categorize your expenses.**

   Speaking of Category Details and Item Details, they have some differences:

   - **Category Details:** This section enables you to document any sort of general expense for your business that isn't related to purchasing an inventory item that you plan to resell later. The Category Details section has three fields:

     - **Category:** In this context, *category* really means choosing an account from your chart of accounts, which Intuit has conflated with tax category, meaning the line on your tax return where the expense will appear. It's an attempt to make the software simpler to use, but in my mind, it folds back on itself and makes things more complex, particularly if you have accounting experience.

     - **Description:** You can use up to 4,000 characters to describe what you exchanged for the money that you're about to send out the door.

     - **Amount:** Enter the amount of money soon to leave your hands.

       REMEMBER

       Plus and Advanced users may also see Customer and Class columns in the Category Details section. You can enter a customer's name if the charge being recorded is reimbursable, and you can use the Class field to associate the expense with a particular class, which I discuss in more detail in Chapter 11.

   - **Item Details:** This section is similar to the Category Details section, but it's used to record the purchase of inventory items, so it has some distinct differences:

     - **Product/Service:** Select the name of the product or service you've procured or click Add Item to add a new inventory item, product, or service. I discuss non-inventory and service items in Chapter 2, and I discuss inventory items in Chapter 10.

     - **Description:** The description should prefill based on the item you chose. If it doesn't, it's a good idea to edit the corresponding item to provide a description to save yourself time in the future and improve the integrity of your books.

     - **Qty:** The quantity of items or services you purchased.

     - **Rate:** The per-unit price of the items or services you purchased.

- **Amount:** The total cost of the goods or services you purchased.

  Most accounting platforms calculate the third field if you fill in any two fields in the Qty, Rate, and Amount sections. QuickBooks, on the other hand, multiplies the quantity by the rate to compute the amount, but it doesn't, say, calculate the quantity if you only fill in the rate and amount fields.

10. **Optional: Click Add Lines as needed to add lines to either section.**

Again, be mindful of the Clear All Lines buttons because they don't ask you if you're sure.

11. **Optional: Provide a memo.**

This can be any sort of notes you want to enter related to the transaction.

12. **Optional: Add one or more attachments.**

You can upload any of the following document types: CSV, DOC, GIF, JPEG, PDF, PNG, TIFF, XLSX, and XML. Each file can be no more than 20MB in size.

13. **At the bottom of the page, you can choose any of the following commands.**

- **Cancel:** Discards the transaction and closes the Expense window if you indicate yes, you would like to leave without saving.

- **Clear:** Discards the transaction and leaves the Expense window open if you indicate that you would like to leave without saving.

- **Make Recurring:** Sets up a recurring expense on a schedule that you choose. This is handy for an automatic bank debit for an insurance payment. I discuss creating recurring transactions in Chapter 7.

- **More:** When you're initially writing a check, this menu contains only a single Void command. Here's a list of all the commands that are available for saved transactions:

  - **Copy:** Creates a duplicate copy of the transaction that you can then edit as needed.

  - **Void:** Marks an expense as voided but keeps it in your accounting records. You have far fewer reasons to void an expense versus a check, but some examples that come to mind are recording an expense to the wrong person and entering a transaction twice.

  - **Delete:** Removes an expense completely from your accounting records.

    Think before you use the Delete command. Deleting an expense that has been marked as reconciled in your bank reconciliation is a surefire way to give whoever reconciles your bank statement a massive headache.

- **Transaction Journal:** Displays a Transaction Drilldown Journal report that enamors you to any accountant. The report breaks down the transaction into the nitty-gritty details of debits and credits.

  - **Audit History:** Displays a Transaction History report that reflects when the transaction was first entered and any subsequent edits.

- **Save and Close or Save and New:** Saves the transaction and closes the Expense window or makes way for a new transaction. The Save and . . . button in QuickBooks is a sticky preference. Whichever choice you make by way of the drop-down arrow on the button becomes the default for that transaction page until you select something different down the line.

Posting credit card credits

This next transaction type is a borderline tongue twister, "Carol creates credit card credits on her computer." Think of credit card credits as a negative expense, with the twist that you enter them as positive amounts. Here's how to record credits that are posted to your credit card account:

1. **Choose + New ⇨ Credit Card Credit.**

2. **Select a vendor from the Payee field.**

   You can add a new vendor in the unlikely event that a credit appears from a vendor you haven't paid in the past.

3. **Choose a bank/credit account.**

   Credit card credits can only be posted to a credit card account.

4. **Enter the payment date.**

   Use the date that the credit was posted to your account.

5. **Optional: Enter a reference number.**

   You can enter up to 20 characters in the Ref. No. field.

6. **Optional: Enter a permit number.**

   Feel free to honor Barry Bonds home run record by entering 762 in this field, or perhaps leave it blank.

7. **Optional: Enter one or more tags.**

   I discuss tags in Chapter 6.

8. **You see Category Details and Item Details sections if you have a Plus or Advanced subscription and have enabled the Inventory feature; otherwise, you see only a section where you can categorize your credit.**

The Category Details and Item Details sections are different.

- **Category Details:** This section enables you to document any sort of general credit for your business that isn't related to returning an inventory item that you intended to resell. The Category Details section has three fields:

  - **Category:** In this context, *category* really means choosing an account from your chart of accounts, which Intuit has conflated with tax category, meaning the line on your tax return where the refund appears. It's an attempt to make the software simpler to use, but in my mind, it folds back on itself and makes things more complex, particularly if you have accounting experience.

  - **Description:** You can use up to 4,000 characters to describe the money that has been returned to you.

  - **Amount:** Enter the credit amount as a positive number. This may feel oxymoronic, but just trust me here. After you save your transaction, use the Search command at the top of the screen to bring the credit card credit transaction back up on the screen, and then click More ⇨ Transaction Journal. Positive amounts entered on the Credit Card Credit screen debit (reduce) your credit card account balance and credit (reduce) the account that you posted the refund to.

    Plus and Advanced users may also see Customer and Class columns in the Category Details section. You can enter a customer's name if the refund being recorded should be paid back to them, and you can use the Class field to associate the refund with a particular class, which I discuss in more detail in Chapter 11.

- **Item Details:** This section is similar to Category Details, but it's used to record the return of inventory items, so it has some distinct differences:

  - **Product/Service:** Select the name of the product or service that you've procured, or click Add Item to add a new inventory item, product, or service. I discuss non-inventory and service items in Chapter 2, and I discuss inventory items in Chapter 10.

  - **Description:** The description should prefill based on the item that you chose. If it doesn't, it's a good idea to edit the corresponding item to provide the description to save yourself time in the future and improve the integrity of your books.

  - **Qty:** The quantity of items or services you returned, as a positive number.

  - **Rate:** The per-unit price of the items or services you returned, as a positive number.

- **Amount:** The total cost of the goods or services you returned, once more, with feeling, as a positive number.

  Most accounting platforms calculate the third field if you fill in any two fields in the Qty, Rate, and Amount sections. QuickBooks, on the other hand, multiplies the quantity by the rate to compute the amount, but it doesn't, say, calculate the quantity if you only fill in the Rate and Amount fields.

9. **Optional: Click Add Lines as needed to add lines to either section.**

Be mindful of the Clear All Lines buttons because they don't ask you if you're sure.

10. **Optional: Provide a memo.**

This can be any sort of note you want to enter related to the transaction.

11. **Optional: Add one or more attachments.**

You can upload any of the following document types: CSV, DOC, GIF, JPEG, PDF, PNG, TIFF, XLSX, and XML. Each file can be no more than 20MB in size.

12. **At the bottom of the page, you can choose any of the following commands:**

- **Cancel:** Discards the transaction and closes the Expense window. If you indicate Yes, it means you want to leave without saving.

- **Make Recurring:** Sets up a recurring refund on a schedule that you choose. It's extremely unlikely you'll ever encounter that need.

- **More:** When you're initially writing a check, this menu contains only a single Void command. Here's a list of all the commands that are available for saved transactions:

  - **Copy:** Creates a duplicate copy of the credit card credit, which you can then edit as needed.

  - **Void:** Marks the refund as voided but keeps it in your accounting records. You have far fewer reasons to void a credit card credit than a check, but some examples that come to mind are recording a refund to the wrong credit card account and entering a transaction twice.

  - **Delete:** Removes a credit card credit completely from your accounting records.

    Be careful using the Delete command because deleting a credit card credit that has been marked as reconciled in your bank reconciliation is a surefire way to give whoever reconciles your credit card statement a massive headache.

- **Transaction Journal:** Displays a Transaction Drilldown Journal report that will have you saying, "See? I knew I was supposed to enter the credit amounts as positive numbers."

- **Audit History:** Displays a Transaction History report that reflects when the transaction was first entered and any subsequent edits.

- **Save and Close or Save and New:** Saves the transaction and closes the Credit Card Credit window or makes way for a new transaction. The Save and . . . button in QuickBooks is a sticky preference. Whichever choice you make by way of the drop-down arrow on the button becomes the default for that transaction page until you choose a different selection down the line.

Paying down credit cards

Although it's not strictly necessary, QuickBooks provides a page from which you can ensure that you record your payment to your credit card company properly. Bear in mind that this page assumes that you made your payment via bank transfer because you can't print a check from the transaction window. I give you the alternate steps to use if you want to print and mail a physical check to your credit card company instead of paying through the company's website.

Here's how to use the Pay Down Credit Card page:

1. **Choose + New ⇨ Pay Down Credit Card (in the Other column).**

   The Pay Down Credit Card page appears, as shown in Figure 3-2.

2. **Choose a credit card from the Which Credit Card Did You Pay drop-down menu.**

3. **Optional: Choose a payee.**

   You aren't required to establish your bank or credit card company as a vendor, but doing so does enable you to run additional reports if needed.

4. **Enter the amount you paid in the How Much Did You Pay field.**

5. **Enter the date that you made the payment in the Date of Payment field.**

6. **Optional: Enter a permit number.**

   Just kidding. Unlike most payment-related screens in QuickBooks, you won't find a Permit No. field here.

7. **Choose the bank account you used from the What Did You Use to Make This Payment field.**

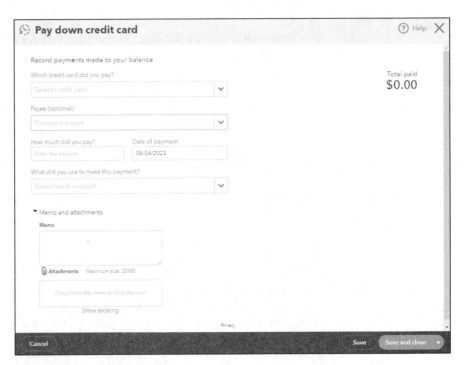

FIGURE 3-2:
A blank Pay Down
Credit Card Page.

8. **Optional: Expand the Memo and Attachments section and enter a memo in the Memo field.**

   Perhaps write an affirmation here, something like, "Yes, I can pay this credit down; yes, I will pay this credit card down."

9. **Optional: Add one or more attachments.**

   You can upload any of the following document types: CSV, DOC, GIF, JPEG, PDF, PNG, TIFF, XLSX, and XML. Each file can be no more than 20MB in size.

10. **At the bottom of the page, you can choose any of the following commands.**

    - **Cancel:** Discards the transaction and closes the Pay Down Credit Card window if you indicate yes, you would like to leave without saving.

    - **Save:** Saves and keeps the transaction onscreen just in case you want to, say, download a PDF version of your credit card statement to attach.

    - **Save and Close or Save and New:** Saves the transaction and closes the Credit Card Credit window or makes way for a new transaction. The Save and . . . button in QuickBooks is a sticky preference. Whichever choice you make by way of the drop-down arrow on the button becomes the default for that transaction page until you select something different down the ine.

IN THIS CHAPTER

Payroll

» **Understanding how to prepare payroll**

» **Knowing how to manage payroll taxes**

» **Paying contractors and filing 1099s correctly**

Chapter **4**

Paying Employees and Contractors

A s an employer, you have a responsibility to pay both your employees and any contractors who work for you. In this chapter, I explore both responsibilities. Running payroll is more than just issuing paychecks to your employees. After you've prepared paychecks, you need to remit amounts withheld for deductions and benefits to the appropriate parties. QuickBooks Payroll is a subscription service that offers automated payroll, tax deposits, and tax forms, but you can manually pay your employees, remit payroll taxes, and file your returns if you prefer. At the end of this chapter, I explore the ways that QuickBooks users typically pay — and report on paying — contractors who are vendors who perform work for a company but don't qualify as employees.

TIP

I discuss time tracking in Chapter 9. The QuickBooks Time service integrates seamlessly with QuickBooks Payroll if you have a QuickBooks Online Essentials, Plus, or Advanced subscription.

Getting Started with QuickBooks Payroll

When you prepare payroll, the process involves doing setup work so that payroll amounts are computed accurately. You must also account for payroll taxes withheld from each employee's paycheck. The payroll service can remit federal, state, and (in some cases) local payroll taxes to the appropriate tax authorities. You, however, must remit to the appropriate institutions any required deductions and contributions that affect each employee's paycheck, such as 401(k) contributions, health insurance, and other deductions.

TIP

You can add employees to QuickBooks without a payroll subscription if you want to use a QuickBooks Time subscription for time tracking but process payroll by hand or through another payroll service.

Subscribing to QuickBooks Payroll

Intuit tries hard to get you to subscribe to QuickBooks Payroll when you start your QuickBooks Online subscription, so you may already be signed up. Here's how to tell:

1. **Choose Payroll from the sidebar menu on the left.**

   You see either a list with the heading Finish Tasks on Your Own Pace or a page showing the QuickBooks Payroll options.

   You can skip to the next section if your payroll subscription is already active.

2. **If you need a subscription, choose the options that appeal to you and clear the ones that don't so that QuickBooks recommends a plan that best fits your needs.**

   Alternatively, scroll down to compare the Core, Premium, and Elite payroll processing options. You're returned to the Welcome to QuickBooks Payroll page after you complete the trial or subscription process.

3. **Click Get Started to launch the payroll wizard.**

4. **Choose No, I'm Not Sure, or Yes when asked if you've incurred payroll expenses this year, and then click Next.**

5. **Select a date for your next payday, and then click Next.**

6. **Complete the series of contact and address screens, and then click Next.**

   The contact information you provided when you initially set up your company appears, which you can override if needed.

7. **Edit the contact information fields if necessary.**

   After you finish this part of the wizard, you're returned to a Setup Tasks list.

8. **Click Finish Up to begin adding your employees.**

   The Your Team page appears.

Setting payroll preferences

In addition to adding employees, you should review payroll preferences and set up payroll taxes. You can't process your payroll and payroll tax returns fully until you complete all the setup fields.

To review payroll preferences, choose Settings ⇨ Payroll Settings. The Payroll Settings page includes a series of sections you can use to review or establish various settings related to payroll. Understanding this page may make you feel less overwhelmed by what you see:

>> General Tax allows you to edit your company type, filing name, and filing address, as well as change your first payroll date if necessary.

>> Federal Tax allows you to indicate your employer identification number (EIN), opt out of workers' comp offers from Intuit partners, and specify a filing requirement and deposit schedule.

>> Special federal programs such as the CARES Act may appear here if payroll tax deferrals or other relief is available.

>> A state tax section allows you to specify your state EIN, payroll tax deposit schedule, and state unemployment rates.

>> The Auto Payroll option indicates whether you have any employees set up on automatic payroll.

>> The Federal Forms Preference enables you to designate third parties and paid preparers authorized to represent you before the Internal Revenue Service.

>> Email notifications allow you to opt in or out of payroll-related email notifications.

>> Early pay allows employees to access a payday lending program. It's free for you, but they have to pay for it.

>> Shared Data allows you to give your employees the option to import their W-2 data into TurboTax.

>> Bank Accounts requires you to connect your bank account to remit deductions, pay your employees via direct deposit, and e-file and e-pay your taxes.

>> Printing allows you to specify whether you want to print checks on plain paper (assuming that your printer allows you to use a MICR cartridge to generate the row of numbers at the bottom of a check) or on preprinted QuickBooks-compatible checks. This section also offers a link for ordering checks.

>> The Accounting preference enables you to map payroll tax payments, expenses, and liabilities to your chart of accounts.

TIP

Be sure to set aside a few minutes to review every section in Payroll Settings. This review helps you avoid surprises and frustration when you make a tax payment or attempt to e-file near a deadline.

QuickBooks also offers a Fill In Your Tax Info wizard that can walk you through some of these choices, although most sections in the Payroll Settings screen are limited to a few fields at a time.

Adding employees

You can't pay your employees through QuickBooks Payroll until you set them up in QuickBooks. Furthermore, you may need some paperwork from your employees, such as a Form W-4 form to document their withholding preferences. You may also need to get their approval to opt into any benefits that your company offers.

REMEMBER

Form W-4 is the Internal Revenue Service form that employees complete to specify their withholding allowance. If you need to complete Form W-4 for any employee, visit www.irs.gov and click the W-4 link in the Forms & Instructions section or use this link: www.irs.gov/pub/irs-pdf/fw4.pdf. You can confirm your state's payroll tax requirements by visiting your state's website and searching for *payroll taxes*. I live in Georgia, so I would search the Georgia Department of Revenue's site.

Setting up an employee can result in what feels like sorting through a blizzard of documentation, but you can minimize that by asking your employees to set themselves up in QuickBooks Workforce. Some of the information that either you or your employees need to enter includes the following:

>> Personal information, which includes the employee's address, Social Security number, birth date, gender, and phone number.

>> Tax withholding, which includes the employee's tax federal filing status (single, married, head of household, and so on) and withholding amount as well as their state income tax, if applicable. QuickBooks prompts you to supply information for the state in which your business operates.

TIP

WARNING

» The method you want to use to pay the employee (such as paper check or direct deposit). If you choose direct deposit, specify the bank account information for the employee (account type, routing number, and account number).

For direct-deposit checks, you can choose to deposit the paycheck in its entirety in a single account, deposit the check into two accounts, or deposit a portion of the check directly and pay the balance as a paper check.

» Employment details, which include employee status, hire date, pay schedule, work location, job title, employee ID, and workers' comp class.

» Pay types, which include the amount you pay the employee (hourly, salaried, or commission only), along with time-off pay policies and additional pay types.

Make sure to pay close attention when working in the How Much Do You Want to Pay section. For hourly employees, QuickBooks makes it easy and intuitive to enter regular time. Scroll down on this page and enable any other types of pay that the employee might accrue, such as overtime, holiday pay, bonuses, and so on. If you don't enable the fields here, you can't enter the amounts when you process payroll.

» Deductions or contributions. (Add in whether the employee has any.)

Here's how to add employees to QuickBooks:

1. **Choose Payroll⇨Employees.**

2. **Click Add an Employee.**

   If you haven't yet opted in to a QuickBooks Payroll subscription, click the Add Employee link at the top of the page.

3. **Click Add an Employee.**

   A Say Hello to Your New Employee dialog box appears.

4. **On the first part of the screen, provide the employee's name, email address, and hire date, and then click Add Employee.**

   Notice the option to allow the employee to enter their data directly in QuickBooks Workforce. You can deselect this option, but you may prefer to push the data entry work to your employees, which enables them to ensure that the information is entered correctly.

5. **An invitation to QuickBooks Workforce is sent to your employee, and their employee record appears onscreen.**

   If you change your mind, you can toggle Employee Self-Setup off at the top-right corner of the screen and then complete the employee profile manually.

6. **Click Edit or Start in the corresponding sections of the employee profile to establish payment methods, pay types and deductions, and contributions.**

Most employers don't let an employee enter their compensation details directly, so I'm going to assume that you, too, want to retain control over this.

WARNING

If you enter data in a field incorrectly, the wizard can appear to be broken or frozen. Scroll back up to look for any fields marked in red. You can't progress through the wizard until you clear up input errors, such as indicating that you have an employee who works 40 hours a day or 8 days a week (instead of 8 hours a day and 5 days a week).

7. **Click Employee List at the top of the screen if you want to return to the Employee List so that you can add another employee.**

TIP

Click Action ⇨ Delete if an employee ghosts you, as unlikely as that may seem these days, or if you have other reasons for removing an employee from the list. This is a true deletion, as opposed to making an employee inactive, which is generally the case for list items in QuickBooks.

Setting up payroll taxes

Before you start using payroll, keep tabs on the to-do list on the Payroll Overview page that you can access by choosing Payroll ⇨ Overview. It provides the following preflight checklist for processing payroll:

» **Setup Task 1: Get Ready to Pay Your Team**

Here you confirm the date of your next payday, enter your business contact details, add employees, and connect your bank if you opt into using direct deposit.

» **Setup Task 2: Let's Handle Your Taxes**

In this section, you enter your state and federal tax ID numbers, connect your bank so that you can remit payroll taxes, and set your tax preferences.

» **Setup Task 3: Take Care of Your Team**

Here Intuit offers to help you secure workers' compensation insurance, a 401(k) plan, and health insurance.

At a minimum, make sure that you complete Setup Tasks 1 and 2 of the checklist.

TIP

The date you start using QuickBooks Payroll determines the "as of" date of historical information you need to collect and determines that date to be the first day of the current quarter. Try to start using QuickBooks on January 1 of any year; that way, you don't need to enter historical information. If you can't start using QuickBooks on January 1, try to start using it on the first day of a quarter to make filing certain payroll tax returns easier. Historical payroll transactions can be summarized before that date but must be entered in detail after that date.

Preparing Payroll

Processing payroll in QuickBooks Online involves a three-step process:

1. Record paycheck information.

2. Review paycheck information.

3. Generate paychecks.

TIP

Mobile users should consider trying the QuickBooks Payroll mobile app to pay employees. You can optionally pay payroll taxes and file payroll tax forms electronically if you opt out of letting Intuit do this for you, and review employee information and paycheck history. Data syncs automatically between the mobile app and your Intuit payroll account. I discuss the mobile app in more detail in Chapter 7.

Recording payroll information

Choose Payroll Link ⇨ Employees and click the Run Payroll button to start processing payroll. The Run Payroll wizard appears and lists all your employees.

WARNING

The Run Payroll button doesn't appear until you've completed the tax setup step, entered your payroll history, and, depending on your automation choices, connected your bank account. Check the bottom of the setup list for any required tasks you haven't completed. If you try to do an end-run by choosing + New ⇨ Payroll, you're simply returned unceremoniously to the payroll setup list.

TIP

Click the arrow next to Run Payroll to review a Bonus Only option for generating bonus checks. You can enter bonus amounts as net pay, meaning that you specify how much you want the employee to receive, and QuickBooks works backward to figure out the gross pay, or you can choose the As Gross Pay option and have QuickBooks calculate the net pay.

Verify the bank account from which to pay employees and double-check the pay period and pay date. By default, a checkmark appears to the left of each employee scheduled to be paid, but you can remove the check if appropriate. Enter the hours that any hourly employees worked during the pay period.

TIP

You can squeeze more employees onscreen by choosing Settings ⇨ Compact just above the top-right corner of the employee list.

Reviewing and generating payroll checks

When everyone's favorite days of the month, known as paydays, come around on the calendar, it's time to process payroll:

1. **Choose Payroll from the left menu bar.**

    The Payroll Overview page appears.

2. **Click the Let's Go button beneath the large It's Time to Run Payroll banner.**

    QuickBooks really doesn't want you to miss payday. Your employees don't either. The Run Payroll page appears to help you with this process.

3. **Enter regular pay hours and an optional memo.**

    Your active employees appear in individual rows. If you need to override federal or state withholdings for a single paycheck, click Edit at the right side of an employee's row.

    REMEMBER

    QuickBooks only shows you fields for pay types that you've enabled within each employee's record. Infrequent pay types, such as holiday pay or bonuses, can suddenly feel like a pop quiz when there's no place to enter the information. To enable additional pay types on the fly, click the employee's name on the Run Payroll page, and then scroll down to the How Much Do You Pay section. Within this page, you see checkboxes for enabling additional pay types.

4. **Click Preview Payroll.**

    If you need more time, click the arrow on the Preview Payroll button and choose Save for Later to save your work in progress rather than abandoning a payroll run completely.

5. **Use the Review and Submit page to make sure everything looks in order.**

    Click Edit next to each employee's Net Pay amount if you need to edit their check, or click the Compare to Last icon to display a chart that compares this paycheck to the employee's previous check.

If you use the Compare to Last Payroll page, make sure you click the Close (X) button in the upper-right corner. If you're like me and press the Escape key to close windows on your computer, you not only close the Compare to Last Payroll page, but cancel your payroll run as well.

6. **Optional: Click Preview Payroll Details.**

This command is a little tricky because it doesn't look clickable but is. A detailed report shows every aspect of your employee's compensation, withholdings and deductions, and any employer costs such as the employer portion of payroll taxes.

7. **Click Submit Payroll to finalize your payroll.**

If you have any issues that you need to resolve before submitting your payroll, you can click the arrow beside Submit Payroll and choose Save for Later.

8. **The Payroll Is Done page appears.**

Hold your horses, though; you might not be completely done yet. If you use direct deposit and don't need to print pay stubs, you can skip the next two steps. Otherwise, you still have some unfinished business to attend to.

9. **Optional: Click Auto-Fill to assign check numbers, or manually enter check numbers if you use handwritten checks.**

If you happen to catch a last-minute issue, you can click an employee's pay amount to display a screen from which you can edit their check. Payroll isn't over until it's over.

10. **Optional: Click Print Pay Stubs to preview paychecks and stubs and print them.**

This report appears in an additional browser tab.

11. **Optional: Click View Payroll Reports.**

The Your Payroll Reports Are Ready page allows you to pick the reports that you want to export to Excel. Each report is placed on a separate worksheet that you can open in Microsoft Excel or Google Sheets. Click OK to close this page.

When you open your payroll report workbook, you might encounter a warning prompt in Excel that informs you that the file format and extension don't match and that the file could be corrupted or damaged. You can safely click Yes to open the report. The geeky details are that the programmers at Intuit are generating a workbook that has an XLS file, but the workbook itself is in the modern XLSX format. In short, you have nothing to worry about here. Click Yes and move along.

12. **Click Finish Payroll.**

Take a deep breath. Now, my friend, you're truly done with payroll.

TIP

You can click Edit at the right edge of the line for any employee to see the details associated with the employee's paycheck. If necessary, you can change certain paycheck details, such as hours worked and federal/state tax amounts.

TIP

If you pay your employees by direct deposit, expect next-day deposits for Payroll Core, or same-day deposits for Premium or Elite for transactions initiated by 7 a.m. Pacific time.

Establishing or correcting payroll exemptions

Although it's most likely unnecessary, you can establish payroll tax exemptions when necessary by following these steps:

1. **Choose Payroll ⇨ Employees and select the name of the employee whose status you need to change.**

2. **Click the Edit link in the Tax Withholding section of the Employee Details page that appears.**

3. **On the What Are [Employee's] Withholding page, scroll down, and expand Tax Exemptions.**

4. **Click Done when you finish editing.**

TIP

To void or delete a paycheck, click Paycheck List in the top-right corner of the Employee page, select a paycheck, and then click the Void or Delete button above the list. A series of questions helps you get the job done.

Printing payroll reports

When you complete payroll, you may want to print payroll-related reports. Choose Reports ⇨ Reports (Business Overview ⇨ Reports) on the left menu bar to display the Reports page. Scroll down to the payroll reports. Along the way, you may see an Employees section that has reports related to time tracking. You can click any payroll report to print it to the screen and, subsequently, to your printer. See Chapter 6 for more details.

Managing Payroll Taxes

As I mention at the beginning of this chapter, the payroll process doesn't end with preparing and producing paychecks. You need to remit payroll taxes and file payroll tax returns on schedules mandated by the Internal Revenue Service, your state, and possibly your locality.

Paying payroll taxes

Using rules established by the IRS, most employers pay payroll taxes semiweekly, monthly, or quarterly, depending on the amount owed (called your *payroll tax liability*). All versions of QuickBooks Payroll now include the option of automated tax deposits and forms, so your payroll tax compliance can be automated, or you can file your returns on your own. Payroll Premium and Elite handle local taxes where applicable.

To manage how payroll taxes are paid:

1. **Choose Settings ⇨ Payroll Settings ⇨ Taxes and Forms, and then click the Edit button.**

2. **Clear the Automate Taxes and Forms option if you *don't* want QuickBooks to handle your taxes and forms for you.**

3. **Optional: If you're handling taxes on your own, choose between I'll Initiate Payments and Filings Using QuickBooks and I'll Pay and File the Right Agencies through Their Website or by Mail.**

WARNING

Don't wait until the 11th hour to file payroll tax returns because you may end up with late filings due to buffers needed for both electronic filing and electronic payments.

You must make federal tax deposits by electronic funds transfer by connecting your bank account to QuickBooks Online. If you opt out of this service, you need to make federal tax deposits using the Electronic Federal Tax Payment System (EFTPS; www.eftps.gov), a free service provided by the U.S. Department of the Treasury. QuickBooks Payroll doesn't use EFTPS but pays directly on your behalf. For this reason, you need to complete and sign IRS Form 8655 (Reporting Agent Authorization) before your tax deposits and form can be filed on your behalf.

Choose Taxes➪Payroll Tax to display the Payroll Tax Center, which keeps you in the loop on the amount of taxes slated to go out the door. Once you've paid employees, the Payroll Tax Center displays taxes that are due, along with their due dates and e-payment cutoff dates. You can preview how much you owe by printing the Payroll Tax Liability report; click the View Your Tax Liability Report link on the Payroll Tax Center page.

Viewing payroll tax forms

Quarterly, you must complete and submit a federal payroll tax return by using Form 941, which identifies the total wages you paid, when you paid them, and the total taxes you withheld and deposited with appropriate taxing authorities throughout the quarter. The IRS permits you to file the form electronically or to mail it. If you connect your bank account, QuickBooks Payroll automatically files these returns for you. When you click Filings on the Payroll Tax Center page, the reports you need to prepare and submit appear.

TIP

If you live in a state that imposes a personal income tax, you typically also must file a similar form for your state; check your state's website for the rules you need to follow for payroll tax reporting. Your state probably has a state unemployment form that you need to prepare and submit as well.

Paying Contractors

In this section, I focus on setting up 1099-eligible contractors, paying them (without using direct deposit), reporting on 1099 payments you've made, and preparing 1099s for your contractors who need them. You don't need to change anything if you've already set up a contractor as a vendor. The contractor list just makes it easier to identify the contractors you work with and pay them if you opt for an Intuit service that I mention later in this chapter.

Paying contractors is generally a straightforward experience. You can wait until you receive a bill from a contractor, enter it, and then pay it, as described in Chapter 8 if you have an Essentials, Plus, or Advanced subscription. QuickBooks Simple Start users can't enter bills, but they can write checks to pay contractors. Either way, you need to ensure that contractors are set up as vendors who will receive Form 1099-NEC. I call these folks 1099-eligible contractors going forward. Previously, nonemployee compensation was reported in Box 7 of Form 1099-MISC.

I use the term *1099-eligible* because if you hire someone as a contractor but don't pay that person at least $600 — the threshold established by the IRS — technically, you don't have to produce a 1099 for that contractor. Further, if you don't pay a contractor more than $600, QuickBooks doesn't show payments to that contractor on certain reports.

1099-eligible contractors are people who work for you but who aren't your employees. Specifically, the IRS distinguishes between 1099-eligible contractors and employees based on whether you, the employer, have the means and methods of accomplishing the work or simply have the right to control and direct the result of the work. If you have the means and methods to accomplish the work, the person who works for you is an employee, not an independent 1099-eligible contractor. If you're at all uncertain, ask your accountant, or visit `https://quickbooks.intuit.com/find-an-accountant/` to engage an expert.

If you use QuickBooks Payroll, you can pay contractors (as well as employees) via direct deposit for a fee of $5 per contractor per month after you complete the direct-deposit setup for your company's payroll subscription. To set up a contractor as a direct-deposit recipient, choose Workers ⇨ Contractors. Click Check It Out, and follow the onscreen directions to add a contractor's banking information. Keep in mind that it may be far less expensive to add ACH capabilities to your bank account and pay contractors directly unless you have only one or two contractors you want to pay this way. Or you can subscribe to Contractor Payments for $15/month to pay up to 20 contractors, plus another $2/month for each additional contractor you add. All plans include 1099 e-filing.

Setting up 1099-eligible contractors

You can set up 1099-eligible contractors in two ways, with the same result:

» You can use the information in Chapter 3 to set up a new vendor. Make sure that you select the Track Payments for 1099 checkbox.

» You can use the Contractors page to set up a contractor. Any contractor you add from this page becomes a 1099-eligible contractor.

Follow these steps to create a contractor (as opposed to a vendor):

1. **Choose Payroll ⇨ Contractors.**

   The Contractors page appears.

2. **Click the Add Your First Contractor button.**

3. **Provide the contractor's name, and if you want the contractor to complete their profile, enter their email address.**

If you provide the contractor's email address, Intuit contacts the contractor and gets their 1099 information for you, including the contractor's signature on the W-9 form that the IRS requires you to keep on file. Intuit uses the form information to populate the contractor's record and leaves a PDF of the W-9 form for you on the Contractors page (Documents section).

4. **Click Add Contractor.**

The contractor's details page appears.

5. **Click Add (or Waiting for Info if you opted to send the contractor an email) to provide details about the contractor type.**

This information is used when you prepare 1099s for the year.

6. **Click Save.**

The contractor's details page appears again, showing the details you just provided.

Paying contractors

You can pay contractors the same way you pay any other vendors; see Chapter 3 for details on expense transactions and checks, or Chapter 8 for entering and paying bills. As noted elsewhere in this chapter, you must have a QuickBooks Online Essentials, Plus, or Advanced subscription if you want to enter contractor bills to pay later. You can use check or expense transactions in any version of QuickBooks to make an immediate payment.

Alternatively, if you opt into one of QuickBooks Payroll or Contractor subscriptions that offers direct deposit, you can choose Payroll ⇨ Contractors ⇨ Pay Contractor to display a page that enables you to pay all contractors from a single screen.

Filing 1099 Forms for Contractors

At the end of each calendar year, the Internal Revenue Service expects you to provide an accounting of every person you've paid $600 or more to during that period. QuickBooks makes the process relatively painless, albeit for a $15/month fee for the Contractor Payments subscription, which enables you to pay up to 20 contractors by direct deposit, plus $2 for each additional contractor, and includes e-filing of 1099 forms.

Reviewing your vendor list

As the end of each year approaches, review your vendor list and make sure you've tagged all the vendors who should receive a 1099 form. The IRS takes these information returns seriously, and in 2024 can charge the following penalties for each 1099 that's filed late or not at all:

>> **Up to 30 days late:** $60

>> **31 days late through August 1:** $120

>> **After August 1 or not filed:** $310

>> **Intentional disregard:** $630

As the saying goes, the best defense is a strong offense, so here's how to review your vendor list to determine which should receive 1099s. This is going to be a bit of a ride because the New Enhanced Experience version of the report is far from enhanced, and in fact you have to return to Classic View to get to the information you need.

REMEMBER

QuickBooks reclassifies vendors whom you click the Track 1099 checkbox for within their vendor record as contractors. Such vendors still appear on your vendor list, as do contractors you set up through the Contractors command.

Here's how to audit your vendor list to identify contractors who have missing information and to identify vendors you should classify as contractors:

1. **Choose Reports⇨Reports.**

The Reports page appears.

2. **Use the Search box to find the Vendor Contact List report.**

You can also find this report in the Expenses and Vendors section.

3. **Click Switch to Classic View.**

We need to add two columns to this report: Track 1099 and Tax ID. In a perfect world, you would click Customize, scroll down the list, and click the icons for Track 1099 and Tax ID. Unfortunately, only the Track 1099 field is available on the list. A crucial aspect of a 1099 audit is to ensure that the Tax ID, meaning Federal ID or Social Security Number, has been entered for every vendor who should receive a 1099.

REMEMBER

A secondary part of a 1099 audit is to look at every vendor and determine if the Track 1099 checkbox should be turned on if it currently isn't.

4. **Click the Settings button in the upper-right corner of the report and then click Show More.**

   This enables you to add columns to the report.

5. **Click the checkboxes for Track 1099 and Tax ID, and then click anywhere on the report to close the Settings dialog box.**

   Track 1099 and Tax ID columns should now appear.

TIP

In Chapter 20, I discuss how you can export reports like this to Excel and then use Filter to display only records where Track 1099 is set to Yes. This makes for an easy way to identify any missing Tax IDs. However, you still need to do a line-by-line review of your vendors to identify any that should have the Track 1099 checkbox turned on within their vendor record.

REMEMBER

The Track 1099 field is automatically selected for all contractors who also appear on the Vendor Contact List, so you at least get a two-for-one with regard to reviewing contractors and vendors in one fell swoop.

Preparing 1099s

Typically, you prepare 1099s each January. Here's how to start the process:

1. **Choose Taxes⇨1099 Filings.**

   The Get Ready to File Your 1099 Forms page appears. It's not quite as fun as hearing "The ice cream truck is coming!" but hey, we're talking about filing a tax form.

2. **Click the button to start or continue your 1099s.**

   Confirm that all information is correct on the Review Your Company Info, and then click Next.

3. **Click the pencil icon for any section where you need to add or edit information.**

4. **Map your accounts (notice how suddenly QuickBooks refers to them as accounts instead of categories) to the 1099 form.**

   Typically, you click the Non-Employee Compensation checkbox and then choose the accounts(s) where you've posted expenses that should be reported on Form 1099. You may need to click the checkbox for Rents and do the same, as well as for any of the items in the Other Payments or Federal Tax Withheld sections, and then click Next.

TIP

If you suddenly feel an overwhelming sense of dread, click Save and Finish Later. This may be an indication that you're best served by outsourcing this task, and perhaps other bookkeeping tasks, to an accountant. This page is a great place to start: `https://quickbooks.intuit.com/find-an-accountant/`.

5. **The next page displays all contractors. It includes vendors you've clicked the Track 1099 checkbox for within their Vendor profile. Click Next once you've completed your review.**

    Such vendors are automatically reclassified as contractors by QuickBooks. Don't worry; any such vendors still appear on the Vendor list, as do any contractors you add to QuickBooks by way of the Contractors menu.

6. **Check that the Payments Add Up page appears and enables you to review the contractors who were paid $600 or more.**

    The list shows you contractors who met the criteria for needing a 1099, but you can filter the list two other ways:

    - Show 1099 Contractors Below Threshold

    - Show Contractors Not Marked for 1099

    The second choice presents all vendors on your vendor list who aren't currently flagged as 1099 vendors. You can click the vendor name to display their record and change their 1099 status, if needed.

7. **Once you've completed your review, click Finish Preparing 1099s to get to the page where you're walked through the filing or printing process.**

    If you've missed the e-filing window for a given year, QuickBooks enables you to print your 1099s on preprinted forms that you can purchase online or find at most office supply stores. You may also order up to a hundred 1099 forms from the IRS at `www.irs.gov/businesses/online-ordering-for-information-returns-and-employer-returns`. Then you need to submit the paper copies through the U.S. Postal Service.

Chapter **5**

Carrying Out Banking and Account Reconciliations

I n this chapter, I show you not only how to set up bank and credit card accounts in QuickBooks but also how to reconcile bank and credit card accounts. If you're wondering how to record credit card transactions in QuickBooks, see Chapter 3; you record credit card transactions in the same fashion as you record expense transactions that post to your bank account.

Establishing Bank or Credit Card Accounts

In Chapter 1, I discuss adding new accounts to your chart of accounts, which QuickBooks sometimes confusingly refers to as categories. The steps for adding a bank or credit card are similar to creating a revenue or expense account but have an extra tweak of requiring you to enter an opening balance. Here's how to add an account to your chart of accounts:

1. **Click the New button on the Chart of Accounts page to open the New Account task pane, shown in Figure 5-1.**

2. **Choose Banks or Credit Cards at the top.**

3. **Select either Bank Accounts or Credit Cards from the Save Account Under list.**

WARNING

   If you choose an account name from this list, rather than Bank Accounts or Credit Card Accounts, then your new account will be a sub-account of the parent account that you chose. However, you can turn off the sub-account status by editing the account, which I discuss in the next section.

4. **Specify a tax form section.**

   Depending on the choice you make in Step 3, this field may default to an appropriate value, or you may have to select from the list.

5. **Enter an account name.**

   You can use up to 100 characters to describe your bank account. Folks who have more than one bank account at a bank sometimes like to include the last four digits of the bank account in the description so that they can distinguish one from the other.

6. **Optional: Enter a description.**

   Describe the account further here if you want.

7. **Expand the Starting Date and Opening Balances section.**

8. **Choose an option from the Date to Start Tracking This Account in QuickBooks list.**

   Always defer to your accountant or bookkeeper if you're unclear how to answer a question like this. Options include Beginning of the Year, Beginning of This Month, Today, and Other, which allows you to specify any date you want. Make sure to choose a date that coincides with the day after your bank statement. For instance, if you're going to use your 12/31/2023 bank statement as your opening balance, choose Beginning of This Year if the current calendar year is 2024.

9. **Enter the account balance from your bank statement.**

   Enter the ending balance from your bank statement, which should be one day prior to the date you entered in Step 8.

10. **Click Save.**

    QuickBooks redisplays the Chart of Accounts page, and your new account appears in the list.

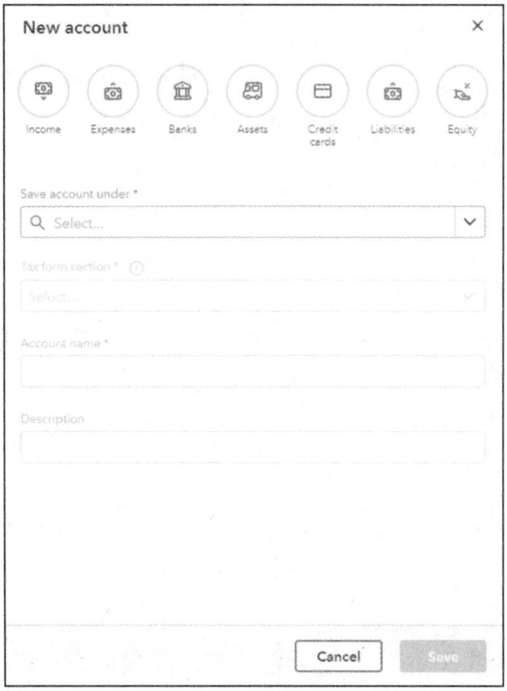

FIGURE 5-1:
The task pane
you use to create
an account.

Making a Bank Deposit

In Chapter 2, I discuss using the Payments to Deposit (or Undeposited Funds) account to record payments from customers. I strongly recommend that you use that when you record Receive Payment transactions as well. As you may surmise from the name, Payments to Deposit is simply a stopover along the way to your bank account. To create a bank deposit transaction, follow these steps:

1. **Choose + New ➪ Bank Deposit.**

    The Bank Deposit transaction window appears, as shown in Figure 5-2. Existing payment transactions appear in the Select the Payments Included in This Deposit section. You can use the lines in the Add Funds to This Deposit to add new payment transactions that aren't associated with an outstanding invoice, such as refund checks, reimbursement payments, the check for $1.63 that you received from a class-action lawsuit settlement, and so on.

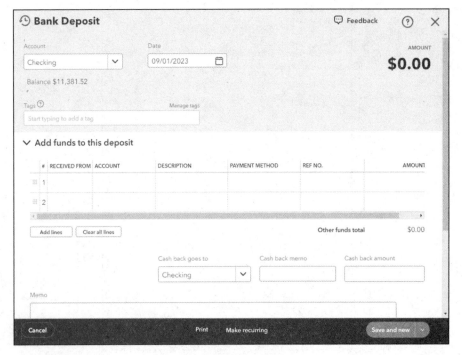

FIGURE 5-2:
The Bank Deposit
page does not
include the Select
Payments to
Include in This
Deposit section
unless you have
entered one or
more Receive
Payment or Sales
Receipt
transactions.

WARNING

Although it may look tempting to do so, do not record invoice payments from customers in the Add Funds to This Deposit section. Instead, create a Receive Payment transaction (which I discussed in Chapter 2). A new section titled Select the Payments Included in This Deposit will appear on the Bank Deposit page. Recording a customer payment in the Add Funds to This Deposit section doesn't mark the invoice as paid, which inflates your accounts receivable balance and means you may annoy your customer by trying to collect payment from the customer a second time.

2. **Choose the bank account into which you plan to deposit the payments, using the From Account drop-down list at the top of the window.**

3. **Select each transaction you want to include in the deposit in the Select the Payments Included in This Deposit section.**

4. **Optional: Specify a payment method for each transaction you intend to deposit.**

TIP

Intuit Payments automatically posts deposits in a QuickBooks Payments section, which is collapsed by default for the benefit of users who don't rely on that service. If you have your own merchant account, credit card transaction receipts may be deposited in your bank account as often as daily. Make sure to record a separate deposit for each day so that the amounts mirror what's hitting your physical bank account. Then create a separate deposit to group any checks and cash payments into a bank deposit.

5. **Optional: Enter a memo and a reference number.**

   The total of the selected payments — and the amount you intend to deposit unless you add entries in the Add Funds to This Deposit section — appears below the Select the Payments Included in This Deposit list.

6. **Optional: Add any or all of the following:**

   - Memo for the deposit transaction itself, which is an additional level of documentation you can add apart from the memo field available on each line of the transaction.

   - Cash-back amount, account, and memo.

   - An attachment, such as a scanned copy of the paper deposit ticket. To do so, click in the Attachments box and navigate to the document, or drag the electronic copy into the Attachments box.

TIP

   Each attachment must be no more than 20MB in size, and one of the following document types: CSV, DOC, GIF, JPEG, PDF, PNG, TIFF, XLSX, or XML.

7. **Click Save and Close.**

   The Payments to Deposit (or Undeposited Funds) account balance is reduced by any checks you chose in this deposit. Payments to Deposit has a zero balance whenever you've deposited all the checks you have in hand.

All that's left to do is to take a trip to the bank. Or, if you're mobile-savvy, ask your banker whether you can deposit checks remotely via your mobile device or via a check scanner.

Synchronizing with Financial Institutions

What does it mean to synchronize your QuickBooks accounts with a financial institution? The activity that posts to a bank or credit card is automatically entered into your books, which greatly simplifies your reconciliation process. Ideally, you can connect directly, but if your bank doesn't offer a direct integration with QuickBooks, you can manually import transactions by way of QuickBooks Web Connect or by importing transactions stored in a Microsoft Excel or Google Docs file.

TIP

See Chapters 2, 3, and 4 for details on entering transactions that affect a bank or credit card account. You typically use an Expense transaction to record credit card purchases and a Credit Card Credit transaction to record refunds to a credit card. You can also use the Pay Down Credit Card transaction to record payments you make to reduce your credit card balances.

REMEMBER

You must set up your bank and credit card accounts in QuickBooks *before* you can connect to your financial institution.

Connecting directly with your bank

Use the following steps to connect your bank or credit card account directly to QuickBooks. Before you get started, make sure you have a few minutes to allow the transactions time to download. Because QuickBooks downloads recent transactions as part of the connection process, it can take some time. It doesn't offer a meaningful progress indicator, so it's hard to forecast exactly how long the initial download will take.

1. **Choose Transactions ➪ Bank Transactions.**

    A Connect Account button appears if you haven't connected any accounts yet.

You create faster access to this page by clicking Edit next to the Menu or Bookmarks headings in the sidebar. Choose Bank Transactions from Bookmarks list, and then click Save to create one-click access to your Bank Transactions page. If you change your mind later, return to the Bookmarks tab, clear the Bank Transactions checkbox, and then click Save.

Before you get further into the process, retrieve your online banking credentials from your password manager so that you have the information handy. Personally, I am a fan of 1Password (https://1password.com/), and millions of other users rely on Dashlane (www.dashlane.com). I no longer recommend LastPass (www.lastpass.com) due to repeated hacking incidents.

There are no perfect solutions when it comes to internet security, so there is always risk involved in storing all your passwords in one place. However, I contend that there is *much greater risk* in not using a password manager at all. Identity thieves make hay from users that reuse the same password across multiple platforms. Unlike the other two platforms that I recommend, LastPass was guilty of storing certain user information, including passwords, in an unencrypted form. 1Password has integrated two-factor authentication into their product, which means logging into sensitive platforms is much more secure and easier than having a verification code emailed or texted to you.

I resisted using password management software for far too long. One day, I was struggling to remember a password when the guy I was meeting with said, "My password manager software saves me so much time." I heard that advice at the right moment, and writing this reminds me that I need to get my two teenagers set up on a password manager as well. You do have a choice: reusing passwords on more than one site, which is a huge identity-theft risk, or using a password manager to have unique and complex passwords for each site that you need to log into, which includes QuickBooks. You install the password manager app on each of your devices and then create a passphrase to serve as a master key. You'll be shocked at the number of sites you're logging into once you have them all in one list.

2. **Choose a logo from the list if your financial institution is one of the eight choices; otherwise, type a name in the Search box and then select a match from the list.**

When I searched on one of my banks, QuickBooks returned 9,869 choices until I removed the word *Bank* from my search. That narrowed the list to 141 choices. The list shows the website address for each bank to ensure that you're making the correct choice.

Don't worry if you can't find your bank on the list or if you have any trepidation about connecting QuickBooks to your financial institution. First, it's a one-way feed, meaning *their* transactions come into *your* books, not the other way around. See the section "Connecting indirectly to your financial institution" later in this chapter if you want or need an alternative to a direct connection.

3. **Follow the onscreen instructions, which vary.**

   You may be directed to go to your bank's website and sign in, after which you're returned to the connection process. Or if you're connecting to PayPal, you're walked through a three-step process.

   You may have to prove your "nonrobotness" by way of a reCAPTCHA. Who doesn't like looking for stoplights in grainy photos? Fortunately, this method is falling out of favor, so you may be prompted instead to authorize an OAuth connection. Just follow the onscreen prompts.

   If all goes as expected, a new page displays the accounts you have at the financial institution and lets you choose which ones you want to connect to QuickBooks.

4. **Choose the accounts you want to connect.**

   For each account you choose, QuickBooks asks you to select an existing Bank or Credit Card account or create a new account. QuickBooks also asks you how far in the past you want to pull transactions for the account. Depending on your bank, options may include Today, This Month, This Year, or Last Year, or you may be able to specify a custom range.

5. **Click Connect, and then wait while your accounts download.**

   The Connect button is disabled until you select an account, specify a type, and choose a date range for downloading transactions.

6. **Follow any additional onscreen prompts you see to finish setting up the account.**

The automatic download of transactions is only the first phase of the process; you must still review and accept the transactions, which I discuss in the "Reviewing Bank and Credit Card Transactions" section later in this chapter.

In Chapter 7, I discuss how you can use the Rules feature to automatically process transactions as they are synchronized with your books.

Facilitating indirect banking connections

You can manually import your banking and credit card transactions if your bank doesn't support direct connections or if you have discomfort about setting up such a connection. Ideally, you'll be able to download a QuickBooks Web Connect file, but as long as you can download the transactions to an Excel spreadsheet or text file, you can then transform the data into a format that QuickBooks will enable you to upload. The end result is the same automatic synchronization, assuming that you're willing to carry out the necessary repetitive actions.

Do not use a public computer to download Web Connect or transaction files from your bank. The files are not encrypted and contain sensitive information about your bank or credit card account. Deleted files are not ever truly deleted on your computer until other data has been saved over that location.

Follow these steps to download transactions from your financial institution:

1. **Log in to your financial institution's website and look for a link that enables you to download to QuickBooks or to a text file.**

   Some websites have a Download button associated with each account, whereas others offer a Download to QuickBooks or CSV/TXT link. Others may offer a QuickBooks Web Connect link. If you can't find a link, odds are that your financial institution doesn't offer this functionality, but check with the customer service department to make sure.

   If you can't download the transactions, try copying and pasting your banking activity into a Microsoft Excel workbook or Google Sheets spreadsheet and then carry out the instructions in the "Processing Non-Standard Download Files" section. You truly can get there from here.

2. **Select any of the following file formats that your financial institution offers:**

   - QBO (QuickBooks)
   - QFX (Quicken)
   - OFX (Microsoft Money)
   - Any file format that references QuickBooks or QuickBooks Online
   - CSV (comma-separated value file)
   - TXT (tab-delimited text file)

   I've listed these files in priority order, meaning you should always choose one of the first four types if available so you don't have to edit the file. The last two types are last-resort options that may require some editing before you can import them into QuickBooks.

3. **Specify a date range for the transactions you want to download.**

   The account's opening balance changes if you download transactions with dates that precede the opening balance, so double-check the dates you choose here, and don't go too far back in time.

4. **If prompted, save the file to a location on your computer where you can find it later.**

   The file will appear in your Downloads folder if you're not given a choice to save the file in a specific location.

   If you downloaded a Web Connect file, which includes QuickBooks (QBO), Quicken (QFX), or Microsoft Money (OFX) files, skip ahead to the "Uploading Web Connect and CSV files" section. Otherwise, read on to see the hopefully minor changes you may have to make to the text file that you download.

Opening non-standard download files

If you have your transactions in an electronic form, such as a CSV or TXT file from your financial institution, you need to transform the data into a format that QuickBooks will allow you to upload. You can skip over this next part if your data is already in an Excel workbook — for instance, you were able to download that format, or copy and paste into it. If not, and you have a text file on your hands, here's how to get the data to appear in Microsoft Excel:

1. **Choose File ⇨ Open.**
2. **Change the File Type field to Text Files.**
3. **Browse to the folder where your CSV or TXT file resides, select the file, and then click Open.**

Meanwhile, in Google Sheets, you do this instead:

1. **Create a blank spreadsheet.**
2. **Choose File ⇨ Import ⇨ Upload.**
3. **Click Select a File from Your Device, browse for the file, and then click Open.**
4. **Make a choice from the Import Location list, and then click Import Data.**
5. **Change the File Type field to Text Files.**
6. **Browse to the folder where your CSV or TXT file resides, select the file, and then click Open.**

Read on to see how to edit your text file to conform to what QuickBooks expects.

Transforming the transaction files

You can upload your transactions into QuickBooks if you can rearrange the data into the three or four columns formats shown in Tables 5-1 and 5-2. You need to save the data to a text file format, but let's build out the format first. What's key is to create a single row of titles and specify the column headings shown. The order of the columns itself does not matter.

REMEMBER

Keep in mind that these columns are the minimum required. QuickBooks ignores any extraneous columns, so don't obsess about making the file just so. What you do need is a single row of titles and the columns shown here. The order doesn't matter.

TABLE 5-1   **An Acceptable Three-Column Format**

Date	Description	Amount
1/1/2025	Example check, fee, or credit card charge	–100.00
1/1/2025	Example deposit or credit card payment	200.00

TABLE 5-2   **An Acceptable Four-Column Format**

Date	Description	Debit	Credit
1/1/2025	Example check, fee, or credit card charge	200.00	
1/1/2025	Example deposit or credit card payment		100.00

REMEMBER

Deductions from your bank account need to be listed as negative amounts in the three-column format and as positive amounts in the Debit column of the four-column format. Credit card charges need to be formatted in this same fashion. Conversely, bank deposits and refunds posted to your credit card account need to be entered as positive amounts in the three-column format and credits in the four-column format. If this feels counterintuitive, remember the bank reports your transactions from their perspective rather than yours.

In either case, edit the spreadsheet to conform with the format in Tables 5-1 or 5-2 by adding or removing columns. Remember, QuickBooks ignores any additional columns beyond the minimum requirements.

FLIPPING THE SIGN ON NUMBERS

You can use spreadsheet formulas to flip positive numbers to negative or vice versa. Here are two approaches:

Microsoft Excel: Enter **–1** in a blank worksheet cell, such as cell E1. Select cell E1 and then choose Home ⇨ Copy. Next, select the numbers that you want to flip the sign on and then choose Home ⇨ Paste ⇨ Paste Special ⇨ Multiply ⇨ OK.

Google Sheets: Let's say that column C contains positive amounts that you want to make negative. If the first amount appears in cell C2, enter **–C2** in any blank cell, such as D2, and then copy the formula down as many rows as needed. Select and then copy the formulas from Column D and choose Edit ⇨ Paste Special ⇨ Values Only. At this point, you can delete column D or erase the worksheet cells to avoid confusion.

You must resolve three special situations before saving your text file:

>> **Amounts:** Make sure your transaction amounts are positive or negative or appear in the proper columns, meaning Debit or Credit, as shown in the tables.

>> **Date formats:** Make sure the date column only contains dates as opposed to dates and times. Let's say that cell A2 contains 01/01/2025 08:00 AM. In Microsoft Excel, you can enter **=ROUND(A2,0)** in a blank cell, such as E2, and then copy the formula down. You can then copy the formulas in Column D, choose Home ⇨ Paste ⇨ Paste Special ⇨ Values, and then click OK. You can use this same formula in Google Sheets and use the Paste Special method described for amounts.

WARNING

Dates within spreadsheets are serial numbers that represent the number of days that have elapsed since December 31, 1899. That means that 1/1/2025 may appear as 45,658 instead. If so, in Excel, select the date serial numbers and then choose Home ⇨ Format ⇨ Format Cells, select a date format from the Date section of the Number tab, and then click OK. In Google Sheets, choose Format ⇨ Number ⇨ Date. QuickBooks rejects dates that appear as serial numbers as opposed to formatted dates.

>> **Splitting columns:** You can remove extraneous text by splitting description or memo columns and then discarding the extraneous text. Copy the data in question to an unused area of your spreadsheet and then select the cells. Choose Data ⇨ Text to Columns in Microsoft Excel, and then work through the wizard, or choose Data ⇨ Split Text into Columns in Google Sheets, and then select or enter a separator from the list that appears.

The next step is to save your work ss a comma-separated value (CSV) file.

Saving comma-separated value (CSV) files

A comma-separated value (CSV) file is simply a text file that has a comma between each field. This format is an alternative to the Web Connect formats that do not require any transformation.

Here's how to save your three- or four-column format as a CSV file in Microsoft Excel:

1. **Choose File ⇨ Save As.**

2. **Change the File Type field to CSV (Comma Delimited).**

3. **Browse to the location where you want to save the file, and then click Save.**

   Make sure you choose a location you can remember because you'll be choosing this file in QuickBooks.

4. **Choose File ⇨ Close.**

   This step is crucial to a successful upload. First, it ensures that your changes are saved. Second, your operating system may lock open files and prevent you from uploading.

To save the CSV format in Google Sheets, use these steps:

1. **Choose File ⇨ Download ⇨ Comma Separated Values (.csv).**

2. **Browse to the location where you want to save the file, and then click Save.**

   Make sure you choose a location you can remember because you'll be choosing this file in QuickBooks.

3. **Choose File ⇨ Close.**

   It's not as crucial to close a Google Sheets spreadsheet as it is in Excel but doing so ensures that you don't make any changes onscreen that aren't in the copy you downloaded.

WARNING

Don't be fooled by QuickBooks' assertion that you can upload TXT files. Most TXT files use tab-delimited or fixed-width formats, although you can certainly save a comma-separated value file with a .TXT file extension.

You're now ready to upload your transactions to QuickBooks.

Uploading your transactions into QuickBooks

At this point you should either have a Web Connect file — meaning a .QBO, .QFX, or .OFX file — in hand or a .CSV file that you have formatted in either the three or four column formats described earlier in this section. Here's how to upload:

1. **In QuickBooks choose Transactions⇨ Banking Transactions.**

   The Bank Transactions page appears.

2. **Click Upload Transactions or else click the Link Account drop-down menu and choose Upload from File.**

   The Import Bank Transactions page appears.

3. **Click the Select Files link, and then browse and select your transaction file.**

4. **Click Continue in the bottom-right corner.**

   Depending upon your screen resolution you may need to scroll the Import Bank Transactions page down to locate the Continue button.

5. **On the next page, select the bank or credit card account where the transactions should appear, and then click Continue.**

   Your transactions are imported, which may take seconds or minutes, depending on the speed of your internet connection and the number of transactions you're importing.

6. **At this point, the steps differ between Web Connect and CSV files.**

   - **Web Connect:** Click Done and move on to Step 7.

   - **CSV file:** The Let's Set Up Your File in QuickBooks screen appears. From here, you do the following:

     (a) Confirm if the first row of your file is a header.

     (b) Indicate whether your file has one amount column or two.

     (c) Select a date format.

     (d) If needed, map the columns in your CSV file to the corresponding QuickBooks fields.

     (e) Click Continue.

(f) Click Yes to confirm that you want to import the transactions.

In some cases, QuickBooks shows you the list of transactions and allows you to pick which ones you want to import. In other cases, a simple confirmation prompt appears.

(g) Click Done.

7. **You're now ready to review and accept the transactions by following the instructions in the next section, "Reviewing Your Bank and Credit Card Transactions."**

Always delete Web Connect files after importing them because they contain sensitive information about your financial accounts that anyone who gains access to the file can view.

When you import transactions from a CSV file, the bank balance in QuickBooks may be reported as zero. Don't panic! This simply means that the balance amount isn't available in the CSV file.

Customizing your Bank Transactions page

Any accounts to which you've uploaded or downloaded activity appear as connected accounts on the Banking Transactions page. You determine the schedule for files that you upload, whereas QuickBooks typically downloads activity from your financial institution nightly, but your financial institution controls the pace of any updates.

You can control the following aspects of the transaction listing on the Banking page by clicking the Settings button above the Action column. Available customizations include:

>> Displaying or hiding the following fields:

- Check numbers

- Payee names

- Tags

- Bank details

- Class names (Plus or Advanced companies only)

- Location names (Plus or Advanced companies only)

>> Grouping transactions by month

>> Viewing 50, 75, 100, or 300 transactions per page

>> Displaying a single Amounts column or separate Spent and Received columns.

>> Making the Date field editable.

>> Copying bank detail information into the Memo field.

>> Suggesting categories (meaning accounts from your chart of accounts) based upon your past transaction history.

REMEMBER

You can also adjust the column widths with the transaction list. Any adjustments you make are a sticky preference that will be remembered going forward.

Reviewing Your Bank and Credit Card Transactions

Your bank and credit card transactions do not post directly to your books but rather land in a holding area, where you must explicitly accept the transactions. This is the same for direct feeds from your bank, where the synchronization is automated, and for indirect feeds, where you manually upload the transactions into QuickBooks.

Accordingly, here are the steps you'll need to carry out on an ongoing basis to match, exclude, or add bank and credit card transactions:

1. **Choose Transactions ⇨ Banking Transactions.**

   The Banking Transactions page appears.

2. **Choose a bank or credit card account to display any related transactions you need to review.**

   Three tabs appear just below your account(s).

   - **For Review:** Unreviewed transactions that await your attention.

   - **Categorized:** Transactions that you've reviewed and accepted or confirmed, either manually or by way of a rule. I discuss rules in Chapter 7.

   - **Excluded:** Transactions that you've opted not to post to your books at the present time. You can select one or more transactions and choose Undo to return the transactions to the For Review list, or you can choose Delete to remove the transactions from QuickBooks.

TIP

Note that the Delete command doesn't ask you if you're sure, so think twice before clicking Delete. See the section "Facilitating indirect banking connections" earlier in this chapter if you inadvertently delete transactions directly downloaded into QuickBooks. You may be able to recover what you deleted by manually downloading the transactions from your financial institution again and then uploading them into QuickBooks.

3. **QuickBooks automatically classifies as many transactions as it can, based on built-in rules that you can override with your own specifications.**

   (a) **When you select one transaction at a time, you can use the following commands:**

   - **Accept (or Confirm):** Accepts the category/account that QuickBooks assigned the transaction to and posts the transaction to your books.

   - **View (Review, or click on the transaction):** Displays a page from which you can do the following:

     - Choose the Categorize radio button to change the vendor/customer, category, location, class, tags, or memo.

     - Choose the Find Match radio button to view potential matches or search for other matches.

     - Choose the Record As Transfer radio button to select an offsetting account for the transfer.

     - Add an attachment, such as a PDF copy of a receipt.

     - Create a rule, which I discuss in Chapter 7.

TIP

     - QuickBooks may ask if you want to create a rule to automatically apply the transactions in the future. Click Don't Show Me This Again if you don't want QuickBooks to suggest creating rules.

     - Exclude a transaction so that it doesn't post to your books.

     - View the categorization history for similar transactions when you choose the Categorize option.

     - Split a transaction that you're categorizing among two or more categories.

   (b) **When you select two or more transactions on the list (using the checkboxes along the left), you can then confirm, update, or exclude them.**

   - **Confirm:** Accepts the transactions, which means that they post to your books and appear on the Categorized tab.

- **Update:** Displays the Update Selected dialog box.

- **Exclude:** Moves the transactions to the Excluded tab. As noted previously, you can later select one or more transactions and choose Undo to move transactions back to the For Review tab, or you can delete the transactions.

4. **Keep working the list until you've reviewed all transactions.**

   You may be able to speed up the process by making one of the following choices from the All Transactions filter:

   - **Recognized:** View transactions that have been recognized. (You updated the category manually.)

   - **Matched:** See transactions in which a match was made between the transaction downloaded from your financial institution and your accounting records.

   - **Transferred:** See transactions that are deemed to be a transfer between accounts, such as a credit card payment, or a transfer of funds between two bank accounts.

   - **Rule Applied:** View transactions that are automatically updated by a rule, which I discuss in Chapter 7.

   - **Missing Payee/Customer:** See a list of transactions for which the payee or customer can't be identified.

   - **Unassigned:** View a list of transactions that have a status other than Add and haven't been processed yet.

Reconciling Bank or Credit Card Accounts

Some people's least-favorite task is reconciling their bank statement, but I like knowing that my books are aligned with my bank; it's a great way to avoid surprises. I'm not a fan of reconciling credit card statements, but I guess it's important to face the music. Fortunately, if you're diligent about entering transactions in QuickBooks and recording bank deposits and credit card payments as described in the preceding section, then reconciling your bank or credit card statement should be a fairly easy process. Grab your most recent statement, and follow these steps:

1. **Choose Settings ⇨ Reconcile from the Tools section.**

   Make sure you click the Settings button and not the + New button.

2. Select the account you want to reconcile.

The fields related to recording service charges and interest don't appear for accounts you've connected to your bank because this information downloads automatically.

You may see a Get Started button that you can click to view a summary, road map–style, of the reconciliation process. At the end of the wizard, click Let's Get Reconciled to continue and display the page.

3. Enter the ending date and balance from your statement and click the Start Reconciling button.

The Reconcile page appears.

Enter bank and credit card balances so they're the same as the balance on your credit card statement. For example, if the bank says you owe $750 on your credit card, enter **$750** in the Ending Balance field. However, if you overpaid and your credit card statement reports a balance of –$125, enter **–125** as the ending balance. Typically, you always enter a positive number for your bank account balance — that is, unless you're reconciling an overdrawn or overpaid account.

Click the Edit Info button if you need to return to the initial screen to correct your ending bank balance or to record a service charge or interest. Click Save to return to the reconciliation window.

4. Select each transaction that appears in your statement and on the Reconcile page by clicking the rightmost column.

Paychecks divided between two bank accounts show up as two distinct transactions in QuickBooks, so they should be easy to match up during reconciliation.

By selecting a transaction, you're marking it as having cleared the bank. Your goal is to have the Difference amount at the top-right corner of the Reconcile page equal $0. If your account is connected to your bank, many transactions might already display a checkmark in the rightmost column because the transactions have been downloaded from the bank and matched with your accounting records, as I discussed in the "Synchronizing with Financial Institutions" section earlier in this chapter.

By default, the Reconciliation page displays all uncleared transactions dated before the statement ending date, but you can click Payments or Deposits to filter by either of those options, like the way most bank statements are organized. Any transactions with dates later than the statement ending date are hidden by default. If, after you select all the transactions you see, the Difference amount isn't $0, click the X next to Statement Ending Date to look for additional transactions to mark as cleared. You can also take advantage of the Filter icon (which looks like a funnel) to limit the transactions in a way that works best for you. Be sure to compare the total payments and deposits with the corresponding numbers on the bank statement. This comparison can help you determine whether deposits or payments are missing.

TIP

You can click the Bank Register or Credit Card Register link in the top-left corner of the page to view the register for the account you're reconciling. When you finish viewing the register, click the Reconcile button in the top-right corner of the register page. If you want to see more transactions on the reconciliation page, click the upward-pointing arrow to collapse the header.

5. **Click the Finish Now button when the Difference equals $0, as shown in Figure 5-3.**

A Success message gives you the opportunity to view the Reconciliation report by clicking the View Reconciliation Report link. The Reconciliation report is broken into a summary section and a detail section that lists all transactions you cleared.

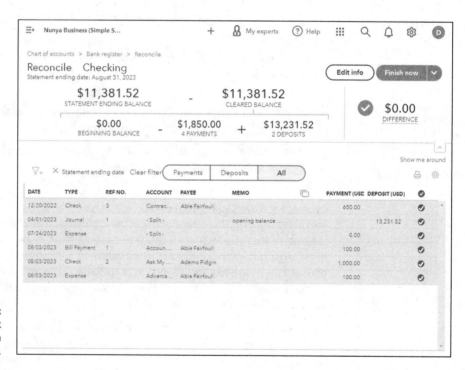

FIGURE 5-3:
The Bank
Reconciliation
page.

REMEMBER

You don't have to finish your reconciliation in a single sitting. Click the drop-down arrow on the Finish Now button and then choose Save for Later if you get interrupted or you simply can't get the reconciliation to zero out. Returning with a fresh eye can often make discrepancies jump off the screen. You can also choose Close Without Saving if you want to abandon the entire process.

TIP

There's an age-old bookkeeping trick that calls for dividing the unreconciled difference by 9. If it divides cleanly, the chances are exceedingly high that your difference is caused by a transposition. For instance, if your unreconciled difference is $90, you may have entered $450 when you should have entered $540 for a transaction.

WHEN THE OPENING BALANCE DOESN'T MATCH THE STATEMENT

It happens sometimes. You go to reconcile an account, and its opening balance doesn't match the ending balance of the previous reconciliation period. You need to fix the beginning balance before you can reconcile the account.

Good news: QuickBooks provides a tool that helps you fix the problem. This tool is in the form of a Reconciliation Discrepancy report, which lists transactions associated with the erroneous beginning balance. When you select an account to reconcile that has a beginning-balance problem, a prompt identifies the amount by which the account beginning balance is off and offers a Let's Resolve This Discrepancy link. Click the link to display a Reconciliation Discrepancy report that lists the transactions affecting the erroneous beginning balance. Typically, the report contains transactions that were changed after they were reconciled or that weren't reconciled when they should have been. The Reconciliation Discrepancy report also contains a Difference amount, and your goal is to make that amount $0. You accomplish that task by handling the transactions in the Reconciliation Discrepancy report.

If you want to explore what happened to the listed transactions that caused the discrepancy, click the View link of the transaction (in the right column of the report) to display an Audit report for the transaction, detailing the changes that were made in the transaction.

To correct a transaction, click it in the report to see ways to correct it. When you correct the transaction in the Reconciliation Discrepancy report, the account is ready to reconcile.

You can click any transaction in the report to view it in the window where you created it. To produce a paper copy of the report, click the Print button in the top-right corner of the report window.

You can view the Reconciliation report at any time. Just redisplay the Reconcile page by choosing Settings ➪ Reconcile. After you reconcile an account, a History by Account link appears in the top-right corner of the page. When you click the link, the History by Account page appears, listing earlier reconciliations for an individual account. Click the View Report link beside any reconciliation on this page to see its Reconciliation report.

To view reconciliations for other accounts, choose a different account from the Account drop-down list.

Chapter **6**

Utilizing QuickBooks Reports

ccounting reports help you keep tabs on the pulse of your business by enabling you to do a deep dive into the details whenever warranted. In this chapter, I walk you through the accounting reports that are available to all subscribers and show how you can export reports to Microsoft Excel, PDF files, or Google Sheets and in some cases to comma-separated value (CSV) files. QuickBooks Online Simple Start subscribers have 57 reports to choose from. An Essentials subscription adds another 28 reports for a total of 85 reports, whereas a Plus or Advanced subscription offers 124 reports. Advanced subscribers can also use a custom report writer and built-in charts, which I discuss in Chapter 14.

TIP

A detailed listing of the reports available to each subscription level is available at https://quickbooks.intuit.com/learn-support/en-us/help-article/purchase-orders/reports-included-quickbooks-online-subscription/L0s4KrGgr_US_en_US.

I used the QuickBooks Online sample company at https://qbo.intuit.com/redir/testdrive to provide an easy way for you to generate reports that contain actual data in case you don't have a meaningful number of transactions entered into your accounting records just yet. This company lets you test drive a Plus subscription and defaults to Accountant View. This means that you may see more reports in the sample company than are available if you have a Simple Start or Essentials subscription.

Looking at the Reports Page

Click Reports on the sidebar to display the page shown in Figure 6-1. Reports are organized into three tabs: Standard, Custom Reports, and Management Reports.

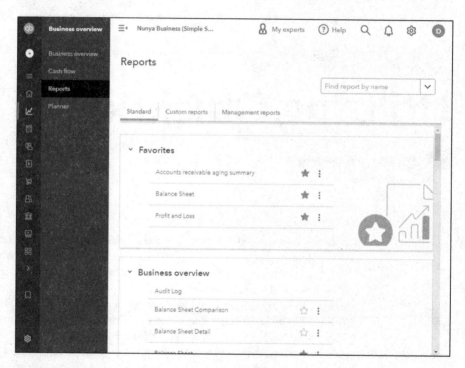

FIGURE 6-1:
The Reports page.

Exploring standard reports

Basic reporting is organized into the following categories:

>> Favorites

>> Business Overview

- » Who Owes You
- » Sales and Customers
- » What You Owe
- » Expenses and Vendors
- » Sales Tax (if the Sales Tax option is enabled)
- » Employees
- » For My Accountant
- » Payroll (if you have a payroll subscription)

TIP

I find it easiest to locate reports by typing a portion of the report name in the Find a Report field. You can also toggle the star next to any report name on or off to determine if a report appears in the Favorites section.

You also can use the Search tool, in the top-right corner of the screen, to search for a report from anywhere in QuickBooks.

Comparing classic versus enhanced reports

All reports are classic reports unless the words *New Enhanced Experience* appear next to the report name. You can toggle to the classic version of any enhanced report by clicking the Switch to Classic Version button at the top of the report. Table 6-1 offers a bird's-eye comparison of the differences between these two types of reports.

Customizing classic reports

Classic reports have some distinct differences from enhanced reports:

- » You can export classic reports to Excel or to PDF files.
- » You can't group classic reports the same way that you can group enhanced reports.
- » Filtering is limited to choosing item types, such as All Income/Expense Accounts, or by way of individual selections, such as specific customers or accounts.

TABLE 6-1

Classic Reports versus Enhanced Reports

Task	Classic Reports	Enhanced Reports
Sort report	Yes	No
Group report	No	Yes
Specify filter operations	No	Yes
Enable/disable header/footers	Yes	No
Company Name field	100 characters	Not available
Column limit	No limit; you may display all available columns	You may not display more than 20 columns
Report Title field	192 characters	250 characters
Hide/display active rows/columns	Yes	No
Number formatting options	Yes	No
Annotate report	Yes	No
Export to Excel	Yes	Yes
Export to CSV	No	Yes
Export to PDF	Yes	Yes
Share reports with other users	Yes	No

The following steps for creating a 12-month Profit and Loss report give you a better sense of what's possible:

1. **Choose Profit and Loss by Month Report from the Business Overview section.**

   A Profit and Loss report appears with a column for each month for this year-to-date.

2. **Scroll up to display the customization options shown in Figure 6-2.**

3. **Change the Report Period field to This Year instead of This Year-To-Date.**

   Alternatively, you can change the start and end dates for the report.

4. **Click the Customize button to display the task pane (see Figure 6-3.)**

   Customization options may vary by report and QuickBooks Online subscription level.

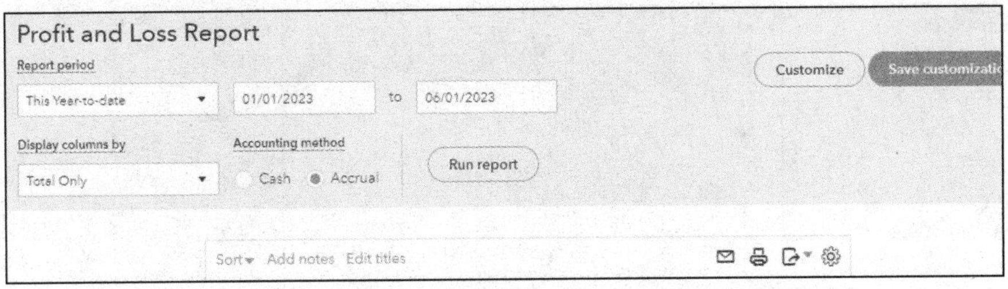

FIGURE 6-2:
Customization
options available
for the Profit and
Loss report.

FIGURE 6-3:
Additional
customization
options for classic
reports appear in
a task pane.

5. **Click the Run Report button on the report screen or in the Customize Report task pane to apply your customizations.**

6. **Click the Save Customization button to display the dialog box shown in Figure 6-4.**

   Modify the report name if you want, and choose whether you want to share the report with other users in your company. Report names can be up to 70 characters in length.

7. **The report now appears on the Custom Reports tab.**

FIGURE 6-4:
The Save
Customization
dialog box.

Investigating enhanced reports

Enhanced reports enable you to group data based on a single criterion and allow you to apply more levels of filtering. You can export enhanced reports to Excel, CSV (comma-separated value) files, or PDF files. The following steps walk you through customizing the Transaction List by Date report:

1. **Choose Transaction List by Date from the For My Accountant section.**

   Alternatively, you can type **by date** in the Find Report by Name field and then press Enter.

2. **Optional: Choose a time period from the This Month to Date drop-down list shown in Figure 6-5.**

   Scroll to the top of the time period list and choose Custom if you don't see the time period you want on the list.

TIP

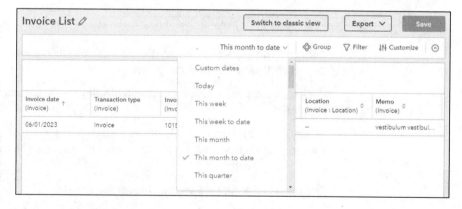

FIGURE 6-5:
Time period
drop-down list on
an enhanced
report.

3. **Optional: Click Group and choose one of 25 criteria from the Group drop-down list, as shown in Figure 6-6.**

   The Add button that appears in the Group task pane is disabled in all subscription levels except for Advanced, so it may simply be a tease for you. Advanced subscribers can specify a group and up to two subgroups.

FIGURE 6-6:
Enhanced reports can be grouped by one level, such as customer, vendor, account, and so on.

FIGURE 6-6:
Enhanced reports can be grouped by one level, such as customer, vendor, account, and so on.

4. **Optional: Click Filter and choose from 28 criteria (see Figure 6-7).**

   You must specify an operation and value for each filter that you apply. All subscription levels can add multiple filters to a report.

FIGURE 6-7:
Filter task pane for enhanced reports.

5. **Optional: Click Customize to choose between Cash and Accrual for the report basis and to manage the columns on the report.**

   As shown in Figure 6-8, you can hide or display columns by toggling the eye icon to the right of each column name. You can reorganize the report by dragging column names into a new position on the list.

6. **Optional: Click the pencil icon to the right of the report title to assign a new name.**

7. **Optional: Click Save to save your customized report to the Custom Reports tab.**

   The report title that appears at the top of the report also appears on the Custom Reports tab.

FIGURE 6-8:
Accounting basis
and column
choices task pane
for enhanced
reports.

REMEMBER

No dialog box appears for enhanced reports. If you inadvertently save an enhanced report, choose Reports from the sidebar menu and then activate the Custom Reports tab. Click Delete in the Action column for the report that you want to remove, as shown in Figure 6-9.

Working with custom reports

You can share customized classic reports with other users in your QuickBooks Online company. This means your Custom Reports tab may display custom reports that other users have elected to share. Conversely, enhanced reports that you've created are available on your Custom Reports tab but no one else's. You can do the following from the Custom Reports tab (see Figure 6-9):

>> **Customized enhanced reports:** A blue CUSTOM label appears next to the name of enhanced reports that you have customized. You can carry out the following actions with such reports:

   • Click the report name to display the report on screen. You can modify the report and then click Save Customizations. Keep the report name intact if you want to overwrite the previously saved custom report.

REMEMBER

- Click Delete to remove the report from your Custom Reports list.

- Click the arrow next to the report and choose Add to Management Reports.

You cannot share enhanced reports that you have customized. You also cannot schedule these reports to be sent via email. If you need either of these capabilities, you must delete the enhanced report from your Custom Reports list and then choose the enhanced report from the Reports list again. Click Switch to Classic View to create a classic report that you can share and email.

» **Customized classic reports:** No label appears next to the report name for classic reports that you have customized. You can carry out the following actions with customized classic reports:

- Click the report name to display the report on screen. You can modify the report and then click Save Customizations. Keep the report name intact if you want to overwrite the previously saved custom report.

- You can click Edit to change the name of the report or add the report to a group. Essentials, Plus, and Advanced users can also share the report with other users in your company and set an email schedule.

- You can click the arrow next to the Edit command and choose Export as PDF, Export as Excel, Save as Management Report, or Delete.

FIGURE 6-9:
Custom
Reports tab.

Reviewing management reports

The Management Reports tab, shown in Figure 6-10, lists three predefined management report packages that you can prepare and print by selecting the View link in the Action column.

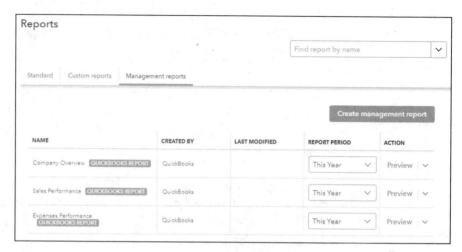

FIGURE 6-10:
The Management
Reports tab.

These report packages are quite elegant. Each package contains a professional-looking cover page, a table of contents, and several reports that correspond to the report package's name:

>> The Company Overview management report contains the Profit and Loss report and the Balance Sheet report.

>> The Sales Performance management report contains the Profit and Loss report, the A/R Aging Detail report, and the Sales by Customer Summary report.

>> The Expenses Performance management report contains the Profit and Loss report, the A/P Aging Detail report, and the Expenses by Vendor Summary report.

Click Preview in the Action column to display the Print Preview window shown in Figure 6-11. You can click the Download or Print buttons on the toolbar to save the report in PDF format. Alternatively, you can click the arrow on the Action column on the Management Reports tab (refer to Figure 6-10) to reveal these options:

>> Edit allows you to add your logo to the cover page, add more reports to the package, include an executive summary, and add endnotes to the package. Click the icons along the left side of the screen to modify each section of the report.

>> Send allows you to email the report package as a PDF file.

>> Export as PDF allows you to save your report package as a PDF file.

>> Export as DOCX saves your report package in a format compatible with Microsoft Word, Google Docs, and other word processing platforms.

>> Duplicate creates a new version of the report package while keeping the original intact. QuickBooks adds a number to the report name, such as Company Overview–1, but you can change the name if you want.

>> Delete appears only next to management reports that you've copied. You can't delete the three default report packages.

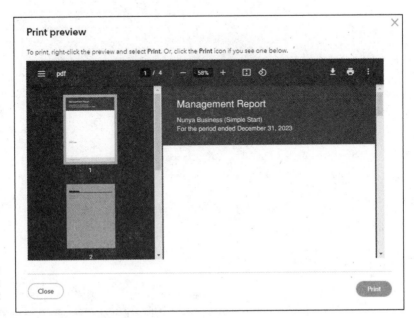

FIGURE 6-11:
Print Preview of a management report.

Interacting with Reports

Some reports enable you to manage information overload by collapsing sections of the report, and most every report allows you to drill down into the underlying details. Let's look at a report that offers both of these features:

1. **Choose Balance Sheet from the Business Overview section of the Reports page.**

2. **Click the triangle icon to the left of any major report category (see Figure 6-12) to collapse that level of the report or click the triangle a second time to expand the report again.**

3. **Click any amount on the Balance Sheet report to display the Transaction Drilldown Report shown in Figure 6-13.**

   Category names and account names on the Balance Sheet report aren't clickable.

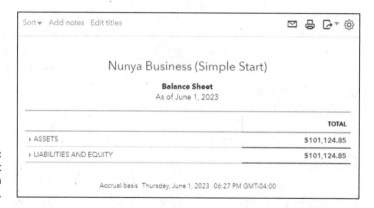

FIGURE 6-12:
A balance sheet collapsed down to two rows.

FIGURE 6-13:
Some reports allow you to drill down to a Transaction report.

4. **Click an account name on the Transaction report, such as Checking, to display the Account dialog box, which I discuss in Chapter 1, or click any other field in the report to display the underlying transaction screen (see Figure 6-14).**

FIGURE 6-14:
You can drill your way down to individual transactions, registers, or lists.

To redisplay the original report — in this case, the Balance Sheet report — close any open transaction window and then click Back at the top of the Transaction Drilldown report shown in Figure 6-13. Alternatively, click Reports on the sidebar to return to the Reports page.

TIP

Duplicating a browser tab before you drill down ensures that you're always just a click away from the original report that you're reviewing. To duplicate a tab in Google Chrome, right-click a tab and choose Duplicate from the shortcut menu. For all other browsers, consult the browser's Help menu for instructions on duplicating a tab.

Charting Your Business

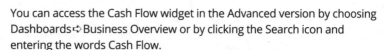

For most QuickBooks users, charts present a good news/bad news scenario. Let's get the bad news out of the way first. Unless you have an Advanced subscription, your ability to create charts is limited to a handful of widgets on the Business Overview page. The good news is that your accountant can create up to 25 charts based upon your accounting records and share these charts with you in PDF form. With that said, here's how to access the limited charts that are directly available:

1. **Choose Dashboards⇨Business Overview.**

The Business Overview page appears.

Widgets appear that show the following information:

- Cash Flow Forecast widget, which projects your cash flow if you link your bank account to QuickBooks

You can access the Cash Flow widget in the Advanced version by choosing Dashboards⇨Business Overview or by clicking the Search icon and entering the words Cash Flow.

REMEMBER

The Cash Flow Planner page is available by choosing Dashboards⇨Planner. Curiously you cannot access this feature by way of the Search tool.

- Profit and Loss for the past 30 days or selected time periods

- Bank balances

- Expenses for the past 30 days or selected time periods

- Unpaid invoices for the past year, and paid invoices for the past 30 days

- Sales for the past 30 days or selected time periods

2. **Optional: Click the Customize button and then hover your mouse over any widget to reposition or delete the object.**

    The Add/Remove Widgets button enables you to turn widgets on or off but not move them.

TIP

The Recommended Charts feature on the Insert tab of Microsoft Excel's ribbon suggests charts suitable for presenting data that you've exported from QuickBooks. The Analyze Data command appears on the Home tab of the Microsoft 365 version of Excel and enables you to create charts by asking plain-English questions.

Tagging Transactions

Tags offer an additional dimension for categorizing and reporting on related transactions. They're similar to the project tracking feature that's available to Plus and Advanced subscribers. You can tag just about every type of transaction except for transfers and journal entries. Tag groups are collections of one or more tags, for which you can run a Profit and Loss by Tag report or a Transaction List by Tag Group report. You can also view lists of transactions by individual tags, sometimes referred to as flat tags.

I recommend that you keep the Profit and Loss by Tag report in mind when planning your tags. For example, let's say that you're completing a project for a customer named Amy's Bird Sanctuary. You can create a tag group called Amy's Bird Sanctuary, which you can apply to any invoices that you send to Amy, as well as to any expenses that you incur related to Amy. You don't need to create a Revenue tag or Expense tag for two reasons:

» The Profit and Loss by Tag report automatically groups revenue and expenses and gives you a net income figure by tag.

» You can assign the Revenue and Expense tags I'm discussing only to a single tag group. You can create Amy's Revenue and Amy's Expense tags, but doing so makes your tracking harder because the Profit and Loss by Tag report contains two columns: one for Amy's Revenue and one for Amy's Expenses — each with separate net income amounts.

However, maybe you're building a fence for Amy, and you're separately installing a gravel sidewalk. This is the level where tags (subtags) makes sense, because then on the Profit and Loss by Tag report you see one column for the fence and a second column for the sidewalk.

In short, tags are beneficial when you want to group related accounting transactions in a manner that isn't already available. For instance, you likely don't need an Insurance tag because you're probably already grouping insurance expenses into one or more accounts and perhaps sub-accounts. On the other hand, if you're sponsoring a booth at an industry conference, you likely have an array of expenses that you want to group into something like a 2024 Conference Sponsorship tag group. If you gain new business from the conference, you can tag invoices for those customers with that tag group as well. You can then use tags (subtags) to group related expenses, such as Booth Materials, Customer Swag, and so on.

REMEMBER

Tags can only be assigned at the transaction level, which means you cannot assign a tag to individual rows within the transaction itself.

Creating tag groups and tags

You can quickly add tags on the fly when creating new transactions by typing a tag name in the Tags field of a transaction window and then clicking Add. However, you need to create any tags in advance that you want to assign to existing transactions:

1. **Choose Settings ⇨ Tags to display the Tag list.**

2. **Click New, and then choose Tag Group or Tag.**

In QuickBooks vernacular, tag groups are parent tags, whereas tags are treated as children tags, or subtags. Each tag group can optionally have one or more subtags associated with it.

3. **Create a tag group or tag.**

You can choose one of the following:

- **Tag Groups:** As shown in Figure 6-15, you assign a tag group name, optionally assign one of 16 colors to the tag group, and then click Save. You can then fill in the Tag Name field and click Add as needed to add subtags to the group. Click Done to close the Tag Group task pane.

TIP

  Simple Start, Essentials, and Plus users can create 40 tag groups while Advanced users can create unlimited tag groups.

- **Tags (subtags):** As shown in Figure 6-16, the Create New Tag task pane has only two fields: Tag Name and Group. You're returned to the Tag list when you click Save. Accordingly, it's more efficient to use the Tag Groups command when you need to create multiple tags. All versions of QuickBooks, including Advanced subscriptions, are limited to assigning 300 tags across all tag groups.

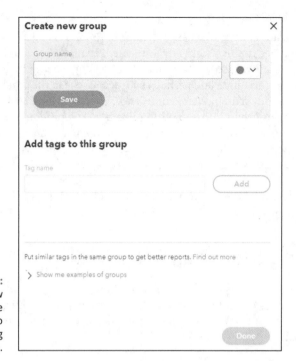

FIGURE 6-15:
The Create New
Group task pane
enables you to
establish new tag
groups and tags.

TIP

REMEMBER

REMEMBER

Plus and Advanced users can use the project tracking capability that I discuss in Chapter 11 instead of tags to track projects that are completed on behalf of customers.

You can associate each tag with only a single group. For instance, if you sell fruit baskets internationally and domestically, you might create tag groups for Domestic Sales and International Sales. In this case, a Fruit Basket tag (subtag) can be associated only with Domestic Sales or International Sales, but not both. One solution might be to have Fruit Baskets be the tag group and to set up Domestic Sales and International Sales as tags (subtags). Fortunately, you can delete tags and tag groups (as opposed to marking them inactive, which is what QuickBooks requires for most list items).

- **Tags (flat tags):** Flat tag are tags that aren't associated with a tag group. To create a flat tag, simply leave the Group field blank in the Create New Tag task pane shown in Figure 6-16, and then Click Save.

  You can't choose flat tags in your reports, but you can use the various transaction filter options in QuickBooks to unearth transactions that have flat tags assigned.

FIGURE 6-16:
The Create New
Tag window
enables you to
assign subtags
to groups or
add flat tags.

Tagging existing transactions

After you have at least one tag or group created, you can start tagging existing transactions:

1. **Choose Settings⇨Tags if necessary.**

2. **Click Start Tagging Transactions in the Money In or Money Out sections or choose See All Untagged Transactions.**

   A list of your transactions appears.

3. **Use the checkboxes to the left of the transactions to select one or more transactions that you want to tag (see Figure 6-17), which causes an Update Tags button to appear (not shown in Figure 6-17).**

   You can use the Filters button to select groups of transactions if you like.

4. **Choose Update Tags⇨Add Tags.**

   You can also choose Remove Tags from the Update Tags drop-down menu if you want to untag one or more transactions.

5. **Choose or type the name of the tag and click Apply.**

   Tags appear in the new Tags column.

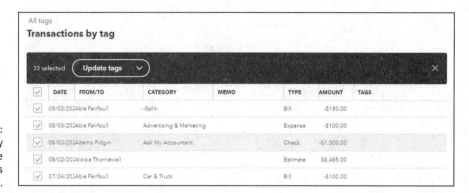

All tags
Transactions by tag

FIGURE 6-17:
You can apply
tags to multiple
transactions
at once.

REMEMBER

You can assign as many tags as you want to a transaction, but you can choose only one tag (subtag) per tag group (parent tag). The nuance goes further: You can't assign a tag group (parent tag) to a transaction. You must choose a tag (subtag) that's associated with a tag group (parent tag).

Figure 6-18 shows the Opening A/R tag added to the Opening Balance Transactions group. Each tag (subtag) can be assigned to one group only, so if I use Opening Balance Transaction as a tag, I can't distinguish Opening A/R (Accounts Receivable) from other types of opening balance transactions.

FIGURE 6-18:
Tags (subtags)
have been added
to two tag groups
(parent tags).

Tagging new transactions

The Tag field appears on just about every transaction screen except for transfers and journal entries. When creating a new transaction, simply choose one or more tags from the Tags field or start typing the name of a new tag, and then choose Add Tag from the drop-down menu.

REMEMBER

You can assign only tags, versus tag groups, to transactions.

Running tag reports

You can choose between two tag-related reports:

>> **Profit and Loss by Tag Group:** The report generates a profit and loss report for the time period of your choice.

>> **Transaction List by Tag Group:** This report lists all transactions within a tag group of your choice.

Throughout the following steps, I draw your attention to a couple of nuances related to these reports:

WARNING

1. **Choose Reports from the sidebar menu.**

   Normally I suggest that you click the Search button at the top of the screen and then enter the word **Tags**. Although you can search for most reports in this fashion, inexplicably tag-related reports don't appear here.

TIP

2. **Type the word Tag in the Find Report by Name field and then choose a report name.**

   The report names vanish if you type *Tags* instead of *Tag*.

3. **Select a tag group from the Display Columns By, change the report period if needed, and then click Run Report.**

Removing the Tags field from transaction pages

You can't disable the Tags feature, but you can remove the Tags field from your transaction pages:

1. **Choose Settings ⇨ Account and Settings ⇨ Sales ⇨ Sales Form Content.**

2. **Toggle off the Tags feature and then click Save.**

3. **Choose Expenses ⇨ Bills and Expenses in the Accounts and Settings window.**

4. **Toggle off the Tags feature and then click Save.**

5. **Click Done to close the Account and Settings window.**

REMEMBER

The Tags command still appears in the Live Bookkeeping submenu in the sidebar, and the Tags tab still appears on the Banking page in Accountant view.

» **Establishing automated bank rules**

» **Enabling recurring transactions**

» **Converting paper receipts to electronic transactions**

» **Importing data into QuickBooks**

Chapter **7**

Employing Apps and Automation

Sometimes it seems that our society has gone app-crazy, and QuickBooks Online is a willing participant in the frenzy. In this chapter, I talk about apps that enable you to access your books from your mobile device, as well as apps that add new functionality. I also cover some automation aspects for QuickBooks, including importing certain lists and transactions, adding automatic subtotals to sales forms, making use of recurring transactions, and transforming paper or electronic bills and receipts into transactions.

The automation techniques that I discuss in this chapter are available to all QuickBooks Online users. In Chapter 10, I discuss how Plus and Advanced users can streamline invoicing tasks with pricing rules, while in Chapter 15, I discuss automation features that are only available in companies that have an Advanced subscription.

Investigating QuickBooks Online Apps

QuickBooks Online Apps come in three different varieties. I discuss the first two in this chapter and the third later in Chapter 13:

>> **Mobile app:** You can log into QuickBooks Online through the web browser on your mobile device, but you're likely to have a much better experience if you download and install the mobile app.

>> **Online apps:** Think of these as plug-ins that fill functionality gaps in QuickBooks. Some are free, but you pay for most of them on a subscription basis.

>> **Desktop app:** In Chapter 13, I discuss how QuickBooks Online Advanced users can download and install a desktop app for Windows that enables users to access multiple companies at once and avoid the infuriating situation that arises when you close the wrong browser tab in QuickBooks and have to log in again.

TIP

If you close the wrong browser tab, press Ctrl+H or Cmd+H in many browsers to display the History page, from which you can reopen the errant tab that you closed by mistake.

QuickBooks Online Mobile apps

Your QuickBooks subscription includes mobile apps for iOS/iPadOS and Android devices. These apps are optimized for touch interaction and on-the-go workflows such as customer management, invoicing, estimates, and signatures. You can also use the mobile apps to track the status of invoices, take payments, reconcile bank accounts, capture expenses, record mileage, and check reports. Pinch-and-zoom functionality works in both the apps and browsers on mobile devices.

WARNING

Mileage tracking in QuickBooks Online Mobile is available only to administrative users. This is a whack-a-mole situation where you solve one problem — making it easy for employees to track mileage — and replace it with another: granting employees administrative access to your books.

You can get the mobile apps from the app store for your device or request a link at `https://quickbooks.intuit.com/accounting/mobile`. Alternatively, you can use your browser to log into your books at `https://qbo.intuit.com` without installing anything. Keep in mind that the mobile apps offer a subset of Quick-Books functionality, so you still need to use a web browser to carry out certain tasks, such as customizing templates.

QuickBooks App Store

As I discuss in Chapter 1, QuickBooks is all about the add-ons, such as Payroll, Time, Payments, and E-commerce. You can also choose Apps in the left menu bar and take a gander at the free and paid options that can enhance your QuickBooks experience. The QuickBooks Mileage feature is tucked away on the Apps menu as well. You can use the QuickBooks Mobile app to track mileage, with the caveat that users must have administrative privileges to your company. Fortunately, you can find other mileage-tracking options on the Apps page, albeit on a paid basis.

Taking advantage of QuickBooks Commerce

QuickBooks Commerce started out as an app that could be added to QuickBooks Online, but now it's a feature of the software platform. Presently you can connect the following platforms to your books:

>> Amazon

>> eBay

>> Shopify

Your subscription level governs the number of platforms you can connect to:

>> **Simple Start:** One sales channel

>> **Essentials:** Three sales channels

>> **Plus and Advanced:** Unlimited sales channels

You're probably thinking, hmmm, there are only three channels listed, so why did he write that Plus and Advanced users get unlimited sales channels? Simply put, Intuit is working on additional connections, so Essentials users will be able to choose up to three e-commerce channels, whereas Plus and Advanced users will have access to all added channels.

Here's how to get started with QuickBooks Commerce:

1. **Choose Commerce from the sidebar menu.**

   Three submenus are available — Overview, Orders, and Payouts — but you won't see any data here until you connect to a platform.

2. **Click Connect Sales Channel.**

3. **Choose a channel and then click Next.**

From there you're prompted to provide your sales channel credentials and then configure how you want the information to flow into your books.

Intuit offers the following caveats for its Commerce offering:

>> Your products and services are only sold in the United States and in United States dollars.

>> You don't use a third-party payment processor, like PayPal, Affirm, or Authorize.net.

>> You don't need to bring in customer, product, or inventory data from your sales channels.

If you encounter one or more dealbreakers on this list, read on to see how you can import data into QuickBooks.

Automating downloaded activity with bank rules

In Chapter 5, I discuss how you can automatically or manually import bank and credit card transactions with your books. In turn, the Bank Rules feature instructs QuickBooks how to categorize and record such transactions automatically. Let's say that you often buy gas for your business vehicles at Shell stations. You can either manually categorize such transactions as Fuel Expense, or you can set up a bank rule to automate the process going forward. Bank rules are applied based upon the accounts, transaction types (money in or money out), and criteria that you specify. Bank rules can assign categories (meaning income/expense accounts) and modify other fields as well. This means that you can create a bank rule that updates one or more fields and then leaves the transaction in the For Review list. Or, you can create a bank rule that updates one or more fields and accepts the transaction, which means it posts to your books and then appears in the Catego-rized list. Either way, you can always amend a transaction by choosing it from the Categorized list, using the Search feature to locate the transaction, or by clicking on the transaction within a report.

REMEMBER

You are limited to creating up to 2,000 bank rules in any one QuickBooks Online company.

Creating bank rules

As noted previously, as you manually review transactions, QuickBooks may prompt you to create a bank rule. Or, you can always create a rule directly:

1. **Choose Transactions ⇨ Bank Rules.**

2. **Click the New Bank Rule button to display the Create Bank Rule task pane shown in Figure 7-1.**

3. **Assign a meaningful name to the bank rule.**

   You can't use special characters like the apostrophe (') in a rule name.

REMEMBER

4. **Indicate whether the bank rule applies to money coming in or money going out and select the account(s) to which you want the bank rule to apply.**

   QuickBooks Simple Start users can only create bank rules for connected bank accounts that synchronize automatically. Essentials, Plus, and Advanced users can also create rules for transactions that are manually uploaded.

5. **Set the transaction criteria for the bank rule by using the drop-down lists in the Include the Following section.**

   Use the Add a Condition link to set additional criteria and to specify if a transaction should meet all or any of the criteria. Specifying All is more stringent and makes QuickBooks more selective about applying the bank rule.

TIP

   The first list box in the section enables you to specify whether QuickBooks should compare the transaction description, the bank text, or the transaction amount with a condition you set. For those inquiring minds out there, *Description* (the transaction description) refers to the text that appears in the Description column of the Bank and Credit Cards page. The *Bank Text* option refers to the Bank Detail description the bank downloads; you can view the Bank Detail description if you click any downloaded transaction. The Bank Detail description appears in the bottom-left corner of the transactions being edited. *Transaction Amount* is the dollar amount of an individual transaction.

6. **Click Test Rule to determine how many unreviewed transactions the bank rule will apply to.**

   QuickBooks won't show you the actual transactions, but you'll at least know that you've specified the criteria correctly to match one or more transactions.

7. **At the bottom of the Create Rule panel, set the information you want to apply to transactions that meet the bank rule's criteria.**

   You can do one or more of the following:

   - *Select a transaction type to assign to the transaction.*

   - *Select a category and (optional) split to use for classifying the transaction.* Splits can be based on percentages or dollar amounts.

- *Select a payee to apply the transactions that meet the bank rule's conditions.*

- *Specify one or more tags for grouping related transactions.*

- *Optional: Click Assign More to add a memo to each transaction that meets the bank rule's conditions. For more on ways to use the Memo field, see the nearby sidebar, "The Memo field and transaction rules."*

- *Toggle off Automatically Confirm Transactions This Rule Applies To if you do not want to automatically add transactions that meet the bank rule's conditions to your company.*

REMEMBER

This setting instructs QuickBooks to bypass the For Review list and post transactions directly to your books. Such transactions appear on the Categorized tab, along with any transactions that you manually post, and you can make changes later if you experience an unexpected outcome with a bank rule.

8. **Click Save in the bottom-right corner of the Create Rule panel.**

   Your bank rule appears on the Rules page going forward and will be applied to any matching transactions in the For Review lists for your accounts.

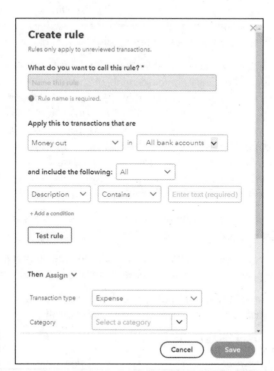

FIGURE 7-1:
The Create Rule
task pane.

You cannot manually run a bank rule because they can only be triggered when new transactions are synchronized or imported into your company.

Choose Copy in the Action column of the Rules page to replicate a bank rule to use as a starting point (instead of starting from scratch). You can also edit, disable, or delete bank rules.

See the section, "Exporting and importing bank rules," later in this chapter to see how to transfer rules between QuickBooks companies.

THE MEMO FIELD AND BANK RULES

QuickBooks uses special icons in the register to identify transactions posted automatically with rules, but you can't filter a register to see only transactions that were added via a rule. You can, however, add a search term, such as "Added by Bank Rule" to the Memo field, which you can then use to filter an account register.

THE HIERARCHY OF BANK RULES

QuickBooks processes your bank rules in the order in which they appear on the Rules page on a first come, first served basis. This means the first bank rule with criteria that match a given transaction gets applied, and no other rules are processed for that transaction, so you may need to reorder the bank rules in certain instances. To do so, drag the icon that looks like a grid of nine dots to the left of the rule on the Rules page to move a rule up or down in the list.

Suppose that you set up two bank rules in the following order:

- **Bank Rule 1:** Categorize all transactions of less than $10 as Miscellaneous Expenses.

- **Bank Rule 2:** Categorize all Shake Shack transactions as Meals & Entertainment.

If a $12 dollar transaction from Shake Shack appears, Rule 2 applies. But if a $7.50 transaction from Shake Shack appears, Rule 1 applies. Mmm, Shake Shack. Is anyone else hungry?

Exporting and importing bank rules

Bank rules can be exported from one QuickBooks company and then imported into another. This is helpful when you have multiple entities that use the same conventions and chart of accounts. You can also create a set of generic bank rules to use as a starting point for crafting rules in other companies. Here's how to transfer bank rules from one company to another:

1. **Choose Transactions⇨Rules in the company that has the bank rules that you want to transfer.**

   The Rules page appears in the company that you are exporting from.

2. **Choose Export Rules from the New Rule drop-down menu.**

   QuickBooks stores an Excel file containing the bank rules in your Downloads folder. The name of the file includes the QuickBooks company name whose rules you exported and the words Bank_Feed_Rules.

REMEMBER

   The Export Rules command is disabled if a given company doesn't have any bank rules established.

3. **Click Close.**

4. **Switch to the company into which you want to import the bank rules.**

   If you use the same Intuit account to access more than one QuickBooks Online company then choose Settings⇨Switch Companies. Alternatively, in Chapter 17, I discuss how Accountant version users can toggle between sets of books.

5. **Choose Transactions⇨Rules.**

   The Rules page appears in the company that you are importing into.

6. **Choose Import Rules from the New Rule drop-down menu.**

   The first screen of the Import Rules wizard appears.

7. **Select the file you created in Step 2 and then click Next.**

8. **On the second wizard screen, select the bank rules you want to import and then click Next.**

9. **Optional: On the third wizard screen, select categories for the bank rules that match the current company's chart of accounts and make changes as needed.**

10. **Click Import.**

   A message tells you how many bank rules imported successfully.

11. **Click Finish.**

   The Rules page for the company you imported into reappears.

12. **Review the bank rules.**

   You can edit or delete the rules in the same way as if you had created them by hand.

Fixing mistakes in uploaded or downloaded transactions

Whether you're accepting transactions manually or on autopilot with bank rules, sometimes mistakes or mispostings can happen. There's no need to worry; you can use the same steps in either case.

REMEMBER

QuickBooks marks downloaded transactions as having cleared your bank so be sure to edit — as opposed to delete — transactions that have been accepted or confirmed.

Follow these steps to undo an accept transaction:

1. **Choose Transactions ⇨ Bank Transactions.**

2. **Select the bank or credit card that the transaction posted to.**

   QuickBooks maintains separate transaction lists for each account.

3. **Click the Categorized tab on the Bank Transactions page.**

4. **Locate the transaction and click Undo in the Action column to send the transaction back to the For Review list.**

   Alternatively, click on the category name in the Added or Matched column to display the corresponding transaction screen and make your edits there.

5. **Switch to the For Review tab, edit the transaction as needed, and then accept (confirm) or exclude the transaction.**

   If necessary, you can delete transactions from the Excluded tab. To do so, click one or more transactions and then click the Delete button. Remember, QuickBooks does not ask you if you're sure that you want to delete, so move deliberately through the process.

Utilizing Recurring Transactions

Have you ever had that dream where you keep doing the same task over and over again? For some of us, it's more of a real-life nightmare. Fortunately, recurring transactions can eliminate some of the repetitive nature of your accounting transactions in Essentials, Plus, and Advanced companies. Just about every transaction is fair game, except for bill payments, customer payments, and time activities. Here are the types of recurring transactions you can create:

>> **Scheduled:** These types of recurring transactions post automatically to your books based on the schedule you establish. They're ideal for transactions with fixed amounts that rarely change, such as monthly rent payments. For instance, recurring bills scheduled for the first of the month post to your books automatically without any intervention from you and are even emailed automatically if you choose.

>> **Reminder:** This type of recurring transaction prompts you when the scheduled date comes around on the calendar. You can edit the transaction details before posting. This is well suited to transactions where the amount varies from month to month, such as a utility bill.

>> **Unscheduled:** This type of transaction hangs out in the background and doesn't remind you or post to your books but is available for use at any time in posting new transactions. Payroll journal entries or year-end closing transactions are ideal candidates for unscheduled recurring transactions.

With that background in mind, read on to see how to create a recurring transaction. I think it's easiest to click the Make Recurring button at the bottom of the screen the next time you create a transaction that you want to recur, but I also show you how you can purposefully create recurring transactions.

Creating a recurring transaction on the fly

QuickBooks allows you to set most first-stage transactions as recurring, such as invoices, bills, sales receipts, expenses, and so on. Conversely, transactions such as Receive Payment and Bill Pay are second-stage transactions because they offset first-stage transactions, and thus cannot be set to recur.

Follow these steps to make a recurring version of an existing transaction:

1. **Click Save to preserve the transaction that you have onscreen, particularly if you've just entered it.**

2. **Click Make Recurring at the bottom of the transaction screen to display the recurring version of the transaction type you started with.**

    You can only recur transactions that have a Make Recurring button at the bottom of the screen.

3. **Optional: Change the template name.**

4. **Choose Scheduled, Reminder, or Unscheduled from the Type list.**

5. **Fill in the number of days in advance that a scheduled transaction should be created or the number of days before the transaction date that you want to be reminded.**

6. **Ensure that the vendor (or customer) is correct.**

7. **Select the frequency for scheduled or reminder transactions, along with the time frame.**

    -   **Daily:** Specify the number of days between when this transaction should post.

    -   **Weekly:** Specify the number of weeks between when this transaction should post and the day of the week that you want it to post.

    -   **Monthly:** Specify the interval in months and the day of the month to pay the bill. For instance, you can schedule a transaction to post on a specific day each month or, say, on the last Tuesday of each month.

    -   **Yearly:** Specify the month and day for the transaction to post each year.

    -   **Start Date:** Indicate the first date when QuickBooks should post the transaction, along with an end date if appropriate. For instance, you might set an end date for a rent bill to coincide with the end of your lease.

8. **Confirm that the mailing address and terms are correct, scroll down the window to confirm that the detail section(s) of the transaction are correct, and add any memo information or attachments to the transaction.**

    Any lines in the Category Detail or Item Detail sections that have a value of $0 aren't saved.

9. **Click Save Template in the bottom-right corner of the window.**

Adding to the recurring transaction list

You can also add new transactions directly to the recurring transaction list by following these steps:

1. **Choose Settings⇨ Recurring Transactions to display the Recurring Transactions list.**

2. **Click New to display the Select Transaction Type dialog box, choose a transaction type, and then click OK.**

   Available choices include the following: Bill, Non-Posting Charge, Check, Non-Posting Credit, Credit Card Credit, Credit Memo, Deposit, Estimate, Expense, Invoice, Journal Entry, Refund, Sales Receipt, Transfer, Vendor Credit, and Purchase Order.

3. **Complete the recurring transaction window in the same fashion as described in the preceding section, and then click Save.**

Editing recurring transactions

To work with existing recurring transactions, choose Settings⇨ Recurring Transactions to display the Recurring Transactions list. Click Edit in the Action column to modify a recurring transaction. Any changes you make in recurring-transaction templates affect only future transactions. You have to manually edit any existing transactions that have been posted to your books.

REMEMBER

QuickBooks automatically updates recurring transactions when you modify a customer or vendor record, such as recording a change of address.

The Action column also includes the following options:

» **Use:** Enables you to record a Reminder or Unscheduled transaction to your books.

» **Duplicate:** Creates additional recurring-transaction templates from existing recurring-transaction templates. You might use the template for your rent to create another template to pay monthly insurance, for example. You can also use this option to create backup copies of complex transactions, such as a detailed payroll journal entry.

» **Delete:** Removes unwanted recurring-transaction templates.

REMEMBER

In many areas, deleting a record in QuickBooks translates to making a record inactive. Recurring transactions are deleted, and QuickBooks doesn't offer an undo capability, so think twice before deleting recurring transactions.

Finally, you can print a report of your existing recurring-transaction templates. Choose Reports on the left menu bar, type **recu** in the Search box (that's all you need to type to find the Recurring Template List report), and click the report name to display the Recurring Template List report.

Transforming Paper and Electronic Documents into Transactions

QuickBooks enables you to convert paper or electronic receipts or bills to transactions without having to key in all the details. To get started, choose Live Bookkeeping⇨Banking⇨Receipts or Banking⇨Receipts. You can capture receipts in four ways:

» Upload files from your computer.

» Upload files from Google Drive.

» Forward from email, which means establishing a special @qbodocs.com email address. The benefit of forwarding is that you can establish a filter in your email to automatically forward receipts that you receive by email for automatic posting to QuickBooks.

» Take pictures of receipts onscreen or on paper with the QuickBooks Online Mobile app.

TIP

To create an email address, click Manage Forwarding Email on the Receipts page. You're prompted to create a special @qbodocs.com email address that has a maximum of 25 letters to the left of the @ symbol. Click Next⇨Looks Good, and then click Done to create the email address. Now you can email receipts to that address to have the activity appear in QuickBooks. Keep in mind that you can send receipts only from registered accounts. Click the Manage Forwarding Email button and add new users in the Manage Receipt Senders section. You can choose only users who have credentials for your QuickBooks company. No matter which route you take, receipts appear in the For Review section.

After you click the Review link, you're prompted to review the following information:

1. **Specify a document type.**

   Choose Receipt or Bill.

2. **Optional: Specify a payee, or leave the setting blank.**

3. **Choose a Bank or Credit Card account.**

4. **Confirm the payment date.**

   The date from your receipt or bill should appear, but you can override this setting if necessary.

5. **Confirm the account or category.**

   QuickBooks attempts to classify the transaction for you, but you can change the default value if necessary.

6. **Edit the description.**

   You can override the default description if necessary.

7. **Confirm the amount in the Total Amount (Inclusive of Tax) field.**

   QuickBooks attempts to capture this amount for you, but you can correct the amount if necessary.

8. **Optional: Enter a memo.**

   This field allows you to write a paragraph or more about the transaction if you want.

9. **Optional: Set the following options:**

   - Click Make Expense and Items Billable if you plan for a customer to reimburse you.

   - Choose a customer from a drop-down list.

   - Add a reference number, such as a receipt or invoice number.

10. **Click Save and Next to post the transaction and review the next transaction in the queue.**

Exporting from and Importing to QuickBooks

In addition to importing bank data, which I discuss in Chapter 5, you can import the following types of lists and transactions:

>> Customers

>> Vendors

>> Chart of accounts

>> Products and services

>> Invoices (Plus and Advanced Only)

WARNING

Although an Invoices option appears for Simple Start and Essentials users, you'll likely immediately run into a message that says `Import invoices isn't quite ready to support sales tax`.

Depending on what you're importing, you may or may not be able to import every field that you want to. For instance, you can import only some of the customer and vendor fields that you see on screen when manually creating such records, so be prepared to fill in some gaps by hand.

TIP

If your company has an Advanced subscription, see Chapter 16, where I discuss how you can use Spreadsheet Sync to import and export data between Excel and QuickBooks Online.

REMEMBER

The Apps page within QuickBooks includes subscription options for several apps that allow you to import and export lists and transactions.

Exporting lists to Excel or Google Sheets

You can export customer, vendor, or product lists to Excel or Google Sheets by doing the following:

1. **Click the appropriate link on the side menu:**

   - Customers & Leads ⇨ Customers
   - Expenses ⇨ Vendors
   - Settings ⇨ Products and Services

2. **Click the Export to Excel button just above the Action column.**

   An Excel spreadsheet appears in your Downloads folder.

3. **Double-click on the resulting file in your Downloads folder to open it in Excel, or in Google Sheets choose File ⇨ Import ⇨ Upload to import the workbook.**

4. **If you're using Microsoft Excel, you may have to click Enable Editing to exit Protected View.**

   I talk about how to disable Protected View and streamline opening Excel files exported from QuickBooks in Chapter 20.

Exporting lists from QuickBooks gives you the option to fill any gaps in the records by way of using a spreadsheet. You can then transfer the resulting records to the corresponding import file template.

Accessing the import file templates

You can download template files that you can edit in Microsoft Excel or Google Sheets and then import back into QuickBooks:

1. **Choose Settings⇨Import Data.**

2. **Choose the type of import you want to perform.**

3. **Click Download a Sample File if you're using Excel or Preview a Sample for Google Sheets.**

   The sample file appears in your Downloads folder if you're using Excel.

4. **If you're using Microsoft Excel, double-click the file in your Downloads folder and then click Enable Editing.**

5. **In Excel or Google Sheets, examine the file's contents by scrolling to the right to see the information stored in each column.**

6. **Create your own file, modeling it on the sample file.**

REMEMBER

Your import file can't contain more than 1,000 rows or exceed 2MB. You can save your file as an Excel workbook, as a CSV file, or as a Google Sheets workbook.

TIP

Dates that you import must be in yyyy-mm-dd format. If you have a date entered in cell A1 of an Excel worksheet, you can use this formula to transform a date such as 2/15/2024 into 2024-02-15:

```
=TEXT(A1,"yyyy-mm-dd")
```

Copy the formula down the column, and then select all the cells that contain the formula and choose Home⇨Copy or press Ctrl+C (Cmd+C in Excel for Mac). Next, choose Home⇨Paste⇨Paste Values to convert the formulas to static values in the yyyy-mm-dd format.

THE SAMPLE IMPORT FILE'S LAYOUT

Information in the sample file is in table format, where each row in the spreadsheet contains all the information about a single product or service. Certain columns may require specific inputs, such as inventory, non-inventory, or service in the Type column of the Products and Services import file. I discuss creating inventory items in Chapter 10.

Importing lists and transactions

Here's how to import supported lists or transactions into QuickBooks:

1. Make sure your spreadsheet or CSV file isn't open in Excel or Google Sheets.

2. Choose Settings⇨Import Data.

3. Choose the type of data you want to import.

4. Click Browse for an Excel or CSV file or Connect for a Google Sheet.

5. Navigate to the folder where you saved the file containing your import file.

6. Specify the file and click Open for an Excel or CSV file, or click Select for a Google Sheet.

   The Import page displays the name of the file you selected.

7. Click Next to upload your file to a staging area.

8. Map the fields in your data file to the corresponding QuickBooks fields.

   Use the Your Field drop-down list to match the columns in your file with the import files.

9. Click Next to display the final page of the wizard.

   A confirmation screen displays the records to be imported. You can widen the columns as needed.

10. Review the records to make sure that the information is correct.

    You can change the information in any field by clicking that field and typing. You can also deselect any rows that you've decided you don't want to import.

11. When you're satisfied that the information is correct, click the Import button.

    A status message briefly flashes on the screen to tell you how many records were imported.

TIP

I tried to trip up the process with two opening balance dates that were in *mm-dd-yyyy* format instead of *yyyy-mm-dd*, but the records were still imported. QuickBooks simply ignored the invalid input but imported the valid fields.

WARNING

If the Import button is disabled, some portion of the data can't be imported. Look for a field highlighted in red to identify information that can't be imported. If the problem isn't apparent, contact Intuit support for help, or set up the records manually.

2

QuickBooks Online Essentials Features

IN THIS PART . . .

Process bills, perform accounts payable duties and implement the Multicurrency feature.

Work with bundles and manage timekeeping and user security.

Chapter **8**

Managing Bills, Accounts Payable, and Multicurrency

Chapter 3 covers recording expenses in your books by using checks, expense transactions, and credit card transactions. In this chapter, I cover checks again, but from a different perspective. In QuickBooks Simple Start, any checks or expenses that you enter affect your bank account immediately. Conversely, if you have an Essentials, Plus, or Advanced subscription, you can enter Bill transactions that allow you to post expenses and charges to your books as soon as you know about them and then pay the bills later. This process is known as A/P, or accounts payable.

Entering bills into QuickBooks as soon as you receive them gives you better control over your finances because it's much easier to tell what you owe by running an Aged Accounts Payable report than it is to sift through a stack of bills from your vendors, some of which might end up hidden or misfiled. In this chapter, you find out how to record credits from vendors, which you can apply against future invoices, as well as how to record a refund should a vendor return your money.

TIP In Chapter 4, I discuss paying contractors, who are basically vendors that you've chosen to isolate to a separate Contractors page. I cover creating vendors in Chapter 3, so please refer to that chapter if you're unclear about how to set up or maintain vendor records.

Understanding Accounts Payable

It seems that our society is moving at an ever more frenetic pace, so you may find that you're expected to pay immediately for charges you incur. This means you might use a credit card or an online payment service, such as Venmo or PayPal. If you're hardcore, you can still write paper checks, although the recipient may look askance at you. For these types of payment situations, go to Chapter 3 to find out how to record the transactions in your books.

What I talk about in this chapter is entering bills that you plan to pay later. It may be a rent bill, a car insurance bill, or a social media expert's invoice. The accounts payable process works as follows:

1. A bill arrives or is implied.

   The vendor might send you a paper or electronic bill, or perhaps you're contractually obligated to pay a certain amount periodically, such as for your lease payments.

2. You determine when you're going to pay the obligation and then enter the corresponding transaction.

   If you're planning to pay the amount due within a couple of days, you can save time by not entering a bill, and instead record the transaction by using one of the methods covered in Chapter 3. It simply creates double work to enter a bill into QuickBooks and then immediately pay it. Further, you clog up your financial records and reports with twice as many transactions. On the other hand, if the vendor expects payment, say within 30 days, you may decide to enter a bill.

3. You pay the bill by the appointed due date.

TIP Some companies use purchase orders, which can be thought of as pre-bills, especially since you can convert a purchase order into a bill. Purchase orders require a Plus or Advanced subscription and are discussed in more detail in Chapter 10.

Entering a bill

As you may have noticed, QuickBooks makes a distinction between invoices that you send to customers and bills that vendors send to you. It all depends on which side of the buyer/seller equation you happen to be on at any moment. Here I explain how to enter a bill, which is similar to entering an invoice:

1. **Choose +New⇨Bill to display the page shown in Figure 8-1.**

Alternatively, choose Expenses⇨Bills, and then click Add Bill⇨Create Bill.

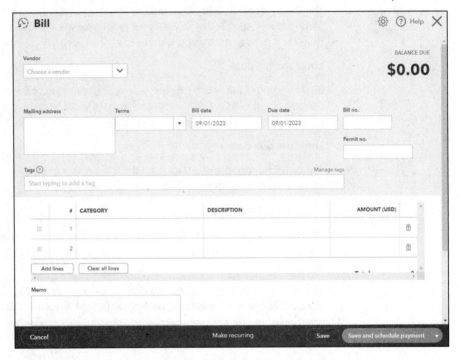

FIGURE 8-1:
The Bill page.

2. **Choose a name from the Vendor list or click Add New to add a new vendor on the fly.**

TIP

Plus and Advanced users who utilize purchase orders in QuickBooks may see an Add to Bill task pane along the right. Click Add All to add all open purchase orders to the bill, or click Add to add an individual purchase order to the bill. I discuss purchase orders in more detail in Chapter 10.

3. **If necessary, enter the vendor's mailing address if you plan to mail the vendor a check or you're planning to use the QuickBooks Bill Pay service.**

Address changes that you made on the Bill page in QuickBooks aren't saved back to the vendor record. If a vendor's address is missing or has changed, it's best to choose Expenses⇨Vendors, select the vendor, and edit the address. This can save you untold time in the future, from not having to enter the address again, to having checks sent to the wrong address or getting lost in the postal system from not having an address.

4. **Optional: Choose the payment terms for this bill.**

Typical terms include Due on Receipt, Net 15, and Net 30. You can also choose Add New to create a new type of payment term.

The Terms list in QuickBooks applies to both customers and vendors. Choose Settings⇨All Lists⇨Terms to view your existing terms. Choose Make Inactive from the Action column if you want to disable a particular payment term.

5. **Enter the bill date.**

Be sure to enter the actual bill date, as opposed to today's date, so that the bill's age is reflected properly on your accounts payable aging reports, and especially in your books if you use the accrual basis financial report.

6. **Enter the due date.**

You can either use the due date from the bill, if one is shown, or enter the date that you plan to pay the bill.

7. **Enter the bill number.**

This is the equivalent of the Ref. No field in the Expense window and the Check No. field in the Checks window. You enter your vendor's invoice number in this space.

8. **You will see Category Details and Item Details sections if you have a Plus or Advanced subscription and have enabled the Inventory feature; otherwise, you'll only see a section where you can categorize your expenses.**

Now I'll go over the differences between the Category Details and Item Details sections:

- **Category Details:** This section enables you to document any sort of general expense for your business that isn't related to purchasing an inventory item that you plan to resell later. The Category Details section has three fields:

  - **Category:** If you want to make a CPA's blood boil, label a column where one should choose an account from the chart of accounts as Category. Yes, I'm looking at you, Intuit. OK, with that off my chest, let me elaborate and say that in Intuit's mind, you're choosing a tax category, or a line from your tax return where the expense will flow. No matter what, it's counterintuitive if you have any accounting experience at all, so just know that you'll pick an account from your chart of accounts in the Category column.

- **Description:** You can use up to 4,000 characters to describe what you exchanged for the money that you're about to send out the door.

- **Amount:** Enter the amount of money that will soon leave your hands.

Plus and Advanced users may also see Customer and Class columns in the Category Details section. You can enter a customer's name if the charge being recorded is reimbursable, and you can use the Class field to associate the expense with a particular class, which I discuss in more detail in Chapter 11.

- **Item Details:** This section is similar to the Category Details section but is used to record the purchase of inventory items, so there are some distinct differences:

  - **Product/Service:** Select the name of the product or service that you've procured, or click Add Item to add a new inventory item, product, or service. I discuss non-inventory and service items in Chapter 2, and I discuss inventory items in Chapter 10.

  - **Description:** The description should prefill based on the item that you chose. If it doesn't, it's a good idea to edit the corresponding item to provide the description to save yourself time in the future and improve the integrity of your books.

  - **Qty:** This is the quantity of items or services you purchased.

  - **Rate:** This is the per-unit price of the items or services you purchased.

  - **Amount:** This is the total cost of the goods or services you purchased.

Most accounting platforms calculate the third field if you fill in any two fields in the quantity, rate, and amount section. QuickBooks, on the other hand, multiplies the quantity by the rate to compute the amount but doesn't, say, calculate the quantity if you fill in only the rate and amount fields.

9. **Optional: Click Add Lines as needed to add lines to either section.**

Be mindful of the Clear All Lines buttons because they don't ask you if you're sure.

10. Optional: Enter up to 4,000 characters in the Memo field.

11. Add one or more attachments.

I cover adding attachments in detail in Chapter 2, so I won't belabor you with reading that information again here.

12. Save the transaction and optionally schedule a payment.

There are two different Save buttons at the bottom of the Bill page:

- **Save:** Saves the transaction but keeps the Bill window and the transaction on the screen.

- **Save and Schedule Payment:** Saves the transaction and then sneakily displays QuickBooks Online Bill Pay service, which enables you to pay five bills for free each month, plus $0.50 per ACH payment and $1.50 per check thereafter. A 2.9 percent fee applies to bills that you want to pay via credit card. Alternatively, you can choose Save and New or Save and Close if you have other avenues you prefer to use for paying your bills.

WARNING

The QuickBooks Bill Pay service can't combine two or more bills for a given vendor into a single check, which means your fees can mount fast if you need to pay multiple bills for a single vendor.

REMEMBER

Bill.com also offers an online bill payment service to QuickBooks users that has a different pricing approach. I discuss apps that can enhance QuickBooks in Chapter 7.

Here are the other buttons at the bottom of the Bill page:

>> **Cancel:** Discards the transaction and closes the Bill window if you indicate yes, you would like to leave without saving.

>> **Clear:** Discards the transaction and leaves the Bill window if you indicate yes, you would like to clear the transaction.

>> **Make Recurring:** Sets up a recurring check on a schedule that you choose, such as annual property tax bills. See the section "Utilizing Recurring Transactions" in Chapter 7 for more information.

Paying one bill at a time

Entering checks and expense transactions offers a one-and-done benefit, in that once you've entered the transactions, you typically don't need to revisit them. That isn't the case with bills unless you chose to schedule online payment in the previous section.

1. **Choose + New ⇨ Check or + New ⇨ Expense.**

   Use the Check option if you need to record a handwritten check or want to print a check. Use Expense for bills that you're paying online, such as through Venmo, PayPal, or via direct deposit through your bank.

2. **Select a payee from the list.**

   Any outstanding bills appear in the Add to Check task pane. You only see this task pane for vendors that have unpaid amounts due.

3. **Click Add All if you want to pay all open bills for the vendor, or click Add below specific bills.**

   The ground may feel like it has shifted on you, because the Write Check screen transmogrifies into a Bill Payment screen. The bill or bills that you've chosen to pay appear in an Outstanding Transactions section, in place of the typical Category Details and Item Details sections.

4. **Optional: Adjust payment amounts as needed or click Clear Payment if you change your mind about paying the bills.**

   Clear Payment returns you to the Check or Expense screen you were on but without the Add to Check task pane. You have to close and then reopen the Check or Expense window at this point to get access to the Add to Check task pane again.

5. **Choose Save and Print if you want to print a check. Conversely, you can choose Save and Close or Save and New to exit the screen or to enter another transaction.**

Alternatively, you can use the Search command or one of the Aged Payable reports to display unpaid bills onscreen, and then click Mark Paid at the top right. A Bill Payment transaction appears, and you can mark other bills as paid. A Print Check command appears at the bottom of the screen for bills that you choose to pay by way of a bank account.

Paying two or more bills at once

Given that bills seem to be coming out of the woodwork constantly, you can thankfully pay multiple bills at once:

1. **Display the Pay Bills page shown in Figure 8-2 by way of one of these choices:**

   - Choose + New ⇨ Pay Bills from the Vendor column.

   - Choose Transactions ⇨ Expenses ⇨ Print Checks drop-down menu ⇨ Pay Bills.

FIGURE 8-2:
The Pay
Bills page.

REMEMBER

The button to the left of the New Transaction button on the Expenses window remembers the last choice you made. This menu enables you to print checks, order checks, and pay bills. Your most recent choice becomes the default state for this button until you make another choice, which means if you choose Pay Bills once, you then have one-click access to the command until you make another selection from the menu.

2. **Choose a payment account.**

An Add New command enables you to add a new payment account on the fly if necessary.

3. **Select a payment date.**

This date applies to all bills that you choose as part of this Pay Bills transaction.

4. **Confirm the starting check number.**

Typically, this automatically increments for you, but you can override the check number shown if needed.

5. **Optional: Click Print Later if you want to print paper checks at a later time.**

This field only applies when you plan to print checks from QuickBooks later on, so skip it if you use the QuickBooks Online Bill Pay service.

6. **Choose one or more bills to pay.**

   Click the checkbox in the first column of the bill list for any bills that you want to pay. The Filter button enables you to display open bills for a specific vendor or range of due dates or to display only overdue bills.

7. **Optional: Adjust the payment amounts.**

   Although QuickBooks assumes that you want to pay bills in full, you can override the payment amounts for any bills to reflect a partial payment.

8. **Choose Print Check, Schedule Payments Online, Save and Close, or Save and New.**

   Print Check appears in the bottom middle of the Pay Bills page when you're making a payment from a bank account. Schedule Payments Online displays the QuickBooks Online Bill Pay service screen, which I discussed earlier in this chapter in the "Entering a bill" section. Choose Save and Close if you want to print later and have finished your work on this screen, or choose Save and New if you want to print later and enter another transaction.

The only other option you have in this window is Cancel, which causes QuickBooks to ask if you want to leave without saving.

Marking bills as paid

It's easy to remit money these days through numerous modalities, such as sending an ACH or using a payment service like Venmo or PayPal. You can also kick it old school and handwrite a paper check. In Chapter 3, I discuss how you can record such transactions as expenses, but you can also mark bills as paid without printing checks, although you will have to assign a check number.

1. **Choose Expenses ⇨ Bills and then click the Unpaid tab.**

   The Unpaid Bills page appears.

2. **Click the checkbox to the left of one or more invoices.**

3. **Click Mark as Paid.**

   The Mark as Paid task pane appears, as shown in Figure 8-3.

4. **Choose a payment account.**

5. **Confirm the Payment Date.**

6. **Optional: Adjust the Payment Amount field if applicable.**

7. **Optional: Click the X adjacent to a bill if you have changed your mind about marking it paid.**

	VENDOR	BILL NO.	OPEN BALANCE	CREDITS	PAYMENT AMOUNT
×	Price Gouger		$1,200.00	Not available	1200.00
×	Price Gouger		$1,835.00	Not available	1835.00
	Total (USD)		$3,035.00	$0.00	$3,035.00

FIGURE 8-3:
The Mark as Paid
task pane.

8. **Clear the Print Later checkbox.**

9. **Enter a number in the Starting Check No. field.**

   This can be a made-up number that should be part of a separate series of numbers from your printed checks.

10. **Click Save.**

    The Mark as Paid task pane closes.

The only other option you have in this window is Cancel, which causes QuickBooks to ask if you want to leave without saving.

TIP

You can also use the Mark as Paid task pane as an alternative to the Pay Bills page. In doing so you would either clear the Print Later checkbox, enter a valid check number in the Starting Check No. field, and then choose Save and Print. Or leave the Print Later checkbox enabled, and then later choose + New⇨ Print Checks to print the physical checks.

Recording Vendor Credits and Refunds

You could consider a vendor credit to be a negative expense. Vendor credits may arise when you return goods that you've paid for or perhaps when a service that was provided didn't meet your expectations and the vendor offers you a credit to be applied against future transactions. Or you may have the good fortune of having a refund check in hand from your vendor. Regardless of the situation, you begin the process by recording a vendor credit transaction.

Recording vendor credits

Use these steps to record a vendor credit:

1. **Choose + New ⇨ Vendor Credit.**

   The Vendor Credit window appears.

2. **Select the vendor that issued the credit.**

3. **Enter the date of the credit.**

4. **Enter the credit amount or refund amount as a positive amount.**

   Don't fall down any rabbit holes here and overthink things. Yes, I know this is basically a negative expense, but the Vendor Credit memo knows that, so you enter a positive amount here, as opposed to a negative amount.

5. **Optional: Select the account used on the original bill in the Category Details section if the credit relates to expenses that aren't related to purchasing inventory.**

6. **Optional: Enter the inventory items that you returned in the Item Details section if appropriate.**

7. **Optional: Attach a digital copy of the credit in the Attachments section.**

8. **Choose Save and Close or Save and New.**

Depending on how you choose to pay your bills, you might not even have to think about applying a credit against a future bill. The Pay Bills window that I discuss earlier in this chapter automatically applies open credits against bills you want to pay.

However, Pay Bills isn't the only way to pay a bill. In the section "Paying one bill at a time," I explain that you can also use the Checks window to pay bills. If you go that route, any open credits appear in the Add to Check task pane. Either way, it's a simple process to apply a credit memo against an unpaid bill.

Recording vendor refund checks

I cover two scenarios here. First, let's assume that you unexpectedly receive a check from your vendor, which means that you do not have an unapplied credit for this vendor. After that, I show you how to apply a refund check against an unapplied vendor credit transaction.

Posting refunds directly to your books

In this scenario, a vendor has sent you a check that you didn't anticipate, which means you don't have a vendor credit pending. You can record such payments in this fashion:

1. **Choose + New ⇨ Bank Deposit from the Other column.**

   The Bank Deposit window appears.

2. **Choose the bank account that you'll deposit the check into, or choose Payments to Deposit (Undeposited Funds) if you plan to take the check to the bank with one or more other checks.**

3. **Enter your vendor's name into the Received From column of the Add Funds to This Deposit section.**

4. **Choose an expense or cost of goods sold account from the Account column.**

   Do not choose Accounts Payable because doing so creates an unapplied open credit.

5. **Optional: Fill in the Description, Payment Method, and Ref No. fields.**

   Don't worry. Mum's the word if you choose to skip these fields.

6. **Enter the refund check amount into the Amount field.**

7. **Optional: Record any other amounts that you want to include on the same bank deposit.**

8. **Choose Save and Close.**

Everything is now accounted for in this scenario where an unexpected refund check arrives.

Offsetting a vendor credit

Our second scenario assumes that at some point in the past you entered a vendor credit because you anticipated applying the credit against a future bill. Perhaps your needs changed, or the vendor no longer provides the product or service you used in the past, so you requested a refund check. Here's how to apply the check in such a way that you can zero out the open vendor credit:

1. **Choose + New⇨ Bank Deposit from the Other column.**

   The Bank Deposit window appears.

2. **Choose the bank account that you'll deposit the check into, or choose Payments to Deposit (Undeposited Funds) if you plan to take the check to the bank with one or more other checks.**

3. **Enter your vendor's name into the Received From column of the Add Funds to This Deposit section.**

4. **Choose Accounts Payable (A/P) from the Account column.**

   Make sure to choose Accounts Payable (A/P) from the list; otherwise, you may end up with some phantom amounts lingering on your Aged Accounts Payable report once you finish posting these transactions.

5. **Optional: Fill in the Description, Payment Method, and Ref No. fields.**

   Don't worry. Mum's the word if you choose to skip these fields.

6. **Enter the refund check amount into the Amount field.**

7. **Optional: Record any other amounts that you want to include on the same bank deposit.**

8. **Choose Save and Close.**

9. **Choose + New⇨ Pay Bills.**

   I know, I know. You're saying, "They just paid *me*, I don't need to pay *them*!" Hang with me here, as all will be revealed momentarily.

10. **Select the bank deposit transaction that you saved in Step 8.**

    The vendor credit appears in the Credit Applied field, and the Total Payment becomes zero.

11. **Choose Save and Close.**

    Whew! You made it! Your vendor refund check or payment is applied and properly accounted for.

Working with Multiple Currencies

The Multicurrency feature — available to Essentials, Plus, and Advanced users — enables you to generate customer and vendor transactions denominated in currencies other than your home currency. You can also track bank accounts in other currencies. This includes the cryptocurrencies Bitcoin and Litecoin, as well as more than 150 global currencies. Use the search term **list of supported currencies** at `https://quickbooks.intuit.com/learn-support/en-us` to see the list of supported currencies. Multicurrency doesn't support customer- or currency-specific pricing, but QuickBooks Desktop does. Accordingly, converting from QuickBooks Desktop to QuickBooks Online can be problematic if you're currently using the Multicurrency feature in QuickBooks Desktop.

WARNING

A word of caution before you go further: You cannot turn the Multicurrency feature off after you enable it. You also cannot change your home currency because the Multicurrency feature affects many accounts and balances. In short, don't turn Multicurrency on unless you need to record transactions in other currencies or have bank accounts denominated in foreign currency, which includes cryptocurrency wallets.

Going forward, you will be required to specify a currency whenever you add an account to your chart of accounts or create a new customer or vendor record. You can assign only one currency to each account, customer, or vendor. QuickBooks automatically creates a new accounts receivable or accounts payable account when you create sales or expense transactions in a given currency.

REMEMBER

You can't change the currency for a customer, vendor, or account once you've posted a transaction to it. If such a need arises, you must deactivate the current record and then create a new customer, vendor, or account for which you can specify the new currency.

WARNING

Certain financial add-ons such as QuickBooks Payroll and QuickBooks Payments require your home currency to be U.S. dollars. You'll also want to confirm that any apps that you install work with the Multicurrency feature. I discuss apps for QuickBooks Online in Chapter 7.

Do I need Multicurrency?

The decision for using Multicurrency comes down to your base currency:

>> **U.S. dollars:** You need to enable the Multicurrency feature if you need to enter customer or vendor transactions denominated in any other currency.

>> **Any other currency:** You need the Global version of QuickBooks Online (https://quickbooks.intuit.com/global/) instead of the Multicurrency feature. This version only offers subscriptions for Simple Start, Essentials, or Plus.

REMEMBER

Income and expense accounts continue to use your home currency — the currency of the country where your business is physically located. You can specify the currency used for asset or liability accounts.

Enabling Multicurrency

Follow these steps to enable Multicurrency:

1. **Choose Settings ⇨ Account and Settings ⇨ Advanced.**

2. **Click the Edit icon in the Currency section.**

3. **Choose your home currency from the Home Currency drop-down list.**

   Choose the currency of your country, meaning don't select USD – United States Dollar as your home currency if your business is based in Canada.

4. **Toggle Multicurrency on to activate the feature.**

   QuickBooks warns you that

   ● You can't turn Multicurrency off.

   ● You can't change your home currency.

   ● Extra fields and columns will appear

   ● Some features may be disabled

5. **Select the checkbox labeled I Understand I Can't Undo Multicurrency.**

6. **Click Save.**

7. **Click Manage Currencies if you want to add one or more currencies now, or click Done if you plan to do that later.**

Setting up currencies

A Currencies option appears on your Settings menu once you've enabled Multicurrency. You can then establish the currencies that you accept:

1. **Choose Settings ⇨ Currencies to display the Currencies page.**

   CAD – Canadian Dollar and EUR – Euro may be automatically established as currencies for you by default.

2. **Click Add Currency.**

3. **Make a selection from the Add Currency list.**

4. **Click Add.**

   The Currencies page reappears with the new currency added.

Revaluing currencies

QuickBooks always records exchange rates, shown on the Currencies page, as the number of home currency units needed to equal one foreign currency unit. QuickBooks downloads exchange rates every four hours from Wall Street on Demand, but you can override this with your own exchange rate:

1. **Choose Settings ⇨ Currencies to display the Currencies page.**

2. **Choose Revalue from the Actions column for the currency that you want to revalue.**

   The Revalue page appears and indicates the currency that you are revaluing against your home currency.

3. **Optional: Edit the Revalue Date if needed.**

4. **Choose Custom Rate.**

5. **Enter the exchange rate.**

6. **Optional: Deselect any accounts that you do not want to revalue.**

7. **Click Revalue and Save.**

Removing currencies

Unlike all other lists in QuickBooks, you can delete currencies, as opposed to simply making them inactive:

1. **Choose Settings ⇨ Currencies to display the Currencies page.**

2. **Choose Revalue from the Actions column for the currency that you want to delete.**

3. **Click Yes to confirm you want to delete the currency.**

   The Currencies page reappears with the new currency added.

Noticing how the Multicurrency feature changes QuickBooks

Several things change about QuickBooks after you turn on Multicurrency:

» A Currencies option appears in the Lists column of your Settings menu.

» A Currency column in your chart of accounts reflects the currency assigned to each account.

» An Other Expense account named Exchange Gain or Loss is automatically added to your chart of accounts.

» Currency-specific accounts receivable (A/R) and accounts payable (A/P) accounts are automatically added to your chart of accounts the first time you create a related transaction.

» Your bank and credit card registers reflect the currency of each transaction (in parentheses) adjacent to any columns that reflect dollar amounts, along with a separate Foreign Currency Exchange Rate column.

» Sales and purchase forms that display your home currency allow you to specify a foreign currency for each transaction. QuickBooks then does all the conversions for you onscreen.

» All foreign currency amounts are converted to home currency amounts on your reports.

Using multiple currencies

This section takes a brief look at the effects of creating a bill transaction that uses multiple currencies. Creating a sales transaction for a foreign customer works in a similar fashion. You can also record journal entries in a foreign currency. You cannot process payroll or enter other types of transactions using foreign currencies.

REMEMBER

Time entries cannot be associated with a foreign currency customer.

Suppose that you have a vendor whose base currency is the Canadian dollar, and your home currency is the U.S. dollar. In this example, when I refer to the "foreign currency," I mean the Canadian dollar. Here's how to set a currency denomination for a vendor:

1. **Choose Expenses ➪ Vendors.**

   The Vendor page appears.

2. **Click New Vendor.**

3. **Select the vendor's currency from the Currency field at the top of the task pane, as shown in Figure 8-4.**

You'll see similar settings when you create a new customer or bank account.

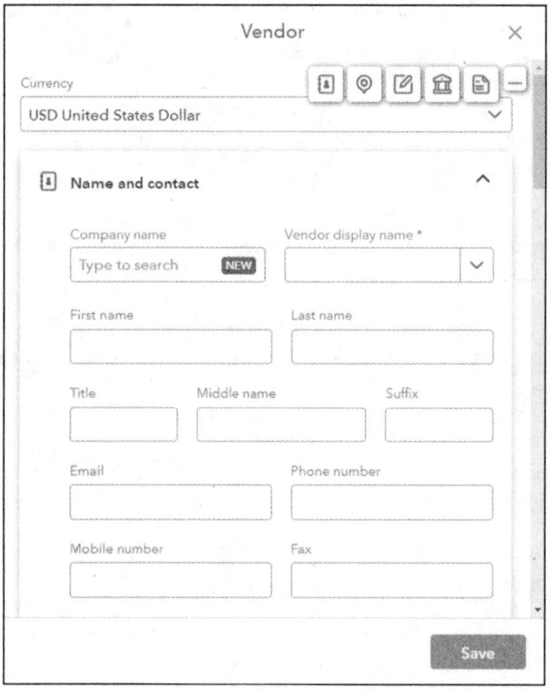

FIGURE 8-4:
Assigning a
foreign currency
to a new vendor.

4. **Click Got It when the Currency Can't Be Changed prompt appears.**

Optionally, click Don't Show This Again if you don't want to be reminded again.

5. **Enter the information for the Vendor Display Name field, along with any other fields you want to complete.**

6. **Click Save.**

The Currency column on the vendor page shows the currency assigned to each vendor. If you don't see the Currency column, click the Vendor List Settings button, click the Currency checkbox, and then click the Vendor List settings button again.

To enter a bill from foreign currency vendor, choose Expenses ⇨ Bills and then choose Add Bill ⇨ Create Bill. After you select your foreign currency vendor, the two currencies (first the foreign currency and then your home currency) associated with the transaction appear, as shown in Figure 8-5. Notice that you can override the exchange rate for this transaction if you want. If you like, you can compare this to Figure 8-2, which is what the Bill page looks like until the Multi-currency feature is enabled.

WARNING

The exchange rate field is erased when you enter a date beyond today. This makes sense because, well, you can't know the exchange rate until you get to that day. If you enter an exchange rate, QuickBooks asks if you want to use that exchange rate just for that one transaction or for all transactions on that date.

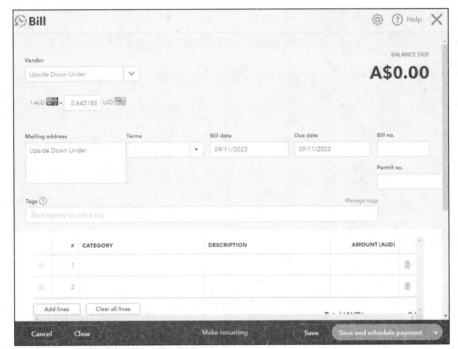

FIGURE 8-5: The Bill page in a company with Multicurrency enabled.

The amounts for each line appear in the foreign currency as you add products or services to the invoice, and totals are presented in both currencies. The balance due on the transaction appears in the foreign currency so that your customer knows how much to pay.

Keep in mind that QuickBooks reports display values in your home currency. For instance, a bill for CAD$93.50 appears as something like USD$69.95 on your Accounts Payable Aging Summary or Detail reports. Similarly, the Accounts Receivable (A/R) – CAD account that QuickBooks automatically adds to your chart of accounts reflects a balance of USD$69.95 on the Balance Sheet report.

Chapter **9**

Creating Bundles, Managing Users, and Tracking Time

An Essentials subscription or higher adds new features and functionality, some of which I discuss in Chapter 8. I lead this chapter off with a discussion of the bundle feature that you can use to streamline your invoicing process by being able to add two or more items to an invoice with a single selection. From there, I show you how to control the amount of access that you can grant to users in Essentials or Plus companies. (I cover managing users in Advanced companies in Chapter 13.)

Then I delve into the Time Tracking feature, which also requires an Essentials subscription or higher and can help streamline both payroll- and invoicing-related tasks. Time tracking enables you to create billable time entries, which I show you how to apply to invoices, along with billable expenses.

Bundling Products and Services

Essentials, Plus, or Advanced subscribers can group two or more items into a bundle, meaning a collection of products or services that a customer buys from you in a single transaction. A company selling fruit baskets might create one or more bundles comprising products at various price points so that they don't have to add the items to sales transactions one by one.

TIP

Bundles in QuickBooks Online are known as *group items* in QuickBooks Desktop.

Follow these steps to create a bundle:

1. **Choose Settings ⇨ Products and Services.**

2. **Click the New button to display the Product/Service task pane and then choose Bundle.**

   The Bundle task pane appears.

3. **Provide a name, a SKU if appropriate, and a description to appear on sales forms for the bundle.**

4. **Optional: Upload a picture of the item by clicking the Upload button, and navigating to the location where you store the picture.**

5. **Optional: Click Display Bundle Components When Printing or Sending Transactions if you want to see the individual components listed on your transaction forms instead of a single line item that uses the description you entered in Step 4.**

REMEMBER

A bundle is *not* an assembly. QuickBooks Online does not create a bill of materials or track bundles as separate items with quantities or cost. The price for a bundle is the sum of the prices for the individual components, which can be modified with pricing rules, as I discuss in Chapter 7.

6. **Use the table at the bottom of the task pane to identify the products included in the bundle, and then add products or services and the associated quantities as needed.**

7. **Click Save and Close, or choose Save and New if you want to create another bundle.**

Managing User Rights

QuickBooks allows you to limit a user's access to different areas of your books in Essentials, Plus, and Advanced companies. Simple Start companies have only a single user who has access to all parts of the company. Depending on your subscription level, you can add up to four types of users to your company.

Exploring the types of users

QuickBooks Online has four user levels, and the number you can have for your account depends on your subscription level. Following are the four levels:

>> **Standard:** Each standard user is assigned a role that determines their level of access to your accounting records. I discuss the roles you can assign to each user later in this section.

>> **Accountant:** Companies are allowed one or two accountant users. The number each company can have depends on the subscription level. (See Table 9-1.) Accountant users have full access to almost every aspect of your company by way of the QuickBooks Online Accountant platform, which I discuss in Part 5.

REMEMBER

The number of standard and accountant users is fixed for each company. You can add more standard users by upgrading to the next subscription level, but you can't add additional accountant users.

>> **Time tracking:** Essentials, Plus, and Advanced companies can have unlimited time tracking users who have access only to time-related features (or QuickBooks Time, if available).

>> **View Company Reports:** Plus and Advanced companies are allowed unlimited View Company Reports users who can view all reports in your company except for those that show payroll or time-tracking contact information.

Table 9-1 shows the number of users that are available at each subscription level.

TABLE 9-1: ## QuickBooks User Types Listed by Subscription Level

Subscription Level	Standard User Limit	Accountant User Limit	Time Tracking Users	View Company Reports Users
Simple Start	1	1	None	None
Essentials	3	2	Unlimited	None
Plus	5	2	Unlimited	Unlimited
Advanced	25	2	Unlimited	Unlimited

Reviewing QuickBooks feature areas

QuickBooks Online groups features by the major categories shown in Table 9-2. With the exception of payroll, reports, and lists, Essentials and Plus users have all-or-nothing access to these categories. In Chapter 13, I discuss how granular access to individual features can be granted in Advanced companies.

TABLE 9-2: **QuickBooks Feature Areas**

Area	Features
Sales	Invoices
	Estimates
	Sales receipt
	Receive payments
	Credit memo
	Refund receipt
	Delayed credit
	Delayed charge
Expenses	Bills
	Checks
	Bill payments
	Print checks
Products and Services	Products and services
Lists	Employees
	Vendors
	Customers
	Currencies
Bookkeeping	Bank deposit
	Transfer
	Bank transactions
	Rules
	Tags
	Receipts

Area	Features
Accounting	Chart of accounts
	Registers
	Reconciliation
	Journal entries
Reports	Payroll reports
	Sales reports
	Expense reports
	Management reports
	Custom reports
Time Tracking	Time tracking
Account Management	Access subscription
	Manage users
	Company info
Payroll	Payroll
	Workers compensation
	Benefits

Reviewing standard user roles

If you have an Essentials or Plus subscription, your ability to regulate access to the major feature areas is controlled by assigning users to one of the following roles:

>> **Primary Admin:** Whoever initiates a QuickBooks Online subscription becomes the primary admin, but you can reassign the primary admin as needed. Think of this as a superuser with unlimited rights to change any aspect of your accounting records, including adding and removing users.

>> **Company Admin:** A company admin has all the rights of the primary admin, except company admins can't edit or remove the primary admin's access.

>> **Standard All Access:** This role gives users access to all areas, including payroll and time tracking. Such users can also carry out these activities:

- View and optionally edit company information

- Optionally view and edit subscriptions

- Optionally view but not edit the user list

» **Standard All Access Without Payroll:** Inexplicably, this role is available in Essentials companies but not Plus. Such users can access all areas, including time tracking but not payroll, and they can view but not edit company information. You can't enable this role to view or edit subscriptions or the user list.

» **Standard Limited Customers and Vendors:** This role has access to the following feature areas:

- Sales

- Expenses

- Products and Services

- Lists (except employees)

- Reports (except payroll)

- Time Tracking

- View and optionally edit company information

- Optionally view and edit subscriptions

- Optionally view but not edit the user list

» **Standard Limited Customers Only:** This role has access to the following feature areas:

- Sales

- Products and Services

- Lists (except vendors and employees)

- Reports (except expenses and payroll)

- Time Tracking

- View and optionally edit company information

- Optionally view and edit subscriptions

- Optionally view but not edit the user list

» **Standard Limited Vendors Only:** This role has access to the following feature areas:

- Expenses

- Products and Services

- Lists (except customers and employees)

- Reports (except sales payroll)

- Time Tracking

- View and optionally edit company information

- Optionally view and edit subscriptions

- Optionally view but not edit the user list

>> **Standard No Access:** This role has access to the following feature areas:

- Time Tracking

- View and optionally edit company information

- Optionally view and edit subscriptions

- Optionally view but not edit the user list

>> **Timekeeping Only:** If you have a Premium or Elite Payroll or Time subscription, choosing this option directs you to QuickBooks Time to manage the user's privileges. Otherwise, this role has access to the basic Timekeeping feature, view-only access to company information, and no other aspects of the company. Timekeeping users do not count toward your subscription limit, so you can create as many timekeeping users as you want.

>> **View Company Reports:** Plus subscribers can assign this role to users you want to allow to view all reports except payroll and reports that contain contact information, such as customer and vendor lists. This role can view but not edit company information and has no access to other aspects of your books. This role isn't available in Essentials companies.

Managing users

Users who have permission to view or edit the user list can choose Settings ⇨ Manage Users to view the user list. Users with edit privileges can add, edit, and delete users.

Adding users

Carry out the following steps to add users:

1. **Click Add User.**

   The Add a New User page appears.

2. **Fill in the First Name, Last Name, and Email fields.**

3. **Choose a role from the Roles list.**

4. **Optionally expand the Account Management section if it appears in the Add Additional Permissions section, and toggle the available checkboxes on or off.**

TIP

The Company Info checkbox defaults to displaying a minus sign, which indicates the user has view access only. Click the minus sign to change it to a checkbox, which enables the user to edit company information as well. Click the checkbox again to toggle back to the minus sign. The Access Subscription and Manage Users checkboxes are even more nuanced. Click the left-most checkbox to grant view and edit access to the user, or leave that checkbox blank and then click the View checkbox to provide view access only.

5. **Click Send Invitation.**

QuickBooks emails the user an invitation to join your team.

Editing users

Here's how to edit a user's profile:

1. **Choose a user from the list.**

The Edit User page appears.

2. **Update the First Name, Last Name, and Email fields if needed, or modify the user's role and optional privileges.**

TIP

Changing the user's email address on the user list doesn't affect their access to your company. The user can still log in using the email address they provided when they set up their email account.

REMEMBER

Unless you're the primary admin for a company, you can't change your own role or security settings.

3. **Click Save and then click Yes to confirm that you want to save the changes.**

Deleting users

You can delete users in the following fashion:

1. **Choose a user from the list.**

The Edit User page appears.

2. **Scroll down and click Delete.**

You see the Are You Sure You Want to Delete This User? prompt.

3. **Click Delete User.**

4. **The User List reappears.**

The user you deleted no longer appears on the list.

You can't make a user inactive, but you can change their status to Standard No Access. Such users still count against the user limits predicated by your subscription level, but this can be a useful way to limit access while an employee is away on vacation or an extended absence.

Reassigning the primary admin role

The primary admin role is exclusive to a single user, and each QuickBooks company is required to have a primary admin user. The primary admin user can relinquish their rights and designate another user as primary admin in the following fashion:

1. **Log into your company as the primary admin user.**

   If you're unable to log in as the primary admin user, visit `https://quickbooks.intuit.com/learn-support/` and search for *Request to be the primary admin or contact* to request that Intuit make this change for you. You're required to provide documentation that you have rightful ownership or access privileges.

2. **Choose Settings⇨Manage Users.**

3. **Confirm that the user you want to designate as the primary admin is already configured as a company admin. If necessary, click Edit adjacent to that user, change their role to Company Admin, and then click Save.**

4. **Click the arrow in the Action column and choose Make Primary Admin.**

In Chapter 17, I discuss how you can assign the primary admin role to your accountant, and how your accountant can return the primary admin role back to you.

Enabling Time Tracking

Time tracking is already enabled if you have a QuickBooks Premium or Elite payroll subscription or a Premium or Elite time tracking subscription. Here's how to tell if you have any of these plans:

1. **Choose Settings⇨Account and Settings⇨Billing & Subscription.**

   The Billing & Subscription page appears.

2. **If both the QuickBooks Online Payroll and QuickBooks Time sections have a Learn More button, you don't currently have a payroll or time tracking subscription; otherwise, the name of your plan is listed in the corresponding section.**

The QuickBooks Core payroll subscription doesn't include the additional time tracking features that the Premium and Elite payroll subscriptions provide.

If you have a payroll or time tracking subscription, you can skip this section and move on to the following section of this chapter, "Creating employees and contractors." Otherwise, you need to enable the time tracking feature. The process for enabling most optional features, such as time tracking, starts with choosing Settings ⇨ Account and Settings, but time tracking is an exception to this rule. Use these steps instead:

1. **Choose Time ⇨ Overview (or Pay and Get Paid ⇨ Time ⇨ Overview).**

   A Supercharge Your Time overview page appears.

2. **Click Check Out Pricing.**

   A sales page appears for the QuickBooks Premium and Elite subscription plans.

   The Premium and Elite payroll and time tracking enable your employees to track their time on a mobile device or via a time kiosk (a tablet computer running QuickBooks Time). You can also establish geo-fencing to remind employees to sign in or out as they enter or leave a job site or location and create customizable reports beyond what's offered in QuickBooks itself.

3. **Click the respective Sign Up button to subscribe to either plan, or scroll down to the bottom of the page and click the Use Basic Time Tracking (Included in Your Current Plan) link.**

   Intuit wants you to think that you have to pay for time tracking, and you may need to in order to get certain features, but a free option exists if you're still figuring out what your time tracking needs are.

If you choose Use Basic Time Tracking, an Overview page displays a misleading checklist indicating that the next step is to add a time entry. If you haven't set up employees or contractors yet, you're prompted to add an employee. Click cancel on this screen and follow the instructions in the next section if you want to add a contractor instead.

Creating employees and contractors

I cover creating employees and contractors in detail in Chapter 4, so I provide only a quick overview here. You can set up an employee as follows:

1. **Choose Payroll ⇨ Employees.**

   If you haven't opted into a payroll plan and haven't created employees yet, you're presented with a page extolling the benefits of the QuickBooks Payroll subscription plans. Otherwise, you see an employee list.

2. **The next step depends on the following variables:**

- *You have an existing payroll subscription but haven't yet created an employee:* Expand the Get Ready to Pay Your Team section and then click Finish Up.

- *You want to purchase a Premium or Elite Payroll subscription:* Click the Sign Up button for the corresponding plan, and then follow the onscreen prompts.

- *You have a Time Tracking subscription or are using the Basic Time Tracking and want to add an employee:* Click the Add Employee link just below the Employee, Contractor, and Workers' Comp tabs.

- *You want to add a contractor:* Click the Contractor tab and then click Add Your First Contractor.

TIP

Depending on the approach you take, you may see a variety of different screens. See Chapter 4 for a more detailed discussion of adding employees and contractors.

REMEMBER

You need to set yourself up as an employee or contractor if you want to track your own time.

Establishing time tracking users

Earlier in this chapter, I mentioned that you can have unlimited time tracking users. Rest assured, time tracking users only see screens related to recording time and don't have any access to the rest of your accounting records. Plus and Advanced users can also add unlimited users who have access to all reports except those that show payroll or time contact information. Once you have created an employee or contractor, you can give them time tracking privileges. The steps vary depending on your situation.

Premium or Elite Payroll subscription

If you have a Premium or Elite Payroll subscription, and you want an employee to track their time, follow these steps:

1. **Choose Payroll ⇨ Employees.**

2. **Click the employee's name.**

3. **Click the Send Invite link for QuickBooks Time.**

If you want a contractor to track their time, use these steps:

1. **Choose Payroll ⇨ Time ⇨ Open QuickBooks Time ⇨ My Team.**
2. **Click on the contractor's name.**
3. **Click Send Invite.**

Premium or Elite Time subscription

If you have a Premium or Elite Time subscription and you want an employee or contractor to track their time, use these steps:

1. **Choose Payroll ⇨ Time ⇨ Open QuickBooks Time ⇨ My Team.**
2. **Click on the team member's name.**
3. **Click Send Invite.**

If you are using the basic time tracking feature, and you want an employee or contractor to track their time, use these steps:

1. **Choose Settings ⇨ Manage Users ⇨ Add User ⇨ Time Tracking Only.**
2. **Complete the First Name, Last Name, and Email fields.**
3. **Choose Track Time Only from the Roles list.**

REMEMBER

   If you choose any role other than Track Time Only the user counts toward the user limit for your subscription level.

4. **Click Sync Team Member.**
5. **Choose an employee or contractor from the list or click Add New.**

   When you click Add New, a Vendor task pane appears, through which you can add a contractor. QuickBooks moves the vendor to your Contractor list even though you are setting them up as a vendor.

TIP

   An Update button appears on the screen so that you can make a correction if you inadvertently select an incorrect choice.

   You have to back out of this screen and set up your employee in the fashion described in Chapter 4.

6. **Click Send Invitation.**

REMEMBER

   Your employees (or vendors) create a QuickBooks Online account if necessary.

Once they log in, they're presented with a summary screen that shows hours for the current week and month. When your employees then click Add Time, they have three options:

>> **Weekly:** Enables employees to complete or add to a weekly time sheet.

>> **Single Activity:** Enables employees to record a single time-related activity.

>> **Go To Report:** Displays the Time Activities by Employee Detail report.

TIP

See Chapter 11 if you want to use the Project feature to track time and other transactions in a QuickBooks Online Plus or Advanced subscription.

You can also add time entries directly by choosing + New ⇨ Time Entry. To run the Time Activity by Employee report, choose the Reports link on the left menu bar and enter the word Time in the Find a Report By Name search box. You can customize the report to display any time frame that you want. I cover reports in more detail in Chapter 6.

Creating Billable Time Entries

Your employees may complete activities required to run your company (such as preparing customer invoices or entering accounting information), and they may perform work related directly to your customers. In the latter case, you may want to track the time that employees spend on client-related projects so you can bill your customers for your employees' time. This section focuses on the time-tracking tools native to QuickBooks Online.

Enabling billable time entries

Once you've set up one or more employees or contractors who will be tracking time, you must turn on two options:

1. **Choose Settings ⇨ Account and Settings ⇨ Time.**

   The General section indicates how many employees or contractors are set up for time tracking.

TIP

   Click the Team Members link in the General section to display a task pane that shows the list of time tracking employees and contractors. You can then enable or disable time tracking on a case-by-case basis.

2. **Click the pencil icon in the Timesheet section.**

3. **Toggle the Show Service field on.**

4. **Toggle Allow Time to be Billable on.**

5. **Click Save and then Done.**

TIP

If your business has time-tracking needs that go beyond the basics, click See Plans to check out QuickBooks Time. This is one of several timekeeping apps that fully integrate with QuickBooks Online to enable your employees to track time on their mobile devices. Time entries that they record sync automatically with your books, with all the appropriate customer, job, and employee information.

Entering time activities

Perhaps you want to record two hours that an employee worked on a consulting project. Follow these steps to open the Add Time For window:

1. **Choose + New ⇨ Time Entry.**

   The Add Time For task pane appears.

   REMEMBER

   If you're working with a project, you can choose Projects (Business Overview ⇨ Projects), select the project, and click Add to Project.

2. **Choose an employee from the Add Time task pane.**

3. **Choose the date when the work was performed.**

4. **Click Add Work Details.**

   The Add Work Details pane opens.

5. **Enter a time amount in the Duration field, such as 2 for two hours.**

   Alternatively, you can enter start and end times by toggling the Start/End Times option.

6. **Select the customer for which the work was performed.**

7. **Select the service that was performed.**

   REMEMBER

   You can't add new services on the fly from the Add Work Details screen, so make sure to set up any new services before you try to create time entries.

8. **Toggle the Billable (/hr) option if applicable.**

9. **Enter any notes, such as a description of the work.**

   You can change the description after adding the time entry to the invoice.

10. **Click Done to save the entry, or click Delete to discard the entry.**

Adding billable time and expenses to an invoice

You can add billable time entries and expenses to an invoice in a couple of ways.

Customers page

Use the following steps to add billable time through the Customers page:

1. **Choose Sales, Sales & Expenses, or Customers & Leads⇨Customers.**

   The Add Time For task pane appears.

2. **Click any customer's name.**

   The customer's page appears and displays a list of transactions.

3. **Choose Action⇨Create Invoice for any Time Charge transaction that hasn't ben invoiced yet.**

   If you have multiple time charges you want to invoice, simply click Create Invoice for any one of the charges. The Invoice window that appears enables you to add the other time entries to the invoice.

TIP

I discuss how to indicate that an expense is billable in Chapter 3.

Invoices page

Use the following steps to add billable time through the Invoices page:

1. **Choose +New⇨Invoice.**

   The Invoice page appears.

2. **Choose a customer's name.**

   Any unbilled time entries or expenses appear on the right side of the screen.

3. **Click Add for any individual time or expenses you want to bill, or click Add All.**

   Each billable time entry's information is added to the invoice as a line with the service, description, quantity, rate, and total amount filled in. By default, time entries appear individually in the invoice, but you can opt to group time entries by service type. You can edit any information as needed. Fill in the rest of the invoice as described in Chapter 2 to add other lines that don't pertain to time entries.

TIP

Don't forget that you can add a subtotal for time entries, or any group of line items on an invoice by clicking the Add Subtotal button. In Chapter 7, I discussed how to automatically group and subtotal time entries.

QUICKBOOKS ONLINE AND GOOGLE CALENDAR

If you use Google Calendar to track your time you can install an app that enables you to pull event details into an invoice. This app is free if you have a Gmail account or a Google Workplace subscription (formerly known as G Suite). Choose Apps ⇨ Find Apps and then search for *Invoice with Google Calendar*. Click Get App Now and then follow the prompts.

When the app is installed, you can click the Google Calendar icon that appears on the invoice form. A panel enables you to set search parameters, such as choosing a Google Calendar, specifying a time frame, and entering any keywords to search on. You can choose events to add to the invoice from the search results, which records the title, description, hours worked, and date from Google Calendar.

3

QuickBooks Online Plus Features

Chapter 10

Tracking Inventory and Purchase Orders

I n Chapter 2, I discuss how to create service items and non-inventory items in any QuickBooks company. In this chapter, I show you how to track physical inventory items, which you can do only in Plus and Advanced companies. I then discuss purchase orders, which are non-posting transactions that document orders for goods and services you've placed with one or more vendors.

Keep in mind that inventory tracking in QuickBooks Online is rather simplistic. My technical editor Dan DeLong sums it up as "I buy some stuff, and then I sell that stuff." For instance, let's say that you buy shoes. It's unlikely that you're altering those shoes in any way; you're probably turning around and simply selling those shoes to someone else, ideally at a higher price than you paid. If this encapsulates your inventory needs, you'll probably be happy with physical inventory tracking in QuickBooks. However, if you manufacture products or transform raw materials into other goods, you'll most likely find the inventory tracking capability in QuickBooks Online to be severely lacking. In that case, look at the App Store for QuickBooks Online, which I discuss in Chapter 7. You may be able to subscribe to an add-on for QuickBooks Online that will fill the gap for you.

Working with Physical Inventory Items

QuickBooks Online requires you to use the first in, first out (FIFO) inventory valuation method. This means that the first items you purchase are the first ones you sell. This doesn't mean you need to physically keep track of the sequence in which items arrived in your storeroom or warehouse; rather, just know that QuickBooks associates the cost of the first items you purchase with the first items you sell.

WARNING

You must file Form 3115, Application for Change in Accounting Method (https://irs.gov/forms-pubs/about-form-3115), with the Internal Revenue Service if you're based in the United States and currently using another accounting method, such as last in, first out (LIFO) or Average Cost for valuing your inventory.

TIP

QuickBooks Desktop Premier and Enterprise versions offer more robust, advanced inventory capabilities, such as to support manufacturing, but only support the average costing valuation method.

Enabling the inventory feature

You can't track physical items in QuickBooks until you enable the Track Inventory Quantity setting by carrying out these steps:

1. **Choose Settings➪Account and Settings➪Sales.**
2. **Click on the Products and Services section, and then enable the Track Inventory Quantity on Hand setting.**
3. **Click Yes to confirm your understanding of your inventory costing method becoming FIFO.**
4. **Click Save and then click Done.**

REMEMBER

Inventory items are always valued and reported on using your home currency. Enabling the Multicurrency feature has no effect on inventory item valuations, even if you buy or sell items in a foreign currency. I discuss the Multicurrency feature in more detail in the Cheat Sheet for *QuickBooks Online For Dummies* at www.dummies.com/.

Adding inventory items

The steps for adding inventory items are similar to creating service and non-inventory items but with some additional fields:

1. **Choose Settings⇨Products and Services to display the Products and Services page.**

   Alternatively, Products and Services appears in the sidebar menu under Sales & Expenses or Sales, depending on whether your menu is set to Business View or Accountant View, respectively.

2. **Click the New button to display the Product/Service Information task pane, and then choose Inventory.**

   The Product/Service Information task pane shown in Figure 10-1 appears.

TIP

   If you didn't click Save when you enabled inventory tracking, you can click Turn On Inventory Tracking, and then click Turn On.

3. **Enter up to 100 characters in the Name field, which is one of only three required fields.**

4. **Optional: Enter up to 60 characters in the SKU field.**

   SKU is short for *stock-keeping unit*. It's another way of referring to a part number or other identifier for your products and services.

FIGURE 10-1:
Use this task pane to create an inventory item.

5. Optional: Upload a picture of the item by clicking the Edit button, and navigating to the location where you stored the image.

Click the Delete button to the right of Edit if you want to remove a picture you've uploaded.

6. Optional: Assign the item to a category.

Assigning items to categories enables you to group related items. I discuss categories in more detail in Chapter 2.

7. Optional: Assign a default class to the item if you've enabled the Class feature.

I discuss the Class feature in Chapter 11.

8. Enter an amount in the Initial Quantity On Hand field.

This amount is the starting inventory count you want to record in your books. Enter zero if you haven't yet procured or produced this item.

9. Enter a date in the As of Date field.

Typically, you want to use the first day of your fiscal year for the As Of Date, entered in mm/dd/yyyy format, or make a choice from the calendar that appears when you click in the field.

REMEMBER

The As Of date should not be any earlier than the start date of your QuickBooks company. Start dates can vary by item, however, which is a way that you can track when you first started buying and selling items.

10. Optional: Enter an amount in the Reorder Point field.

QuickBooks alerts you when the quantity on hand for an item reaches or drops below the amount you indicate here.

11. Confirm the Inventory Asset account (category).

The Inventory Asset account field should be prefilled for you, but you can create a new asset account by clicking the drop-down arrow and then choosing Add Account.

12. **Fill in the Description field for how the item should be described on sales forms.**

Sales forms include invoices and estimates.

13. **Fill in the Sales Price/Rate field.**

Consider this to be the base price you sell your product for. You can override the price manually or employ pricing rules in the upcoming "Using Pricing Rules" section.

14. **Confirm the Income Account (category).**

The Income Account is prefilled, but you can choose or add a different account if you want.

15. **A Sales Tax section appears if you've enabled the sales tax feature. Optionally, click Edit Sales Tax if you want to override the default location-based sales tax calculations for this product.**

A Product/Service task pane appears and asks you to choose a product category. Alternatively, you can choose Taxable or Non-Taxable and then click Done.

16. **Optional: Fill in the Purchasing Information field.**

Enter a description that you want to appear on purchasing forms, which includes purchase orders, bills, and checks.

17. **Optional: Enter the cost of the item.**

This is the cost you last paid when you purchased this item.

18. **Optional: Specify or add a preferred vendor.**

Use the Preferred Vendor field to indicate the vendor that you most frequently purchase this item from. This in no way prevents you from procuring the item elsewhere when needed.

19. **Click Save and Close.**

The Products and Services list appears, displaying your new item.

TIP

Click Settings above the Action column and then choose Compact to squeeze more products and services onscreen.

Editing inventory items

The Products and Services page shows all your active inventory items, as well as services, non-inventory items, and bundles.

TIP

Bundles are combinations of inventory items, services, and non-inventory items you can add to an invoice as a single item or a collection of items. I discuss how to create bundles in Chapter 9.

The following commands in the Action column on the Products and Services pages are specific to inventory items:

>> **Edit:** This command appears in the Action column next to every item on your Products and Services list. Click Edit to make changes to the item itself.

>> **Make Inactive:** Choose this command to make an item inactive. To view items you've marked as inactive, click the funnel icon just above your list of products and services, change Status to Inactive, and then click Apply. This command then becomes Make Active in case you want to reactivate items in the future.

WARNING

QuickBooks enables you to make items inactive even if the quantity on hand isn't zero. The Quantity on Hand field is automatically adjusted to zero when you make such items inactive. Making an item active again doesn't restore any quantity on hand that was present when you marked the item inactive.

>> **Run Report:** Choose this command to run a Quick Report for the past 90 days of transactions for this item.

>> **Duplicate:** Choose this command to display the Product/Service Information task pane that you used earlier in the chapter to create a new item. Some fields are prefilled to ease the process of setting up similar items.

>> **Adjust Quantity:** Choose this command to adjust the quantity on hand of Inventory items, which I discuss in more detail in the section "Adjusting inventory quantities or values."

>> **Adjust Starting Value:** Choose this command to adjust the starting value of Inventory items, which I discuss in more detail in the section "Adjusting inventory quantities or values."

>> **Reorder:** As I discuss in more detail in the section "Reordering inventory items," this command enables you to create a purchase order so that you can reorder Inventory items.

You use the Products and Services list pretty much the same way you use the Customer and Vendor lists. For example, you can search for an item by its name, SKU, or sales description. You can identify the columns you can use to sort the list by sliding your mouse over the column heading; if the mouse pointer changes to a hand, you can click that column to sort the list using the information in that column.

Using Pricing Rules

The pricing rules feature in QuickBooks seems to be in perpetual beta testing. When I tried to create a price rule for an individual customer, QuickBooks acted as if I hadn't created customers yet. If you're willing to work around that constraint, here's how to enable the Price Rules feature:

1. **Choose Settings ⇨ Account and Settings ⇨ Sales.**

2. **Click in the Products and Services section and toggle on the Turn on Price Rules setting.**

3. **Click Save and then click Done to close the Account and Settings page.**

Once you've enabled price rules, follow these steps to create one or more rules:

1. **Click Settings ⇨ All Lists ⇨ Price Rules.**

   The new Price Rules section appears below Products and Services on the All page.

TIP

   Choose Settings ⇨ Switch to Accountant View if you do not see Pricing Rules on the All Lists page after you have enabled the feature.

2. **Click Create a Rule to display the Create a Price Rule page.**

3. **Assign a name to your rule.**

4. **Choose All Customers, Select Individually, or if available, choose a class from the Customer list.**

   If you chose Select Individually, checkboxes appear to the left of your customer names on the page so that you can select the applicable customers.

5. **Choose All Products and Services, All Services, All Inventory, All Non-Inventory, Select Individually, or if available, choose a category from the Products and Services list.**

6. **Choose Percentage, Fixed Amount, or Custom Price Per Item from the Price Adjustment Method list.**

   If you chose Custom Price per Item, your Products and Services list appears along with an Adjusted Price column that you can use to selectively override individual prices.

7. **If you chose Percentage or Fixed Amount, choose Increase by or Decrease from the Percentage or Fixed Amount lists, respectively, and then enter an amount in the adjacent field.**

8. **Optional: If you chose Percentage or Fixed Amount, choose a rounding increment from the list.**

9. **Optional: Provide a start date or an end date for the price rule.**

10. **Click Save and Close, or choose Save and New if you want to create another price rule.**

Intuit recommends that you keep the total number of price rules to 10,000 or less.

You can't assign a price rule to a bundle, but you can assign price rules to individual items within a bundle. I discuss bundles in Chapter 9.

Recording Inventory Transactions

The most common inventory-related transaction is likely reordering inventory, particularly if you purchase products for resale. Of course, any time you have custody of physical goods, discrepancies may arise or products may get damaged, which means you may need to adjust inventory quantities or valuations.

Reordering inventory items

You can also use the Products and Services list to identify inventory items that are below their reorder level or out of stock. Click Low Stock at the top of the list to show only items that have either a quantity below the reorder point you set (see the "Adding inventory items" section earlier in this chapter) or an on-hand quantity of one. Click Out of Stock to view items that have an on-hand quantity of zero or a negative inventory quantity. Click the X that appears to the right of either graphic to display all items again.

You can reorder low-stock or out-of-stock inventory items in two ways:

» Click the arrow in its Action column and choose Reorder from the drop-down menu that appears.

» Select the checkbox to the left of two or more item names you're ordering from a single vendor, and then choose Batch Actions ➪ Reorder to add multiple items to a purchase order.

In either case, a purchase order reflecting the item(s) you chose appears. Complete the purchase order and then send it to your supplier. QuickBooks allows you to generate purchase orders for only one vendor at a time, so you need to repeat these steps for each vendor you want to order from.

REMEMBER The Reorder option is only available in the Action column for Inventory items. You have to manually create purchase orders for Non-Inventory and Service items you purchase from others.

Adjusting inventory quantities or values

On occasion, you may need to adjust inventory item quantities on hand or starting values, particularly after performing a physical inventory count. You can print the Physical Inventory Worksheet report by choosing Reports (Business Overview⇨Reports) and then typing the word **Physical** in the Search field. This worksheet makes it easy to record item quantities on hand as you count inventory. You can then compare the report to your accounting records and make adjustments as needed.

Adjusting inventory quantities

If your physical count results in a discrepancy from your accounting records, you need to create an adjustment to reconcile your books with the reality in your warehouse. Follow these steps to create an inventory adjustment:

1. **Choose New⇨Inventory Qty Adjustment to display the Inventory Quantity Adjustment page.**

   Click Show More if you don't see the Inventory Adjustment command on the New menu. Alternatively, you can click the drop-down menu in the Action column for any item on your Products and Services page and then choose Adjust Quantity.

2. **Optional: Change the adjustment date or the inventory adjustment account.**

   You can also change the reference number.

3. **Click the Product field in Row 1 and choose an inventory item from the drop-down menu.**

   The Description field is populated, along with the current quantity on hand. The New Qty field defaults to the current quantity on hand.

   If you've enabled class and location tracking, you can supply information for those fields as you complete the Inventory Quantity Adjustment window.

REMEMBER

4. **Update either the New Qty or the Change in Qty field.**

   If the Qty on Hand field indicates that you should have 345 giant bows, but you counted only 330 bows in your warehouse, you need to reduce the quantity on hand in QuickBooks by 15. You can do either of the following:

   • Enter **330** in the New Qty field.

   • Enter **–15** in the Change in Qty field.

5. **Repeat Steps 3 and 4 for each inventory item you need to adjust.**

   Click Add Lines if you want to add more items.

   The Clear All Lines button next to Add Lines completely erases the Inventory Quantity Adjustment screen without asking you to confirm. To guard against accidentally clicking this button, you can click the Save button at the bottom of the screen to save your work in progress. Conversely, the Cancel and Clear buttons at the bottom of the screen provide a confirmation prompt.

6. **In the Memo field, enter a description that explains why you made this adjustment.**

   Your accountant, or perhaps your future self, will thank you for your diligence in documenting why the adjustments were made.

7. **Click the Save and Close button.**

You can prefill the inventory adjustment screen by choosing one or more items from your Products and Services page and then choosing Adjust Quantity from the Batch Actions menu.

Entering inventory quantity adjustments

You can review or amend inventory adjustment transactions by carrying out these steps:

1. **Choose + New ⇨ Inventory Qty Adjustment or use the Change Quantity command on the Action menu on the Products and Services page to display the Inventory Quantity Adjustment window.**

2. **Click the Recent Transactions button in the top-left corner of the window, to the left of the words Inventory Quantity Adjustment.**

3. **Choose an adjustment from the list or click View More to display the Search page, where you can provide additional criteria.**

4. **Once you've displayed a transaction, you can make edits as needed or delete the transaction.**

   You can remove a line from an adjustment by clicking its Delete button at the right edge of the row. You can delete the entire transaction by clicking the Delete button at the bottom of the screen.

5. **Click Save and Close in the bottom-right corner of the window.**

Adjusting an inventory item's starting value

Perhaps in spite of your best-laid plans, you made a mistake when you entered the starting value for an inventory item. You can edit the starting value for any inventory item you created subsequent to November 2015.

WARNING

Changing an item's starting value can have wide-ranging effects, and a note to this effect appears when QuickBooks senses you're trying to edit an inventory item's starting value. If you're not sure what you're doing, ask your accountant. Please. They won't mind.

To adjust an inventory item's starting value, follow these steps:

1. **Choose Settings ⇨ Products and Services.**

2. **Click the arrow in the Action column for the inventory item you want to adjust, and then choose Adjust Starting Value from the drop-down menu.**

   A warning appears, explaining that changing an inventory item's starting value may affect the initial value of your inventory.

3. **Assuming that you heeded the preceding warning and know what you're doing, click Got It!**

   The Inventory Starting Value window appears.

TIP

   If you've enabled class and location tracking, note that you can supply information for those fields along with other fields that affect the inventory item's starting value.

4. **Adjust the Initial Quantity on Hand, As of Date, and Initial Cost as needed.**

   Although you can also change the Inventory Adjustment Account, I don't recommend doing so unless you want to *really* get under your accountant's skin.

REMEMBER

   You're in the wrong place if you want to change the inventory asset account. Choose the Edit command in the Action column of the Products and Services page for the item you want to modify. Make the change in the Product/Service Information task pane.

5. **Click Save and Close.**

Working with Purchase Orders

Purchase orders are non-posting transactions that don't appear in your company's general ledger, nor do they affect your financial statements — they simply help you keep track of unfulfilled orders you've placed. Once the goods or services have been provided, you compare the packing slip or other documentation to the purchase order and then convert the purchase order to a bill to be paid or to a check or expense transaction. At this point your books are affected as follows:

>> Bills that you create increase the balance of your accounts payable account. Checks reduce the corresponding bank account balance, whereas expenses may reduce your bank account balance or increase a credit card account balance.

>> If the purchase order includes one or more inventory items, your inventory account balance increases by the cost of the items received.

>> Any other line items on the purchase order typically increase the balance of corresponding expense accounts.

NON-POSTING TRANSACTIONS

Purchase orders and estimates are two examples of non-posting transactions. Non-posting transactions don't affect your accounting records, but they're helpful because they enable you to track potential transaction information you don't want to forget. Other non-posting transactions include delayed charges and delayed credits.

Delayed charges record potential future revenue, much like estimates. In fact, you can convert a delayed charge to an invoice in the same way that you convert an estimate to an invoice. For details, see the section "Converting an estimate to an invoice," in Chapter 2.

Conversely, if you want to stage a credit memo to be posted against an invoice later, you can create a delayed credit. Unlike Credit Memo transactions that affect your books upon entry, Delayed Credit transactions affect your books only when they're applied to an invoice. This is helpful when you want to post a credit to a customer's account on a contingent basis, such as when the credit only applies if they place another order in the future.

Creating either transaction is much like creating an invoice, which I discuss in detail in Chapter 2.

Configuring purchase order settings

Following are the purchase order–related settings you may need to enable or adjust:

1. **Choose Settings⇨Account and Settings⇨Expenses.**

2. **Toggle on Show Items Table on Expense and Purchase Forms in the Bills and Expenses section.**

3. **Click Save to record your change to the Bills and Expenses section.**

4. **Click on the Purchase Orders section, and then toggle Use Purchase Orders on.**

5. **Optional: Toggle on Custom Transaction Numbers in the Purchase Orders section.**

   Enable this setting if you want to assign your own transaction numbers to purchase orders; otherwise, purchase order numbers are automatically assigned to your transactions.

6. **Optional: Fill in the Default Message on Purchase Orders.**

   This allows you to add boilerplate language to appear on every purchase order.

7. **Click Save to record your change to the Purchase Orders section.**

8. **Optional: Click in the Messages section to customize the default email message.**

   You can customize the subject line and email body and then choose to send yourself a copy, as well as copy or blind copy one or more email addresses.

9. **Click Save to record your change to the Messages section.**

10. **Click Done to close the Account and Settings window.**

Now you're good to go and ready to start creating purchase orders.

Creating purchase orders

Follow these steps to create a purchase order from scratch:

1. **Choose + New⇨Purchase Order from the left menu bar.**

   A new purchase order window appears with a status of Open. You can mark purchase orders as Open or Closed.

2. **Choose a vendor.**

   The vendor's mailing address appears.

3. **Optional: Choose a customer from the Ship To field.**

   This enables you to instruct the vendor to deliver the goods or services directly to your customer.

4. **Add at least one line item either to the Category Details or the Item Details section.**

   Category Details gives you the flexibility to order anything under the sun without specifying an inventory, non-inventory, or service item. As you may surmise, the Item Details section enables you to choose existing items or add new items on the fly.

5. **Optional: Fill in the Your Message to Vendor field with any special instructions, or enter a memo, which is an internal note that your vendor can't see.**

6. **Optional: Attach an electronic document to the invoice by clicking the Attachments box. You can then navigate to the document or drag the document into the Attachments box.**

   Supporting documents must be no more than 20MB in size each, and one of these file types: PDF, JPEG, PNG, DOC, XLSX, CSV, TIFF, GIF, or XML. This means you can include pictures of the product, schematics, or blueprints for an item to be manufactured, and so on. If your vendor sends you a sales order or estimate confirming the transaction, you can add a copy of that document here as well.

7. **At the bottom of the window, you can choose any of the following options:**

   - Cancel to discard the purchase order and close the window.

   - Print to display a preview of the purchase order, from which you can print a paper copy or download a PDF version.

   - Make Recurring to schedule the transaction as a recurring invoice.

   - More to copy, delete, or view the audit history of the transaction.

     TIP

     The More button appears at the bottom of the screen after you've saved the purchase order or clicked Print to display the print preview.

   - Save to assign a purchase order number and save the transaction.

   - Save and New to save your transaction and create a new purchase order.

- Save and Close to save the transaction and exit the Purchase Order window.

- Save and Send to assign a purchase order number and save the transaction, after which you can edit the default email message, preview the purchase order, and then email a copy to the vendor.

TIP

Toggle between Save and New, Save and Close, and Save and Send by clicking the arrow on the button. The option you choose becomes the default behavior for purchase orders until you make a different selection in the future.

Converting estimates to purchase orders

In addition to creating purchase orders from scratch, you can also convert estimates into purchase orders. Estimates, which I discuss in Chapter 2, can be considered pre-invoices; they document what a customer has agreed to purchase from you. Once the customer approves the estimate, you may want to convert the estimate to a purchase order. Doing so doesn't close out the estimate because you also likely want to convert the estimate into an invoice. However, converting an estimate to a purchase order minimizes data entry and helps ensure that the purchase order is completed correctly.

WARNING

You can only convert estimates with a Pending or Accepted status to purchase orders or invoices. Converting an estimate to an invoice sets its status to Closed, so convert estimates to purchase orders first if you need both.

Here's how to convert an estimate to a purchase order:

1. **Create and save a new estimate, select an estimate from a vendor's Transaction List, or use the Search command at the top of every QuickBooks page.**

    Alternatively, choose + New ➪ Estimates, and click the Recent Transactions icon to the left of the estimate number in the top-left corner of the screen to see a list of recent estimates.

2. **Click the arrow next to the Create Invoice button and choose Copy to Purchase Order from the drop-down menu.**

    You may see a message that some items on the estimate won't carry over to the purchase order. This situation occurs when one or more items in the estimate don't have the I Purchase This Product/Service from a Vendor option enabled within your item list.

    TIP

    The Create Invoice button appears on the Estimate window after you click Save. So, no, you aren't going crazy if you were just scouring a blank estimate window looking for the button.

3. Click OK if a prompt indicates that some items may not carry over to a purchase order.

4. Edit the purchase order as necessary, selecting a vendor and adding any more items you want to the purchase order.

5. Choose Save and Send, Save and New, or Save and Closed, as appropriate.

Duplicating existing purchase orders

The Copy command on the Purchase Order screen enables you to replicate an existing purchase order. For instance, you may want to reorder a set of items you've ordered in the past. Or you might convert an estimate to a purchase order but need to order items from more than one vendor. Here are the steps:

1. Search for the purchase order if needed.

2. Click the Recent Transactions command in the top-left corner of the Purchase Order page to view recent purchase orders, select a purchase order from a vendor's Transaction List, or use the Search command at the top of every QuickBooks page.

   Click the Copy command at the bottom of the Purchase Order screen.

3. Edit the purchase order as needed and then choose a Save option at the bottom-right corner of the screen.

Receiving items against purchase orders

You can apply all or part of a purchase order to a Bill, Check, or Expense transaction. You record what you've received and later add the remaining items to another transaction as needed until the entire purchase order is fulfilled. QuickBooks can link multiple transactions to the purchase order and automatically close the purchase order when you've received everything or you've clicked the Closed checkbox for any line items that you won't receive in full.

Perhaps you have a purchase order with three items, and you receive one of the three items. Here's how to receive the items against the purchase order:

1. Open the New menu and choose Bill, Check, or Expense.

   For this example, I'm using a check.

2. Select the vendor.

   Open purchase orders for the vendor appear in the panel on the right side of the screen, where you can see some of the lines on the purchase order as well as its original amount and current balance.

3. **Click Add on the purchase order in the panel.**

   This action adds all the lines on the purchase order to the Item Details or Category Details section, starting at the first available line in the appropriate section.

4. **Edit the quantity or amount for each line to reflect the portion you want to record as partially received or paid.**

   Note that you can partially pay a line on the purchase order by changing the quantities on that line from the original number on the purchase order to the number you receive.

5. **Save the transaction.**

If you reopen the purchase order, you see that QuickBooks keeps track of the status of the items on the individual lines of the purchase. The purchase order itself remains open and shows one linked transaction. Repeat these steps as needed until you receive all the items or decide to close the purchase order, which I discuss in the next section.

Clicking Linked Transactions below the purchase order's status in the top-right corner of the Purchase Order window displays any linked transaction types. Click the linked transaction prompt to display the related transaction(s).

Closing purchase orders

Sometimes plans don't work out as expected. When they don't, rest assured that you can close an entire purchase order at any time by changing its status from Open to Closed:

1. **Choose Expenses⇨Vendors.**

   Your vendor list appears.

2. **Click on the vendor whom you issued the purchase order to.**

   The vendor's transaction page appears.

3. **Click Filter, choose Purchase Orders from the Type list, optionally set a Date filter, and then click Apply.**

4. **Click on the purchase order in the list or choose View/Edit from the drop-down menu in the Action column.**

   The purchase order appears.

5. Click the Open button beneath the Vendor field, change the Purchase Order Status to Closed, and then click anywhere on the PO screen to dismiss the status window.

6. Click Save and Close.

TIP

Rest assured that you can always open a closed purchase order and change its status back to Open. Don't fret about closing out the wrong PO.

Tracking open purchase orders

The Open Purchase Orders Detail enables you to keep tabs on the status of your pending purchase orders. Choose Reports ⇨ Reports and start entering **Open Purchase Orders** in the Find Report by Name field. Click the report name from the resulting list. You can also use the Open Purchase Order List report. For more on reports, see Chapter 14.

Chapter **11**

Utilizing Classes, Locations, and Projects

You must have a Plus or Advanced subscription to use the features I discuss in this chapter. Class tracking enables you to categorize transactions into major segments, such as department or product line. Conversely, the Locations feature enables you to categorize transactions by department, office, state, region, and so on. Further, you can configure QuickBooks to display unique sales form titles and company contact information for each location.

I also show you how to use the Projects feature to group revenue and expenses for undertakings that you carry out on a customer's behalf. QuickBooks offers a single Project Profitability Summary report, but you can also use the Projects page to monitor how a project is performing. The Tags feature that I discuss in Chapter 6 is an alternative, especially if you have a Simple Start or Essentials subscription.

Tracking Transactions with Classes

Class tracking is helpful whenever you need to isolate a subset of sales or expenses. For instance, a law firm might create a class for each partner, whereas a medical practice might create a class for each doctor. Classes can be assigned at departmental levels or by service line, such as commercial versus residential. You can then run reports such as Profit and Loss by Class, Sales by Class Summary, and Sales by Class Detail.

Enabling class tracking

You can optionally enable the Classes feature if you have a Plus or Advanced subscription. This feature is turned off by default, but you can enable it as follows:

1. **Choose Settings ⇨ Account and Settings ⇨ Advanced.**

2. **Click the Edit icon in the Categories section.**

3. **Toggle on Track Classes.**

4. **Optional: Click Warn Me When a Transaction Isn't Assigned to a Class.**

   Enabling this setting can improve the integrity of your reports by ensuring that every transaction is assigned to a class.

   TIP

5. **Specify how granular you want your class tracking to be by making a selection from the Assign Class list:**

   • **One to Entire Transaction:** This option enables a Class field at the top of your sales and expense forms so that you can assign the entire transaction to a single class.

   REMEMBER

   Classes apply to the categories (accounts) that you assign in the detail section of the transaction but not the offset, such as any amounts that post to a bank account, accounts payable, or accounts receivable. A check for $300 that allocates $100 each to three different categories generates four different line item entries in your books: one to record the expenditure to your bank account and three to categorize the expenses paid. In this case, the three expense items are associated with the class, but the reduction in your bank account is not.

   • **One to Each Row in Transaction:** This option adds a Class column to the details section of your sales and expense forms so that you can assign each row of a transaction to a different class.

6. **Click Save and then Done.**

You can also enable class tracking for payroll if you have a QuickBooks Payroll subscription:

1. **Choose Settings ⇨ Account and Settings ⇨ Payroll Settings.**

2. **Click Edit in the Accounting section.**

3. Click Edit in the Class Tracking section.

4. Choose how you want to track classes for payroll.

5. Assign a class to each employee, or assign a single class for all employees.

6. Click Continue and then Done.

Creating classes

You can add or remove classes from your company's class list once you've enabled class tracking. Here's how to add classes to the list:

1. Choose Settings ⇨ All Lists.

2. Choose Classes.

3. Click New.

   The Class dialog box appears.

4. Enter a name for the class.

   It isn't apparent based on the size of the Name field that class names can be up to 60 characters long, including spaces.

5. Optional: Click Is Sub-Class. If you do so, choose a parent class from the Enter Parent Class field.

6. Click Save.

REMEMBER

Plus subscriptions are limited to 40 classes, whereas Advanced subscriptions can create unlimited classes.

Editing classes

You can rename classes or change their subclass status by following these steps:

1. Choose Settings ⇨ All Lists.

2. Choose Classes.

3. Click the arrow adjacent to Run Report for the class you want to change, and then click Edit.

   The Class dialog box appears.

4. Revise the class settings as needed.

5. Click Save.

Deleting classes

A tricky aspect of QuickBooks is that most lists don't allow you to physically delete items, which means you must mark them inactive instead. This is also the case for classes. Here's how to mark a class as inactive:

1. **Choose Settings ⇨ All Lists.**

2. **Choose Classes.**

3. **Click the arrow adjacent to Run Report for the class you want to change, and then click Make Inactive (Reduces Usage) in Plus companies, or Make Inactive in Advanced companies.**

4. **Click Yes to confirm that you want to mark the class as inactive.**

TIP

Alternatively, you can mark multiple classes as inactive at once by clicking the checkboxes next to the class names and then choosing Batch Actions ⇨ Make Inactive.

If you change your mind about making a class inactive, you can reactivate a class later by carrying out these steps:

1. **Choose List Settings ⇨ Include Inactive and then click anywhere on the Classes page to close the Settings list.**

2. **Click Make Inactive next to the class you want to activate.**

Exploring Location-based Functionality

Location tracking offers you another dimension by which you can categorize and track transactions. Reporting by location isn't as robust as the class tracking reports are, but I show you how to create location-based reports. You can deposit all the customer payments for a specific location at once. The sleeper aspect of locations is that you can also customize your sales forms by location.

Enabling location tracking

You can optionally enable the Location feature if you have a Plus or Advanced subscription. This feature is turned off by default, but you can enable it as follows:

1. **Choose Settings ⇨ Account and Settings ⇨ Advanced.**

2. **Click Edit in the Categories section.**

3. **Toggle Track Locations on.**

4. **Make a choice from the Location Label list: Business, Department, Division, Location, Property, Store, or Territory.**

   A field with the label that you choose appears on your sales and expenses forms.

5. **Click Save and then Done.**

Creating locations

You can add or remove locations from your company's Location list once you've enabled location tracking. Here's how to add locations to the list:

1. **Choose Settings ⇨ All Lists.**

2. **Choose Locations.**

3. **Click New.**

   The Location dialog box appears.

4. **Enter a name for the location.**

   It isn't apparent based on the size of the Name field that location names can be up to 40 characters long, including spaces.

5. **Optional: Click Is Sub-Location.**

   If you do so, choose a parent location from the Enter Parent Location field.

6. **Optional: Click This Location Has a Different Title for Sales Forms.**

   If you do so, enter the form name in the field that appears.

7. **Optional: Click This Location Has a Different Company Name When Communicating with Customers.**

   If you do so, enter the company name in the field that appears.

8. **Optional: Click This Location Has a Different Address Where Customers Contact Me or Send Payments.**

   If you do so, enter the address in the fields that appear.

9. **Optional: Click This Location Has a Different Email Address for Communicating with Customers.**

   If you do so, enter the email address in the field that appears.

10. **Optional: Click This Location Has a Different Phone Number Where Customers Phone Me.**

   If you do so, enter the phone number in the field that appears.

11. **Click Save.**

Plus subscriptions are limited to 40 locations, whereas Advanced subscriptions can create unlimited locations.

Editing locations

You can rename locations or change their settings by following these steps:

1. **Choose Settings⇨All Lists.**
2. **Choose Locations.**
3. **Click the arrow adjacent to Run Report for the location you want to revise, and then click Edit.**

   The Location dialog box appears.

4. **Revise the location settings as needed.**
5. **Click Save.**

Deleting locations

Any locations that you save become permanent additions to QuickBooks because you can't delete locations. You can, however, make them inactive:

1. **Choose Settings⇨All Lists.**
2. **Choose Locations.**
3. **Click the arrow adjacent to Run Report for the location you want to change, and then click Make Inactive (Reduces Usage) in Plus companies or Make Inactive in Advanced companies.**
4. **Click Yes to confirm that you want to mark the location as inactive.**

Alternatively, you can mark multiple locations as inactive at once by clicking the checkboxes next to the location names and then choosing Batch Actions⇨Make Inactive.

If you change your mind about making a location inactive, you can reactivate it later by carrying out these steps:

1. **Choose List Settings⇨ Include Inactive and then click anywhere on the Locations page to close the settings list.**

2. **Click Make Inactive next to the location you want to activate.**

Running location-based reports

You won't find location-specific reports on the Reports page in QuickBooks. However, you can run a QuickReport:

1. **Choose Settings⇨ All Lists.**

2. **Choose Locations.**

3. **Click Run Report for the location of your choice.**

   A Location QuickReport appears onscreen.

You can customize the Location QuickReport just the same as most other reports. I discuss customizing reports in more detail in Chapter 6. You can also add the Location field to reports that have the New Enhanced Experience:

1. **Choose Reports (or Business Overview⇨ Reports.**

2. **Choose a transaction report with the New Enhanced Experience label, such as Invoice List.**

   The report appears on screen.

3. **Click Customize.**

   The Customize Report task pane appears.

4. **Look for Location on the Layout tab, and click the Show icon if it has a line through it to add a Location column to your report.**

5. **Optional: Click the Filter button and specify criteria for one or more locations.**

6. **Optional: Click the Group button and choose Location.**

7. **Optional: Click Save to add your customized report to the Custom Reports list.**

Most "classic view" reports don't allow you to add a Location column. To confirm, click Customize on the report page and then click Change Columns. If Location appears in the resulting list, it's available to be included on that report.

TIP

Managing Projects

If your business completes projects for your customers, the Projects feature helps you organize, in one central location, all the pieces — that is, associated transactions, time spent, and necessary reports — that make up, well, a project. Also, the reports included in the Projects feature help you determine each project's profitability and keep on top of unbilled time and expenses as well as nonbillable time. You'll still complete all the various sales transaction forms described in this chapter in the same way that I describe them, with one change: Instead of starting from the Sales Transaction list or the New menu, you'll be able (but not required) to start from the Project tab. If you enable the Projects feature before you enter transactions, your picture of a project's profitability will be clearer.

The Tags feature allows you to track revenues and expenses across multiple customers if needed. In fact, you can go wild and use projects and tags together if you need that level of tracking. I discuss the Tags feature in Chapter 6.

Turning on the Project feature

You must have a Plus or Advanced subscription to use the Projects feature, which means this feature isn't available to Simple Start or Essentials subscribers.

The Projects feature is enabled by default in the Plus and Advanced editions of QuickBooks. You must manually enable it in QuickBooks Accountant.

Follow these steps to enable the Projects feature:

1. **Choose Settings ➪ Account and Settings ➪ Advanced ➪ Projects.**

2. **Toggle on the Organize All Job-Related Activity in One Place option.**

3. **Click Save and then Done.**

   A Projects command now appears on the sidebar menu. Otherwise, you find it under Business View ➪ Projects. Either way, you're prompted to start your first project when you choose the Projects command.

The primary admin user in a QuickBooks company can turn the projects feature off. In Step 2, you would toggle Organize All Job-Related Activity in One Place option off instead of on.

Contrasting projects with sub-customers

Simple Start and Essentials subscribers can use sub-customers as a simplistic method of project tracking. (I say *simplistic* because you can only track invoices.) Plus and Advanced subscribers create sub-customers as well, but can also use the Projects feature to track every transaction type. Each project's page has five tabs:

>> **Overview:** Provides a bird's-eye view of income, costs, and profit margin.

>> **Transactions:** Shows every transaction assigned to the project.

>> **Time Activity:** Displays activity by period and then by employee or service.

>> **Project Reports:** Allows you to use three project-specific reports.

>> **Attachments:** Shows files that you've chosen to upload to QuickBooks Online.

The Projects feature keeps all the information for each project in one place. Sub-customers don't offer this centralization — unless you convert them to projects.

>> Any sub-customers you want to convert to projects must be marked as billed to the parent customer. To confirm this setting, edit the sub-customer record and then ensure that Bill Parent Customer is enabled just below the Parent Customer field.

>> You can choose which sub-customers you want to convert to projects and which ones you don't.

>> You can't undo the conversion of a sub-customer to a project.

First I show you how to create a project, and then I show you how to convert sub-customers to projects.

Creating a new project

You can create projects by following steps that are similar to adding records to the other lists I've discussed in this chapter, or you can convert a sub-customer to a project. The steps for creating a project are similar to creating customers or vendors:

1. Choose Projects (Business Overview ⇨ Projects) on the left menu.

2. Click Start a Project if you haven't created a project yet, or click New Project.

3. **At a minimum, fill in the Project Name and Customer fields on the New Project task pane.**

   You can optionally specify start and end dates as well as project status, and you can add notes. You can't add attachments to a project, but you can add attachments to customer records as well as customer-related transactions.

4. **Click Save to display the page for your project.**

   Although you specified a customer, no transactions appear on the Projects page. Newly created projects have no transactions, so there's nothing to see just yet.

To convert a sub-customer to a project, choose Sales ⇨ Customers (Sales & Expenses ⇨ Customers). A message asks whether you want to convert the first level of sub-customers to projects. Click Convert Now in the message window, and select the eligible sub-customers to convert.

TIP

If the Convert Sub-customers to Projects prompt doesn't appear on your Customers screen, choose Projects on the left menu, and then choose Convert from Sub-customer from the New Project drop-down menu.

After you click Convert, a message explains that you're about to convert a sub-customer to a project — and that there's no going back. If you're sure you want to do this, click Continue to convert the sub-customer(s), set the status of the project(s) to "in progress," and then decide whether you want to go to the Projects Center or redisplay the Customer list. Any previous activity for the sub-customer now appears on the corresponding Projects page.

WARNING

If you're thinking about changing the customer name in existing transactions, be sure to pull those transactions into the project. Changing the customer can have repercussions throughout QuickBooks. If you try to change the customer assigned to a payment transaction that you've deposited, for example, you're warned that you must remove the transaction from the deposit before you can change the customer name, which messes up your deposit unless you remember to add the payment to the deposit again. So you see, things can get complicated quickly. Even though a customer and sub-customer or project have a connection, entries in the Customers list are unique list elements.

TIP

You can choose whether to show projects in your customer list alongside sub-customers. To do so, choose Sales ⇨ Customers (Sales & Expenses ⇨ Customers) to display the Customers page. Click the Table Settings icon just above the Action column, and then click Include Projects. You can see projects on the Customers page and in list boxes on transactions, as well as on the Projects Center page.

Adding transactions to a project

You can assign transactions to projects in two ways. First, you can create sales transactions in the manner I discuss in Chapter 2, but you choose the project name from the Customer drop-down list rather than choosing the customer name itself.

Second, you can start most transactions by clicking Add in the Projects Center, which prefills the project name on the transaction. Inexplicably, the Projects Center resolutely doesn't allow you to create a Sales Receipt transaction, so simply choose New➪Sales Receipt instead.

Reporting on projects

The power of projects becomes apparent once a project accumulates some activity, such as invoices, time charges, and expenses. The Project Center allows you to list your transactions on the Transactions and Time Activity tabs, and the Project Reports tab offers three reports:

>> Project Profitability is a Profit & Loss report for the project.

>> Time Cost by Employee or Vendor reflects the labor and external service fees posted to the job.

>> An Unbilled Time and Expenses report shows you time and costs assigned to the project but not yet billed.

The Overview tab of the Project center enables you to manage the status of projects. When you create a new job, the status defaults to In Progress, but you can click the Options button for a given project to change the status to Not Started, Completed, or Canceled. The Options menu also enables you to delete a project if no transactions have been assigned to it.

Updating project status

You can change the status of a job from either the project list or the Overview page for a specific project. Click Options in the Action column on the Project list page, or change the status by way of the drop-down menu adjacent to the customer name at the top-left corner of the Overview page for a project. You can change the status of any project to Not Started, In Progress, Completed, or Canceled. The first drop-down field above your list of projects enables you to filter the project list by status, the second allows you to filter by customer, and then to the right of that, a Search field enables you to search based on a portion of the project name.

Deleting projects

You can delete a project if you haven't assigned transactions to it yet. To do so, click the Options menu next to the project and then choose Delete Project. Click Yes to confirm that you want to delete the project. Remember, though, that in QuickBooks Online, no list items are truly deleted. Contrary to the convention of inactivating unnecessary customers, vendors, and so on, Projects use the term *Delete* as if you can truly delete them. Rest assured, you can always revive deleted projects:

1. Click the Settings button just above your list of projects, and then choose Show Deleted Projects.

2. Choose All Statuses from the Status field above your list of projects.

3. Click Options in the Action column for any deleted project, and then make a choice from the list.

4. Click the Settings button just above your list of projects, and then clear the Show Deleted Projects checkbox.

WARNING

You can't see your active projects until you clear the Show Deleted Projects checkbox from the Project Settings menu.

» Editing your budget

» Uploading budgets from a spreadsheet template

» Running budget-related reports

Chapter **12**

Creating Budgets

B udgets are projections of revenues and expenses for the coming year. As the year rolls on, actual results can be compared to a budget to monitor whether things are going as planned. Plus and Advanced users can create budgets in QuickBooks based on current or prior fiscal year actual results. Users can also assemble budgets in Microsoft Excel or Google Sheets and then save them in a particular comma-separated value (CSV) file format for import into QuickBooks. This chapter wraps up with an explanation of how to use the Budget Overview and Budgets vs. Actual reports to keep tabs on how accurate your projections were.

TIP

In Chapter 16, I discuss how Advanced users can use the Spreadsheet Sync feature to create budgets.

Initiating a Budget within QuickBooks

You can create a budget at any time by using these steps:

1. **Sign in to your QuickBooks company as an admin or a user with correct permission to access budgets.**

   Here's how to determine if you have the proper rights:

   - **Simple Start:** You can't create budgets within this version.

   - **Essentials:** Unfortunately, you can't create budgets with this version either.

- **Plus:** *Standard* users with *All Access* are able to create budgets.

- **Advanced:** Users with *Standard All Access* rights or specific access to the budgeting feature can create budgets.

Choose Settings⇨Manage Users to adjust the access rights for specific users. Admin users have complete access to every element of a QuickBooks company.

2. **Choose Settings⇨Account and Settings⇨Advanced⇨Accounting and confirm that the first month of your fiscal year is set correctly.**

   Click the section or choose the pencil icon to edit the fiscal year if needed.

3. **Choose Settings⇨Budgeting.**

   The Budgets page appears.

4. **The next step depends on whether you've created a budget:**

   - **You haven't created a budget yet:** Click Create a Budget at the bottom of the page.

   - **You've created one or more budgets:** Click Create New at the top-right corner of the page.

5. **The New Budget page appears, as shown in Figure 12-1.**

FIGURE 12-1:
The New
Budget page.

6. Choose a fiscal year from the Period list.

QuickBooks allows you to create a budget for the current year, two prior years, and four subsequent years.

7. Choose Consolidated or Subdivided budget.

A consolidated budget is created at the organization level, whereas subdivided budgets can be created by location, class, department, or customer.

TIP

An onscreen prompt on the Budgets page mentions departments, but QuickBooks doesn't offer a department feature specifically. You can use classes, locations, or projects to track revenue and expenses by department. You can change the caption of the Locations feature to Departments when enabling Locations in the Plus and Advanced versions.

8. Click Next to create your budget.

A blank budget appears, as shown in Figure 12-2.

TIP

If you change your mind about creating a budget, simply click the X in the upper-right corner or press Escape. Click Yes to indicate that you want to leave without saving.

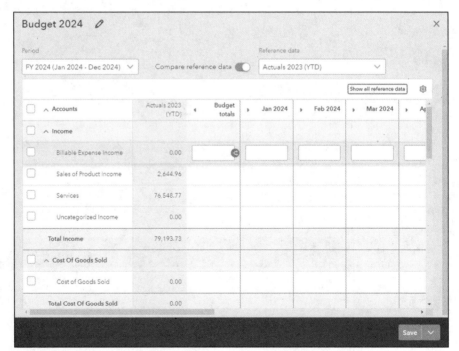

FIGURE 12-2: The Budget input page with a single reference data column.

9. **Optional: Click the pencil next to the budget name at the top-left corner to assign a different name.**

10. **Optional: Make a selection from the Reference Data list.**

You can choose actuals from the current year or any of the four prior years.

11. **Optional: Click Show All Reference Data.**

Initially your reference data appears in a single column, as shown in Figure 12-2. The Show All Reference Data button shows your reference data on a monthly basis (see Figure 12-3).

TIP

Both the Hide All Reference Data button and the Compare Reference Data toggle turned off hide all reference data columns. You can then selectively unhide any reference data columns by clicking the right arrow column in the budget column heading.

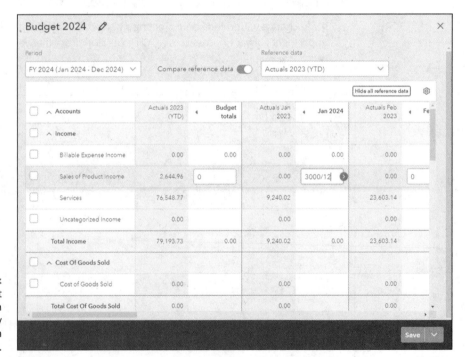

FIGURE 12-3:
The Budget input page with monthly reference data columns.

Populating Your Budget

Figures 12-2 and 12-3 give the impression that you need to type amounts into each budget field, but that's not at all the case.

1. **Populate your budget in one of the following ways:**

   - **Manually type amounts in each field:** Use this approach when the amounts differ from the reference data amounts and vary from month to month.

   - **Enter a calculation in a field:** Type basic mathematic formulas into the amount fields, such as 100*1.05, 1200/100, 100+200, or 300–75, as shown in the January column for the Sales of Product Income account in Figure 12-3.

   - **Copy an amount or calculation to the right:** Click the blue arrow within the active budget field to copy amounts or calculations to any remaining months.

   - **Split the Budget Total across all 12 months:** Enter an amount or calculation in the Budget Totals column and then click the blue button with two arrows to divide the amount by 12 and copy it across all 12 months. The Split icon appears in the Budget Totals column for the Billable Expense Income account in Figure 12-2.

   The Budget Totals column recalculates automatically whenever you change any monthly amount. However, this doesn't automatically work in reverse. If you type an amount in the Budget Totals column, you either need to use the Split the Budget Total button or manually allocate the amount across the months. The Budget Totals field turns red whenever a discrepancy like this arises.

   - **Copy reference data:** Choose one or more checkboxes on the left side of the screen and then choose Batch Actions ⇨ Copy Reference Data.

   The Batch Actions command appears after you click one or more checkboxes. In addition to choosing specific accounts, you can click the checkbox at the top of the list to select all accounts, or choose a group checkbox, such as for Income to populate all income accounts at once.

   - **Clear data:** Choose one or more checkboxes on the left side of the screen and then choose Batch Actions ⇨ Clear Data to erase the activity for selected accounts.

   No undo or restore feature is available for the budget, so be sure to click Save at the bottom-right corner periodically so that you don't lose your work.

2. **Optional: Choose a subdivision level for your budget:**

   - **Add Subdivided Budget For:** Use this list to select the customers, locations, or classes that you want to create a budget for.

     A company level budget is known as a consolidated budget in QuickBooks Online, as opposed to the aforementioned subdivision levels.

   - **View Budget For:** Use this list to choose a specific subdivision level.

3. **Choose Save and Close from the Save drop-down menu when you're ready to leave the budget.**

REMEMBER

Importing Budgets from Outside of QuickBooks

If you need more flexibility than the built-in budget screen offers, you can import consolidated, or company level, budgets from Microsoft Excel or Google Sheets into QuickBooks. You download and populate a template that you then import into your accounting records. You can't import subdivided budgets, such as by customer, location, or class, into QuickBooks.

WARNING

Make sure that you add any new accounts to your chart of accounts before starting the import process. You can't add new accounts to the chart of accounts by importing a budget template.

Creating a budget template

Here's how to create a consolidated budget template that you can use in Microsoft Excel or Google Sheets:

1. **Choose Settings ⇨ Budgeting and then click Import a Budget.**

   The Budgets page appears.

2. **The next step depends on whether you've created a budget:**

   - **You haven't created a budget yet:** Click Import a Budget.

     Advanced users will also see a Create In Spreadsheet button, which initiates the Spreadsheet Sync process that I discuss in the "Creating Consolidated Budgets with Spreadsheet Sync" section later in this chapter.

REMEMBER

   - **You've created at least one budget:** Click the drop-down portion of the Create New button and choose Import a Budget.

3. **Select the period for which you want to import a budget.**

   QuickBooks allows you to import a budget for the current year, two prior years, and four subsequent years.

4. **Click P&L Budget_sample to generate a template that you can populate in a spreadsheet platform.**

5. **Change the name and location of the template file if you want, and then click Save.**

6. **Open the budget template.**

   - **Microsoft Excel:** Choose File ⇨ Open and then change the File Type list to Text Files. Select the .csv file and then click Open.

   - **Google Sheets:** Choose File ⇨ Import ⇨ Upload. Make another choice from the Replace Spreadsheet list if needed, and then click Import.

     The columns in the budget template are based on the fiscal year that you chose, whereas the rows are based on your chart of accounts. Don't add additional rows or columns to the template format.

WARNING

7. **Once you've completed your budget, the next step is to save the .csv file.**

   - **Microsoft Excel:** Choose File ⇨ Save and then File ⇨ Close.

     Make sure that you close the .csv file in Excel; otherwise, an operating system lock can prevent the budget from importing into QuickBooks.

REMEMBER

   - **Google Sheets:** Choose File ⇨ Download ⇨ Comma Separated Value (.csv), specify a name and location for the file, and then click Save. Click the Sheets Home button to the left of the File command to close the spreadsheet so that you aren't tempted to make changes that aren't in the .csv file that you created.

Importing your budget

Once you have created and saved a budget template, the next step is to import your budget:

1. **Choose Settings ⇨ Budgeting.**

   The Budgets page appears.

2. **The Import a Budget command appears in one of two places, depending upon whether you've created a budget:**

   - **You haven't created a budget yet:** Click Import a Budget on the Budgets page.

- **You've created at least one budget:** Click the drop-down portion of the Create New button and then choose Import a Budget.

3. **Select the time period for which you want to import a budget.**

4. **Click Upload Budget, select the `.csv` file that comprises your budget, and then click Open.**

5. **Click Next.**

6. **Your imported budget appears on the same page that you would have used to create your budget within QuickBooks.**

   You can freely modify imported budgets by using the techniques I discussed in the "Populating your budget" section earlier in this chapter.

REMEMBER

7. **Decide whether to save your budget:**

   - **Click Save:** Click the Save button if you want to save and then review or edit the budget.

   - **Click Save and Close from the Save drop-down menu:** Choose Save and Close to save your budget and leave the Budget page.

   - **Click the X in the top-right corner or press Escape:** You're asked if you want to leave without saving. Click Yes to discard the imported data.

Maintaining and Reporting on Budgets

All your active and archived budgets appear on the Budgets page. You then have several options regarding managing budgets and generating budget-related reports:

1. **Choose Settings ⇨ Budgeting.**

   The Budgets page appears and displays a list of your budgets.

2. **The Action column displays one of the following options, and you can click the arrow to reveal the remaining choices:**

   - **View/Edit** displays the budget page shown in Figure 12-2 so that you can continue working on the budget or make other changes.

   - **Run Reports in Spreadsheet Sync** launches the Spreadsheet Sync feature, which I discuss in Chapter 16.

   - **Run Budgets vs. Actuals Report** generates a report that compares your actual results against your monthly budget.

TIP

You can also create a quarterly or annual comparison report by clicking Customize on the Budget vs. Actuals Report page and then choosing Accounts vs. Qtrs or Accounts vs. Total from the Show Grid list.

● **Run Budget Overview Report** generates a report that details your budget.

TIP

The Budget vs. Actuals and Budget Overview reports are also available in the Business Overview section of the Reports page, or you can type the word **Budget** in the Find Report by Name field. You then need to choose the budget you want to reference from the Budgets list at the top of the report.

● **Archive** enables you to archive a budget.

TIP

Toggle the Hide Archive Budgets command to access archived budgets later. An Unarchive command appears on the Options menu for such budgets.

● **Duplicate** enables you to make a copy of a budget.

● **Delete** removes a budget from the list.

TIP

Click one or more checkboxes to the left of the budget names to display a Batch Actions button from which you can choose Delete if you want to remove two or more budgets at once.

4

QuickBooks Online Advanced Features

Chapter **13**

Desktop App, Backups, and Customizable Security

I n this chapter, I cover some features that are specific to the Advanced version of QuickBooks, including the desktop app that offers a number of benefits over accessing your books via a web browser. I then cover how to back up and restore your company, as opposed to trusting that it will be backed up in the cloud. Granted, Intuit is basing its reputation on keeping everyone's accounting data safe, but you can never have too many backups. I close the chapter with a discussion of how you can somewhat customize the access that users have to features and reports, including limited access to certain features by location.

Installing the Desktop App

The QuickBooks Online Desktop app is simply an optional user interface for QuickBooks Online that you can install on your macOS or Windows computer. This app is in no way related to QuickBooks Desktop, which is a part of a separate accounting software line offered by Intuit. The desktop app for QuickBooks Online offers the following benefits versus accessing your books by way of a web browser:

>> You can stay signed in for up to six months, rather than having to log in to the QuickBooks website multiple times a day when your web browser session expires.

>> The app offers a navigation map and drop-down menus that will feel familiar to QuickBooks Desktop users who have migrated to QuickBooks Online.

>> You can open and access multiple QuickBooks companies without having to sign in and out. You can only download the app if you have a QuickBooks Online Advanced subscription, but you can access Simple Start, Essentials, Plus, or Advanced companies within the app.

REMEMBER

You can open multiple companies at once in the desktop app, but all companies have to be tied to the same Intuit account email address.

Here's how to download and install the QuickBooks Online desktop app:

1. **Choose Settings ⇨ Get the Desktop App.**

2. **Scroll down and choose Download for Windows or Download for Mac.**

3. **Double-click the installation file in your Downloads folder and then follow the onscreen instructions.**

TIP

I discuss how to download and install the QuickBooks Mobile app for use on a mobile device in Chapter 7.

4. **Sign into the app in the same way that you log into QuickBooks Online via your web browser.**

5. **As shown in Figure 13-1, choose a company to open if you have multiple entities associated with your Intuit account, and then click Continue.**

You aren't prompted to choose a company if you only have access to a single QuickBooks company. Your company then appears in the first tab of the app.

TIP

I initiated Simple Start, Essentials, Plus, and Advanced subscriptions for the purpose of writing this book. I used the same company name, Nunya Business, across all four subscriptions, and I added the subscription level in parentheses after the company name so that I could keep things straight. As shown in Figure 13-1, the subscription level appears when you choose a company name.

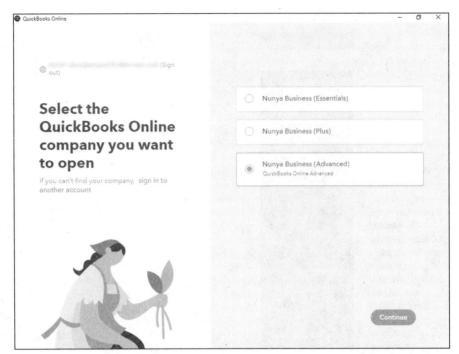

FIGURE 13-1:
You can open
Simple Start,
Essentials, Plus,
or Advanced
companies with
the QuickBooks
Online
desktop app.

6. **Optional: Click the + adjacent to your company's tab to add an additional tab. You then have the following options:**

- Navigate to a different page within your company than you're using on the first tab.

- Display another company by making a choice from the You're Viewing list at the top-right side of the page.

Once you're logged into a company, everything works the same in the desktop app as you're accustomed to in your web browser. You can add as many additional tabs as you want. Although you can't tell from the tab names, in Figure 13-2, I'm accessing two different QuickBooks Online companies at the same time.

7. **Optional: Click the Open Tabs/Windows button at the top-right corner of the app to display the Open Tabs/Windows task pane shown in Figure 13-3.**

A preview of the tab appears in the task pane when you hover your mouse over a tab name. Click the Open Tabs/Windows button again to hide the task pane.

REMEMBER

The QuickBooks Online Desktop App keeps you logged into your companies, so when you launch the app you have immediate access without signing in. Choose File ➪ Sign-Out if you don't want anyone to be able to access your books by simply launching the desktop app.

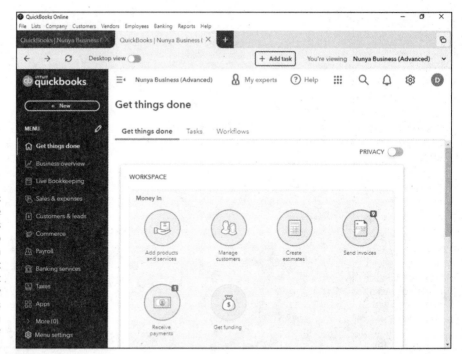

FIGURE 13-2:
Each tab in the QuickBooks Online desktop app can display a different company, or it can display different pages within a particular company.

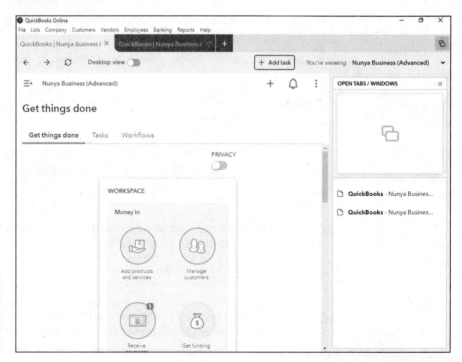

FIGURE 13-3:
The Open Tabs/Windows task pane within the QuickBooks Online Advanced desktop app.

Utilizing QuickBooks Online Backup

If your company has an Advanced subscription, you can choose to back up your data by way of the QuickBooks Online Backup app. You can choose to perform a one-time backup or schedule automatic backups. You can then restore your company back to a date and time of your choice among the backups that are on file.

QuickBooks Online Backup saves a copy of most of your data. Exceptions include

>> Account-based billable expenses

>> Audit log entries

>> Bank feeds and their links to transactions and bank rules

>> Custom form templates

>> Custom reports

>> Customer types

>> Delayed credits and charges

>> Item-based billable expenses with markup

>> Pricing price rules

>> QuickBooks Online Payments information

>> Reconciliation reports

>> Recurring transactions

If you'll allow me a moment of personal commentary, given that all your data is being stored in a database, how on earth can Intuit not create a backup that grabs everything? Regardless, this is a constraint you'll have to work within.

Enabling QuickBooks Online backups

Your company is automatically backed up daily after you enable the backup app by carrying out these steps:

1. **Choose Settings ⇨ Back Up Company.**

2. **Log into the QuickBooks Online Backup & Restore app if prompted.**

3. **Optional: Choose Add Company, choose a company from the Search for a Company list, and then click Next.**

    The Home page for the Online Backup and Restore app reappears, as shown in Figure 13-4.

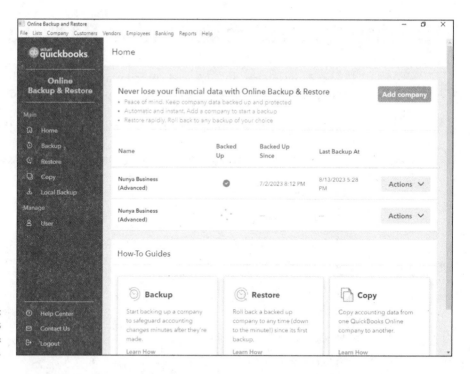

FIGURE 13-4:
The QuickBooks
Online Backup &
Restore app.

REMEMBER

The company list displays all companies associated with your Intuit account, including Simple Start, Essentials, and Plus subscriptions, but you're only allowed to back up Advanced companies. The app displays an error message when you attempt to back up a company that has a Simple Start, Essentials, or Plus subscription.

Going forward, the app automatically backs up your data daily. In the next two subsections, I contrast initiating a manual backup on demand, which you can choose to restore later if needed versus creating a local backup that exports most of your lists, transactions, and settings to files that can be opened in Microsoft Excel or Google Sheets but can't be restored.

Manually backing up your QuickBooks company

You can initiate an on-demand backup by using these steps:

1. **In QuickBooks, choose Settings ⇨ Back Up Company.**

2. **Log into the QuickBooks Online Backup & Restore app if prompted.**

   The QuickBooks Online Backup & Restore app appears.

3. **Choose Actions⇨Run Backup next to the company you want to back up.**

A status page appears and displays the status of the backup.

4. **Click Logout to exit the app once your backup has completed.**

Creating local backups of your data

This feature enables you to export most of the data in your QuickBooks company to comma-separated value (CSV) files that you can then open and work with in Excel. Each local backup is composed of a ZIP file that contains 22 CSV files that contain most of your lists, transactions, and settings. This serves as an alternative to the Spreadsheet Sync feature I discuss in Chapter 16. In Chapter 21, I discuss how you can use Power Query to create links to CSV files to analyze your data. The local backup feature also saves to Dropbox or Google Drive all attachments you've uploaded to QuickBooks. (They're saved in the format you uploaded them in.)

You can't restore local backups to QuickBooks Online.

REMEMBER

The term *local backup* implies that your data is backed up to your local computer, and in a sense, that's true. You must link the backup app to either your Dropbox or your Google Drive account, and then, depending on your settings, the backup files are synced to your local computer. The first step is to link the app to either Dropbox or Google Drive. Here's how:

1. **In QuickBooks choose Settings⇨Back Up Company.**

2. **Log into the QuickBooks Online Backup & Restore app if prompted.**

3. **Choose User from the sidebar menu.**

4. **Click Link Dropbox or Link Google Drive.**

5. **Click Allow to permit the app to store data in your cloud-based drive.**

The User page reappears.

Once you've linked Dropbox or Google Drive, you're ready to create a local backup of your data:

1. **Click Home from the sidebar menu of the app.**

2. **Choose Actions⇨Local Backup next to the company for which you want to create a local backup.**

The New Local Backup page appears, as shown in Figure 13-5.

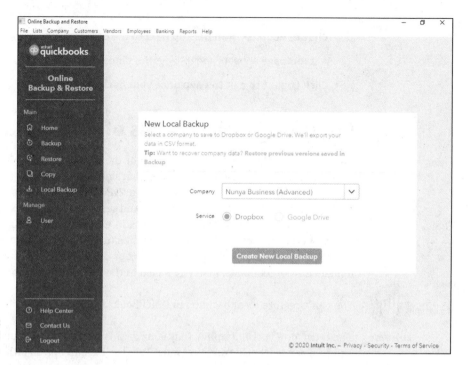

FIGURE 13-5:
The New Local
Backup page.

3. **Choose a company from the list if the company you want to back up doesn't already appear.**

4. **Choose a service if needed.**

5. **Click Create New Local Backup.**

   Within minutes, a ZIP file should appear in the Apps\ChronoBooks folder within your Dropbox or Google Drive account.

As shown in Figure 13-6, local backups are composed of 22 comma-separated value (CSV) files that you can open in Microsoft Excel or Google Drive.

TIP

You can double-click any CSV file to open it in Microsoft Excel, or in Excel choose File⇨Open⇨Browse, choose Text Files from the file type list, and then navigate to the Apps\ChronoBooks folder and open the file of your choice. In Chapter 21, I discuss how you can use Power Query to connect to CSV files.

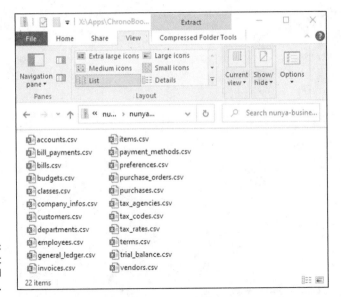

FIGURE 13-6:
The CSV files that
compose a local
backup.

Restoring your QuickBooks company

If necessary, you can restore any previous backup you've made. Keep in mind the exceptions that I laid out at the beginning of this section, and remember that any transactions you've entered subsequent to the backup that you choose to restore are discarded. Here are the steps to restore a QuickBooks backup:

1. **Ensure that all other users are logged out of your QuickBooks Online Advanced company and that they remain logged out until the restore process has completed.**

2. **Choose Settings ⇨ Back Up Company.**

3. **Log in to the QuickBooks Online Backup & Restore app if prompted.**

4. **Choose Actions ⇨ Restore next to the company you want to restore.**

   The Restore page appears and lists any previous restorations you've completed.

5. **Click New Restore.**

   The Restore Your Company task pane appears, as shown in Figure 13-7.

FIGURE 13-7:
The Restore
Your Company
task pane.

6. Choose a company from the Select the Company list.

7. Choose a date from the Date list.

8. Choose a time from the Time list.

9. Type AGREE in the Ready to Restore Your Backup field.

10. Click Next and follow the onscreen prompts.

Duplicating your QuickBooks company

You can copy one company in its entirety to a second QuickBooks Online Advanced company. Before you start the process, you need to have created the QuickBooks Online subscription for the second company. You also need to make sure that QuickBooks Online Backup & Restore hasn't been enabled for the second company. To prevent a company from being backed up, you can choose Actions⇨ Turn Off Backup next to the company you want to prevent from being backed up. From there, you use the following steps to copy the records from a source company to a target company:

1. Make sure all users are logged out of the target company into which you're copying the records from the source company.

2. Choose Copy from the sidebar of the backup app.

3. Enter up to 50 characters in the Note field.

4. Make a selection from the Source Company field.

5. Make a selection from the Target Company field.

6. Click Copy and follow the onscreen prompts.

The Copy page has a status section that keeps you updated about the progress of the copy process.

Disabling QuickBooks Online backup

Unlike many apps for QuickBooks, there's no additional charge for using Quick-Books Online Backup and Restore. However, you can disable the app at any time by carrying out the following steps:

1. In QuickBooks, choose Apps ⇨ My Apps.

2. Click the arrow next to Launch for QuickBooks Online Backup and Restore, and then choose Disconnect.

   A prompt appears asking you to specify why you're removing the app.

3. Choose a reason from the list and then click Disconnect.

You can reinstall the app at a later date by using the steps at the beginning of this section.

Customizing User Security Privileges

Every user in QuickBooks must be assigned a role that determines their level of access to features and reports. In Chapter 9, I discuss how Essentials and Plus users can assign predetermined roles to users. An Advanced subscription offers the ability to somewhat edit the following additional roles:

» **Expense Manager:** Such users have access to expense transactions, vendors, products and services, sales tax, and currencies.

» **Expense Submitter:** These users can submit expense receipts, which I discuss in Chapter 15.

>> **Inventory Manager:** A user with this role can view and edit the products and services list and carry out inventory-related tasks.

>> **Payroll Manager:** This type of user can manage employee records, run payroll, and perform other payroll-related tasks.

>> **Sales Manager:** Assigning this role grants access to sales transactions, customers, products and services, sales tax, and currencies.

You can't customize the built-in roles I discussed in Chapter 9, but you can customize the roles in the preceding list and create new ones from scratch, albeit with major limitations on what you can and can't grant or prohibit access to. I first walk you through the Manage Users page, which you can access by choosing Settings ⇨ Manage Users. You then see three tabs:

>> **Users:** This list displays all the users assigned to the company. QuickBooks Online Advanced companies can have up to 25 billable users. In Chapter 9, I discuss how you can also have unlimited Time Tracking and View Company Reports users.

>> **Roles:** This tab shows the standard roles that are available in Essentials and Plus companies, along with the roles that I mentioned earlier. You can't customize the standard roles, but you can all other roles, and you can add new roles and tailor them to your exact specifications. The number of custom roles you can create is unlimited.

>> **Accountants:** This tab lists any accounting firms that have been invited to oversee your QuickBooks company. Advanced companies are permitted up to two accountant users.

Here's how to edit a prebuilt customizable role and create a role from scratch:

1. Choose Settings ⇨ Manage users if needed to display the Manage Users page.

2. Activate the Roles tab.

3. Click the Edit link adjacent to a role, such as Expense Manager.

4. Click Yes when asked if you're sure you want to edit the role.

   The page shown in Figure 13-8 appears displaying the rights available to that role. As you can see, you have a limited ability to edit the built-in roles.

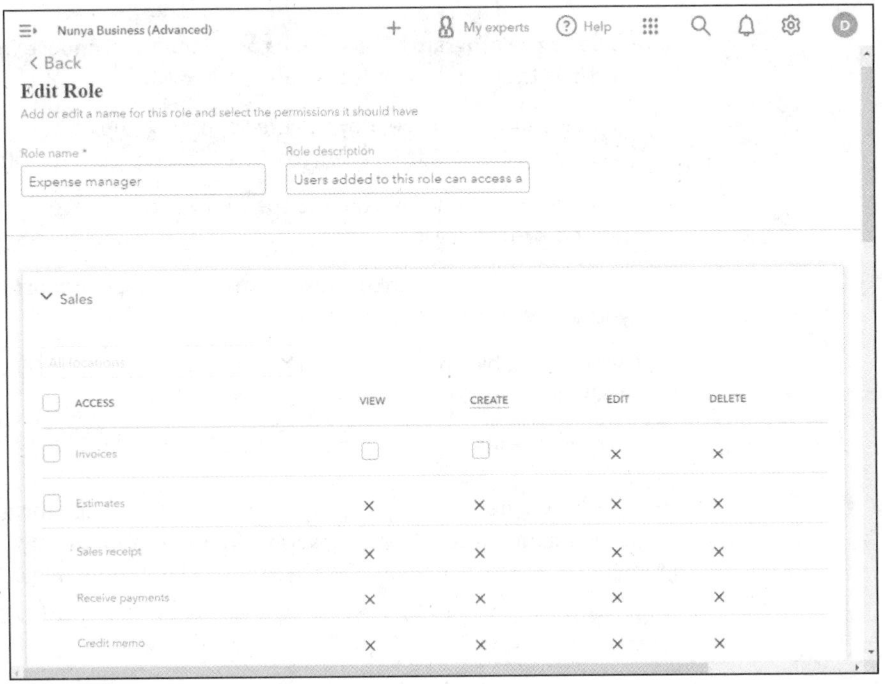

FIGURE 13-8: QuickBooks Online only allows you to enable or disable certain features.

5. Make any adjustments as you see fit, and then click Save Role.

The limitations on the access that you can and can't grant for prebuilt roles extend to new roles as well. You may well find that you're simply unable to create a role that has the exact combination of characteristics you're seeking. Here's how to give it a try:

6. Choose Settings⇨Manage Users if needed to display the Manage Users page.

7. Activate the Roles tab.

8. Click Add Role.

9. Fill in the Role Name field.

10. Recommended: Enter up to 150 characters to describe the role.

The description you provide here appears on the Roles tab of the Manage Users worksheet, which makes it easier to assign proper roles to your users.

11. **Expand the program area sections as needed and choose from the settings that are available for you to customize.**

The description that you provide here appears on the Roles tab of the Manage Users worksheet, which makes it easier to assign proper roles to your users.

TIP

You can limit sales transactions to specific locations. I discuss the Locations feature in Chapter 11.

12. **Expand the sections and choose from the settings that are available for you to customize.**

All customizable options are turned off by default until you enable them when customizing a role.

13. **Click Save Role.**

Once you've created or customized your roles, you manage the users in your company in the same fashion that I described in Chapter 9, albeit with additional role options that aren't available in Essentials and Plus companies.

Chapter **14**

Custom Reports and Charts

I n this chapter, I show you the enhanced reporting capabilities offered for those users who have a QuickBooks Online Advanced subscription. This includes a custom report builder and the ability to add custom fields to records and transactions. You can use the Advanced sample company at https://qbo.intuit.com/ redir/testdrive_us_advanced if you don't have an Advanced subscription or haven't yet added enough transactions to create meaningful reports with.

TIP

Remember to log out of your QuickBooks company before trying to sign into the sample company. You can also open the sample company from an incognito page of your browser or use a different profile in your browser.

Introducing the Custom Report Builder

You can customize the built-in reports for every QuickBooks subscription level to a certain extent. This means that you can hide or display columns, control whether headers and footers are included in the report, and make other minor cosmetic changes. The Custom Report Builder lets you go far beyond what's possible with this basic Functionality, as described here:

1. **Choose Reports ⇨ Reports from the sidebar menu.**

   Scroll down the sidebar menu if you don't immediately see the Reports command.

2. **Click +Create New Report.**

3. **Make a choice from the Select the Report Type dialog box, and then click Create.**

   The following options are available:

   - Blank
   - Invoice
   - Expenses
   - Sales
   - Bills
   - Journal Entry
   - Banking Transactions
   - Transactions List

   For the purpose of this set of steps, use Invoice. You may have to scroll down to see the Create button.

   One of two things happens:

   - A default report format appears, such as Invoice Report. Invoice Report has the following options:

     - *Table View:* This command appears under the report title and is the default view.

     - *Chart View:* This command is adjacent to Table View and presents your report in chart form.

     - *Time Period:* Use this drop-down list to specify the time period for your report.

       The time period for custom reports defaults to Last Month, but you can use this menu to specify a custom date range or choose from dozens of period options.

     - *Pivot:* This command appears in Table View and enables you to create a summary report from your data. I discuss Table View in more detail later in this chapter.

REMEMBER

- *Group:* This command appears in Table View and enables you to group transactions on your report in a variety of ways, just as you can with any built-in reports that offer the Modern report look and feel, as I discuss in Chapter 6.

- *Filter:* This button enables you to filter your report in the same fashion that you can any built-in reports.

- *Customize:* This command displays a task pane that corresponds to the current view, meaning Table, Chart, or Pivot.

- *Collapse Report Title:* Click the button adjacent to the Customize button to hide the report title section so that you can display an extra row or two of your report onscreen. The up arrow toggles to a down arrow that you can click to redisplay the report title.

- A blank My Custom Report appears with two buttons: Start by Report Creation Wizard or Start by Adding Data Columns. I describe both options later in this chapter.

The following controls are also available:

- *Report Name:* Click the Edit icon if you wish to change the name of your report.

- *More Actions*: A drop-down menu offers the following options:

  - Schedule Report: This command creates a workflow, which I elaborate on in more detail in Chapter 15.

  - Email Report: This command displays a Send dialog box that enables you to craft an email by filling in To, CC, Subject, and Message fields. The report is attached as a PDF file.

  - Add to Management Reports: This command adds the report to the built-in and custom reports on the Management Reports tab of the Reports tab.

- *Export:* You can save custom reports that you create as Excel workbooks, comma-separated value (CSV) files, or PDF files.

Unlike standard reports within Advanced companies, custom reports cannot be exported directly to Google Sheets. The indirect approach is to export your custom report as an Excel workbook and then create a blank Google Worksheet. From there, choose File⇨Import⇨Upload.

Now that you have the lay of the land, you're ready to delve deeper into some of the controls.

Configuring Table View

Table View will feel familiar to you if you've worked with any of the standard reports in QuickBooks that have the "New Enhanced Experience" moniker because such reports open in the Custom Report Builder by default. You can dig further into the Table View by way of the Invoice report:

1. **Choose Reports ⇨ Reports from the sidebar menu.**

2. **Click +Create New Report.**

3. **Select an option, such as Invoice, and then click Create.**

4. **Click Customize to display the Customize Report task pane shown in Figure 14-1.**

   The Customize Report task pane has two tabs, which mostly mirror the ones that are available when you're customizing an enhanced standard report, which I discuss in Chapter 6.

   - **Columns:** This tab allows you to select the fields that you want to include in your report by navigating the following hierarchy:

     - *Transaction or List Type:* Choose between Sales, Expenses, or Other.

       - Field List: Available lists are marked in black text, whereas lists that you cannot select from have gray text. Once you select a field list, you can then choose from these lists:

         - Line Items: Add or remove fields that display line-item columns, such as Product/Service names.

         - Attributes: Add or remove fields that display transaction level columns, such as Invoice Date, Transaction Type, and so on.

         - Linked Attributes: Add or remove meta fields, such as Account Type from the Account list, Resale Number from the Customer list, Email address from the Location list, and so on.

   - **Layout:** Drag the six-dot button on the left of a field name to change the position of a column, or click the eye icon on the right side to hide an unwanted field.

TIP

During the time that I wrote this book, a General tab appeared and then disappeared. The tab provided an option to control the formatting of negative numbers and may resurface within the Customize Report tab.

In short, use Table View to control the layout and data presented on your report, which you can then adapt further by using Chart View or Pivot.

FIGURE 14-1:
Customize Report
task pane.

Exploring Chart View

The Chart View tab enables you to present the data you've assembled in Table view into chart form:

1. **Open any custom or enhanced standard report in Table View, as discussed in the previous section.**

2. **Click the Chart View tab, which appears below the report title.**

   A Customize Chart task pane appears, as shown in Figure 14-2, enabling you to build one of three different types of charts:

   - Vertical bar: This is a standard bar chart similar to what you may have created in Microsoft Excel or Google sheets.

   - Trend line: A trend line chart in QuickBooks is known as a line chart in Excel and Google Sheets.

   - Stacked bar: In Excel or Google Sheets, a stacked bar chart has the bars broken down into segments, but in QuickBooks a stacked bar chart is pretty much indecipherable from a vertical bar chart.

FIGURE 14-2:
Customize Chart
task pane.

3. **Optional: Make a selection from the Horizontal (x) Axis drop-down menu.**

   Charts typically display a date field by default, but other options may be available. Any date field can be displayed by day, week, month, quarter, or year.

4. **Optional: Make a selection from the Vertical (y) Axis drop-down menu.**

   Typically this is an amount, but you may be able to choose a different amount based on the fields that you've chosen in Table View.

5. **Optional: Make a choice from the Split By list, when one is available.**

   This drop-down typically defaults to none, but you can check whether you've chosen the proper combination of fields that enable you to dissect your data even further.

The More Actions button for Charts View enables you to add a chart to a package of management reports and to add the chart to your Performance Center, which is a secondary dashboard screen. You can access the primary dashboard by choosing Dashboard ⇨ Business Overview, and the secondary dashboard by choosing Reports ⇨ Performance Center.

The Exports button for Charts view enables you to export charts to PDF or PNG formats.

TIP

PNG stands for Portable Network Graphic. It's similar in nature to GIF and JPG files that are used to display images.

Speaking of the Performance Center, the Quick Add Charts button enables you to add one or more of these charts to the dashboard:

>> Expenses over time

>> Revenue over time

>> Gross profit over time

>> Net profit over time

>> Accounts receivable

>> Accounts payable

>> COGS over time

>> Net cash flow

>> NPM versus industry benchmarks (net profit margin)

>> GPM versus industry benchmarks (gross profit margin)

The +Add Chart button on the Performance Center gives you an additional starting point for creating custom charts.

Pivoting a Report

Before we get started, I'd be remiss if I didn't mention that iconic sitcom scene in *Friends* where Chandler and Rachel are trying to help Ross carry a new couch up the stairs to his apartment, with Ross exhorting "Pivot" all the way. You don't have to yell "Pivot" when using this next feature, but please feel free to do so. I, for one, won't judge.

TIP

QuickBooks-based pivot tables can only sum fields that contain numeric values, so you can't create reports within QuickBooks that, say, count the number of invoices by customer. In Chapter 20, I show you how to use the PivotTable feature in Microsoft Excel to create such reports.

Let's say you want to create a pivot report that summarizes your product sales by item and by customer. The Product/Service field is not part of the default custom Invoice report, so you need to add the field before you can pivot the data:

1. Choose Reports⇨Reports from the sidebar menu.

2. Click +Create New Report.

3. Select Invoice and then click Create.

4. Click Customize to display the Customize Report task pane.

5. Type Product in the Search Columns field and then press Enter.

6. Expand Line Items and then expand Product/Service.

7. Click the Product/Service checkbox.

8. Click the Pivot button.

    A Pivot task pane appears, as shown in Figure 14-3.

FIGURE 14-3:
Pivot task pane.

9. Choose Product/Service field name from the Rows list.

Your report displays a row for each item that you choose, meaning that if you choose an invoice number, you see details on an invoice-number basis.

10. Choose Customer Name from the Columns List.

11. Choose Amount from the Values list.

The pivot table report appears, as shown in Figure 14-4.

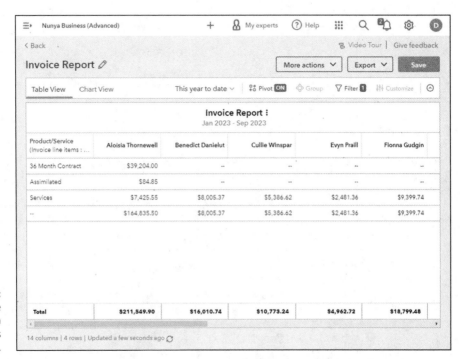

Product/Service (Invoice line items : ...	Aloisia Thornewell	Benedict Danielut	Cullie Winspar	Evyn Praill	Fionna Gudgin
36 Month Contract	$39,204.00	--	--	--	--
Assimilated	$84.85	--	--	--	--
Services	$7,425.55	$8,005.37	$5,386.62	$2,481.36	$9,399.74
--	$164,835.50	$8,005.37	$5,386.62	$2,481.36	$9,399.74
Total	**$211,549.90**	**$16,010.74**	**$10,773.24**	**$4,962.72**	**$18,799.48**

14 columns | 4 rows | Updated a few seconds ago

FIGURE 14-4:
A pivot table report in QuickBooks Online Advanced.

12. Optional: Use the Time Period command to choose a period or specify a custom date range.

REMEMBER

You must turn the pivot table off if you want to return to Table View. To do so, click Customize and then toggle the Show Pivot Table option off, or click Clear All.

» Automating repetitive tasks with workflows

» Overseeing employee expense reports

» Creating, modifying, or deleting multiple transactions

» Automating revenue recognition and depreciation

Chapter **15**

Tasks, Workflows, and Other Advanced Features

n this chapter, I explore more things you can do only in a company that has an Advanced subscription. I start off by showing you how to use the Workflows feature to automate internal and external communication regarding transactions. From there, I show you how you can save time entering data into QuickBooks by using the Batch Transactions feature. I close out the chapter by examining the Revenue Recognition feature, which helps you stay compliant with generally accepted accounting principles (GAAP).

Exploring the Tasks Feature

Simple Start, Essentials, and Plus companies offer a vastly simplified version of the Tasks feature that is available to Advanced users. For those companies, tasks are limited to high-level notifications, such as "x invoices need to be sent."

Accessing the Tasks list

You can access the Tasks list, shown in Figure 15-1, by choosing Tasks (or Get Things Done ⇨ Tasks) from the sidebar menu. From there you can carry out a variety of activities:

>> Click the button in the Action column for a task, such as clicking Send for a Review Invoice task. The button includes an arrow through which you can choose to mark the task as completed, edit it, or delete it.

>> Click the checkbox to the left of two or more tasks and then select Mark Completed or Delete in the Action column.

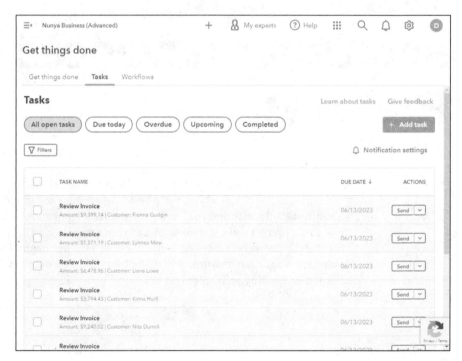

FIGURE 15-1:
The Task page in Advanced companies.

You can filter the tasks list based on the following criteria:

>> All Open Tasks

>> Due Today

>> Overdue

>> Upcoming

>> Deleted

You can also click the Filter button to filter the Tasks list based on multiple criteria. You can optionally click Notification Settings and signify whether you want to receive an email when a task is assigned to you, when a task you assigned to someone else is completed, or when tasks you've created or assigned are updated.

Creating tasks manually

You can manually add a task that you assign to a single user in your company by following these steps:

1. **Choose Tasks (or Get Things Done⇨Tasks).**

   The Tasks list appears.

2. **Click Add Task.**

   The Add Task pane shown in Figure 15-2 appears.

3. **Complete the Task Name field.**

   Task names are limited to 50 characters.

4. **Choose a QuickBooks user from the Assign to list.**

5. **Enter a due date.**

6. **Optional: Toggle Recurring Task on, and then establish a schedule.**

7. **Optional: Describe the task in more detail in the Notes field.**

   Notes are limited to 1,500 characters.

8. **Optional: Attach documents by choosing Upload Document or click Select Document to choose from an attachment previously uploaded to QuickBooks.**

REMEMBER

   Attachments you upload become a permanent part of your QuickBooks company and can't be deleted. Files in any of the following formats can be up to 20 MB in size: PDF, JPEG, PNG, DOC, XLSX, CSV, TIFF, GIF, and XML.

9. **Click Save to add the task to the user's task list.**

FIGURE 15-2:
The Add
Task pane.

Utilizing the Workflows Feature

The Workflows feature serves as an automated tickler and routing system that can create tasks, send emails, and update the Memo field of certain transactions. As of this writing, Advanced users can choose from almost 50 different workflow templates. You can also create workflows for 16 different transaction types and lists.

Reviewing available actions

I walk you through creating a specific workflow in a moment, but at a high level, here are the types of activities a workflow can carry out:

>> **Send Reminder:** This type of workflow can add an item to your Tasklist, send an email externally — say, to a customer or vendor — send an internal email to one or more QuickBooks Online users, or send a push notification to one or more users.

Toggle the Send Consolidated Email option off under Send a Company Email if you want to customize the email message.

TIP

>> **Send for Approval:** This type of workflow can route a transaction through up to four levels, based on conditions that you set, such as transaction amount, location, or customer or vendor name, among other criteria. The transaction doesn't post to your books until the approval process has been completed.

>> **Send Notification:** This is similar to the Send Reminder task, but it's more limited. Notifications are an email message you can customize, whereas Reminders give you additional communication options. You can't include CC or BCC email addresses on a notification.

>> **Send Invoice:** This workflow sends an email to your customer and includes CC and BCC fields.

>> **Update:** This type of workflow can update the memo field of certain transactions.

>> **Scheduled Actions:** This type of workflow enables you to automatically create and send statements and generate email reports.

REMEMBER

The Workflows feature can only send statements and reports as PDF attachments.

Editing a workflow template

Let's say that you want to create a bank deposit reminder. This is a prebuilt task you can edit by carrying out these steps:

1. **Choose Workflows (or Get Things Done⇨Workflows).**

   The Workflows list appears.

2. **Activate the Templates tab shown in Figure 15-3 if necessary.**

3. **Click Set Bank Deposit Reminder in the Workflow Templates section.**

   The Set Bank Deposit Reminder page appears.

TIP

   Click any button within a Workflow Template, such as Bank Deposit, to filter the templates list based on that criteria. You can remove individual filters by clicking the X next to the filter name, or you can click the Filters button, click Rest Filters, and then click Apply Filters.

4. **Update the Name field if needed.**

5. **Fill in the fields for Condition #1 to establish a trigger for the workflow.**

6. **Complete the customizable fields in the Actions section to indicate what you want the workflow to accomplish.**

7. **Click Save and Enable to activate the workflow; otherwise, click Save to keep your changes without activating the workflow.**

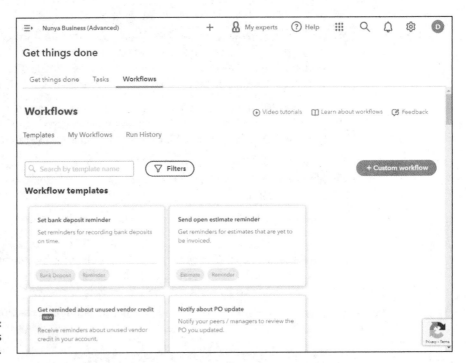

FIGURE 15-3:
The Workflows
Templates page.

REMEMBER

The workflow pages depend on the template that you choose, but all workflow pages have a fairly similar format. The one exception is the approval tasks workflow that presents a flowchart approach so that you can visually see how the approval process will work.

Creating a custom workflow

You're not limited to the built-in workflow templates. Use these steps to roll out your own workflow:

1. **Choose Workflows (or Get Things Done ⇨ Workflows).**

The Workflows list appears.

2. **Click +Custom Workflow.**

The Create Custom Workflow page appears, as shown in Figure 15-4.

3. **Make a selection from the Select Record for Workflow list.**

The row of available actions changes to show you which action(s) can be carried out for a given record type.

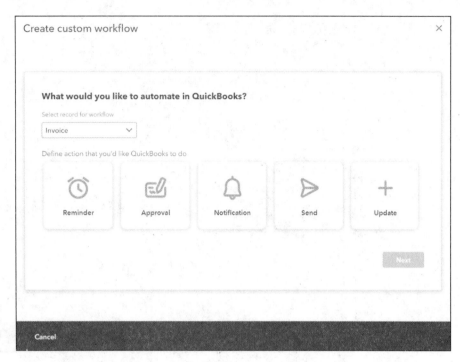

FIGURE 15-4:
The Create
Custom
Workflow page.

4. **Select an action.**

   You must select an action even if only one is available.

TIP

5. **Click Next.**

   The Create Custom Workflow page shown in Figure 15-5 appears.

6. **Fill in the Workflow Name field.**

7. **Optional: Change the source transaction if you realize you made an incorrect choice in step 3; otherwise, leave the field intact.**

8. **Fill out the fields shown onscreen, which vary depending on the type of record and action you've chosen.**

9. **Click Save and Enable to activate the workflow; otherwise, click Save to keep your changes without activating the workflow.**

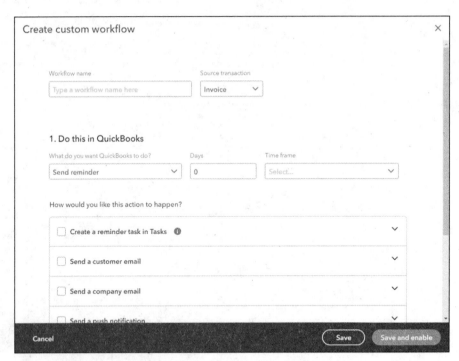

FIGURE 15-5:
The Create Custom Workflow page.

Managing workflows

Workflows you've created appear on the My Workflows tab of the Workflows page. The Workflows list includes the following columns:

>> **Name:** The name assigned to the workflow.

>> **Transaction Type:** The type of record the workflow acts on.

>> **Workflow Type:** The type of action the workflow executes.

>> **Last Updated By:** The name of the user who last updated the workflow.

>> **Updated On:** The date the workflow was created or last updated.

In addition, you can use the On/Off column to enable or disable a workflow. If you click the three-dot menu adjacent to a workflow (in the Actions column), you can access the Edit and Delete commands to manage the workflow.

The Run History tab of the Workflows page provides an audit trail for your workflows.

Recording Expense Claims

The Expense Claims feature allows you to invite employees to submit expense reimbursement requests. Employees can upload a copy of their receipt or initiate an expense claim manually, and then in either case indicate whether they are requesting reimbursement. You must first invite one or more employees or vendors to use the feature, and then you can make some minor customizations. Going forward, expense claim requests will appear on the Expense Claims page for approval. You can then convert the requests into Expense transactions.

Configuring expense claims

Carry out the following steps to invite one or more employees to use the Expense Claims feature and then tailor the feature to suit your needs:

1. **Log into a QuickBooks Advanced company as an admin user.**

2. **Choose Expenses ⇨ Expense Claims.**

3. **Choose Manage Settings and then carry out these steps:**

   a. *Choose Manage Users and add one or more users or adjust their user rights to have access to expense claims.*

   I discuss managing user's roles and rights in Advanced companies in Chapter 13.

   b. *Choose Manage Categories and create nicknames for one or more categories that you want your employee to be able to code expenses to.*

REMEMBER

   QuickBooks confusingly uses the term category in multiple contexts. Many transaction screens in QuickBooks use the word category as a euphemism for account, meaning an account on your chart of accounts.

   c. *Click Manage Expense Form to enable employees to code expenses to customers, projects, classes, and/or locations.*

REMEMBER

   The Add Expense page that your employees use to record expenses includes an optional Customer/Project field your employees can type free form text into, unless you enable the Customers list, which then allows employees to choose a customer from your customer list.

Entering an expense claim

Any employees with access to the Expense Claim feature can record expenditures by logging into QuickBooks Online via their computer or by using the QuickBooks

Online mobile app, which I discuss in Chapter 7. Users can use the following steps to record expenses via their computer:

1. **Choose Expenses⇨Expense Claim.**

2. **Click New Expense Claim and then select Upload Receipt or Enter Expense Info Manually.**

   You will be prompted to select a .PDF, .PNG, .JPG, or .JPEG file if you choose Upload Receipt.

3. **Complete the Amount, Transaction Date, Vendor, and Business Purpose fields, along with any of the optional fields. Click I Need to Be Reimbursed if applicable.**

   If you specified one or more nicknames for categories, the optional Category field is a list that shows the nicknames you created. Otherwise, this is a free-form field, which means you have to categorize each expense claim when you review the transaction.

REMEMBER

   The Vendor field is not tied to your list of vendors but rather is an input field that accepts up to 70 characters. If your company makes direct purchases from Amazon, any reports where Amazon is the vendor do not include expense claim transactions where an employee listed Amazon as the vendor as well.

4. **Click Submit for Review.**

   The expense claim appears on the Expense Claims page. Amounts shown don't appear in your general ledger or on your financial statements until the expense claim is approved.

Approving expense claims

Admin users can approve or delete expense claims by carrying out the following steps:

1. **Choose Expenses⇨Expense Claim.**

   The For Review tab of the Expense Claims page lists any expense claims that need to be processed.

2. **Click Review in the Action column for an expense claim.**

   The Uploaded Receipt page appears, no matter whether your employee actually uploaded a receipt or manually entered the expense claim.

3. **Choose Receipt or Bill from the Document Type field.**

   Choose Receipt if you want to record an expense transaction to your books for a charge your employee made on a company credit or debit card. Otherwise, choose Bill if you need to reimburse your employee.

4. **Complete the required fields for the given transaction type.**

The required fields for Receipt transactions are Bank/Credit Card Account, Transaction Date, Account/Category, and Amount. Alternatively, you must complete the Payee, Transaction Date, Due Date, Category/Amount, and then Amount fields.

5. **Click Save and New.**

6. **Optional: Match the expense claim with an existing transaction in QuickBooks; otherwise, click Create Bill or Create Expense.**

REMEMBER

The Expense Claims feature confusingly uses the terms Receipt and Expense interchangeably, which can further be confused with Sales Receipt transactions, which I discuss in Chapter 2. A simple way to keep it straight is to think of an Expense Claim as attaching a purchase receipt to an expense or bill transaction.

You can pay any bills that you record via the Expense Claims feature in the manner described in Chapter 3.

Batching Transactions

The Simple Start, Essentials, and Plus versions of QuickBooks require you to enter, modify, or delete transactions one at a time. The Advanced version has all the same sales and expenses forms, but it also offers the Batch Transactions feature that enables you to create multiple transactions at once of the following types:

>> Invoices

>> Bank deposits

>> Sales receipts

>> Bills

>> Expenses

>> Checks

You can also import transactions from a CSV file created in Excel or Google Sheets.

TIP

You can also use the Batch Transactions feature to modify or delete existing invoices.

Creating transactions

Here are the steps for creating new transactions by way of the Batch Transactions feature:

1. **Choose +New ⇨ Batch Transactions.**

The Batch Transactions page shown in Figure 15-6 appears.

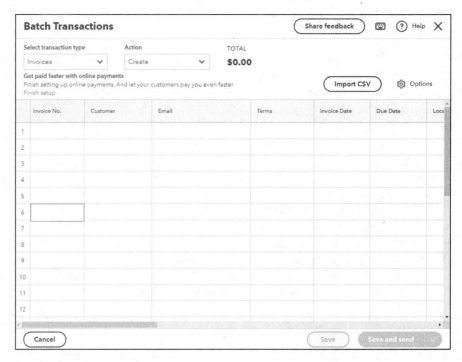

FIGURE 15-6:
The Batch
Transactions
page.

2. **Select a transaction type from the list, if necessary.**

3. **Optional: Click the Options button at the top-right corner of the Batch Transactions page and turn columns on or off as needed.**

You can choose to collapse or expand the Category Details and Item Details sections of the transaction grid by clicking the corresponding buttons in the title row of the grid.

4. **Select a transaction type from the list, if necessary.**

5. **Click the cell for the first column in row 1.**

Default values appear on certain fields, which you can then override.

Click the Keyboard Shortcuts icon to display a list of keyboard shortcuts you can use when working in the Batch Transactions grid.

6. **Complete the relevant columns.**

   Calculated columns are shaded in gray and can't be modified.

7. **Click the three-dot menu in the row number column to reveal choices that vary based on transaction type but include variations on the following choices, among others:**

   - **Duplicate Transaction:** A command generally appears that enables you to duplicate the given transaction type. Some transactions, such as invoices, have an additional command that allows you to duplicate the invoice for multiple customers.

   - **New Transation:** This command inserts a new row into the Batch Transactions grid.

   - **New Line Item:** Batch transactions are assumed to have a single line item unless you use this command to add additional line items as needed.

   - **Delete Transaction:** This removes the transaction from the Batch Transactions grid.

8. **Add additional transactions to the grid as needed.**

9. **Click Save to post the transaction(s) to your books.**

   A second save button appears for some transaction types, enabling you to make choices such as Save and Send or Save and Print.

TIP

The Import Data button on the Batch Transactions page is a shortcut to the Import Transactions screen that I discuss in Chapter 7, which enables you to import transactions into QuickBooks from comma-separated value (CSV) files.

Modifying invoices

You can use the Batch Transactions page to edit multiple invoices from a single screen:

1. **Choose +New ⇨ Batch Transactions.**

   The Batch Transactions page shown in Figure 15-6 appears.

2. **Choose Invoice from the Select Transaction Type field, if necessary.**

3. **Choose Modify from the Actions menu.**

   Transactions dated within the past 30 days appear by default.

4. **Optional: Click the Filter button and enter criteria to fine-tune the list of transactions presented on screen.**

5. **Click the checkboxes associated with the invoices you want to modify.**

   Click the checkbox in the header row of the Batch Transactions grid to select all invoices on the list at once.

TIP

6. **Click the Edit button to display a version of the Batch Transactions page that shows all the invoice details, and then make changes to the invoices as needed.**

   Fields that you edit or that are affected by changes to other fields are marked with a red border so that you can keep track of the changes you've made.

   You can't undo changes that you made by way of the Batch Transactions page.

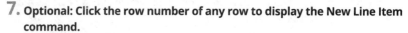

REMEMBER

7. **Optional: Click the row number of any row to display the New Line Item command.**

   You can't delete rows or invoices when using the Modify version of the Batch Transactions page, but you can insert new rows.

8. **Optional: Click Previous to return to the full transaction grid if you want to select other invoices to edit.**

9. **Click Save to post the invoices(s) to your books.**

10. **Click Cancel to close the Batch Transactions page.**

Deleting invoices

You can delete one or more invoices by way of the Batch Transactions page by carrying out these steps:

1. **Choose +New⇨Batch Transactions.**

   The Batch Transactions page shown in Figure 15-6 appears.

2. **Choose Invoice from the Select Transaction Type field, if necessary.**

3. **Choose Delete from the Actions menu.**

   Invoices dated within the past 30 days appear by default.

4. **Optional: Click the Filter button and enter criteria to fine-tune the list of invoices presented on screen.**

5. **Click the checkboxes associated with the invoices you want to delete.**

6. **Click Delete and then confirm the deletion.**

7. **Click Cancel to close the Batch Transactions page.**

Recognizing Revenue

Accounting programs such as QuickBooks Online can help ensure that your business follows generally accepted accounting principles, also known as GAAP. Think of these standards as being similar to the rules of the road when you're driving. When everyone follows agreed-upon and often legally mandated traffic rules and conventions, for the most part, we all stay safe and avoid crashes. Similarly, GAAP ensures that businesses are keeping their books in a similar fashion, which makes peer comparisons within an industry possible and facilitates the purchase and sale of businesses.

Some businesses, particularly public firms and large firms with more than $25 million in revenue, are required to follow additional standards, such as those promulgated by the Financial Accounting Standards Board (FASB). ASC 606 is one of many rules that FASB has issued. (ASC is short for accounting standards codification.) This rule specifically relates to revenue recognition, meaning that revenue should be posted to your books in a timeline commensurate to when the goods or services are being provided. Maybe your customer pays you $36,000 upfront on July 1, 2024, for a three-year service contract. Both GAAP and ASC 606 direct that you don't recognize $36,000 in revenue in July 2024 and then zero revenue for August 2024 through June 2026. Instead, you record the $36,000 to a liability account, such as prepaid revenue, and move $1,000 of the contract per month to something like service revenue until the contract has been fulfilled.

The Advanced version of QuickBooks Online offers a Revenue Recognition feature that can automatically allocate service revenue evenly on a monthly basis over the entire contract. From a GAAP standpoint, this both smooths out spikes in revenue and matches revenue with ongoing expenses that are incurred to fulfill the contract.

Let me share some caveats before I show you how to enable this feature:

>> The Revenue Recognition feature cannot be turned off once it has been used to record a transaction.

>> You can only use Revenue Recognition with Service type items on your invoices.

>> The Service Dates listed on your invoices cannot be in the past.

>> You cannot preview or edit the journal entries that Revenue Recognition generates.

Phew! Writing all of that out made me feel like one of those voices at the end of a drug commercial that discloses all of the potential side effects.

Enabling revenue recognition

Oh, hi! You're still here? Great! Let's see how to turn on the Revenue Recognition feature:

1. **Choose Settings ⇨ Account Setting ⇨ Sales.**

    The Account and Settings page appears.

2. **Click Edit in the Products & Services section.**

3. **Toggle Revenue Recognition on.**

4. **Click Save and then Done.**

Enabling the feature here turns on the fields you need elsewhere to utilize revenue recognition.

QuickBooks automatically posts revenue recognition entries at the end of each month.

REMEMBER

Establishing a service with revenue recognition

The next step is to add a service item to your products and services list that utilizes revenue recognition. You need to create an item for each time span that revenue needs to be recognized over by following these steps:

1. **Choose Settings ⇨ Products and Services (or Sales or Sales & Expenses ⇨ Products and Services).**

    The Products and Services page appears.

2. **Choose New ⇨ Service.**

    The Product/Service task pane appears.

3. **Fill in the requisite fields to create a service item.**

    I discuss creating service items in Chapter 2.

4. **Click the I Recognize Revenue for This Product Monthly checkbox shown in Figure 15-7.**

5. **Make a selection from the Liability Account list, such as Deferred Revenue, or create a new liability account where the revenue for the service will initially post.**

    Each month QuickBooks automatically moves a portion of the service into the income account that you specify for the service.

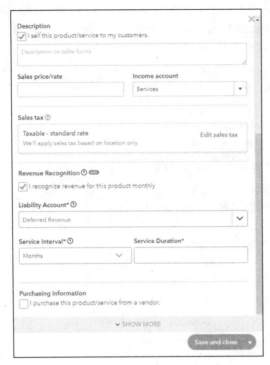

FIGURE 15-7:
Revenue
Recognition
option for service
items.

6. **Specify a service duration in months.**

   As of this writing, QuickBooks Online only supports revenue recognition on a monthly basis.

7. **Complete any other fields needed, and then click Save and Close.**

You can now use the service you created on invoices you generate for your customers.

Creating invoices that use revenue recognition

QuickBooks automatically allocates the revenue for service items that are tagged as utilizing revenue recognition. I discuss creating invoices in more detail in Chapter 2, so I offer streamlined instructions here:

1. **Choose +New ⇨ Invoice.**

   The Invoice page appears.

2. **Fill out the top portion of the invoice in the usual fashion.**

   See Chapter 2 for all of the gory details.

3. **Fill in the Service Date column on each row that includes a service entailing revenue recognition.**

REMEMBER

QuickBooks won't carry out automatic revenue recognition if you leave this field blank or choose a service item that doesn't have the Revenue Recognition option enabled.

4. **Choose a revenue recognition-enabled service from the Product/Service list for that row.**

5. **Complete the rest of the invoice in the usual fashion, and then click Save.**

6. **Click the View Revenue Recognition link in the Product/Service field to display the Revenue Recognition task pane shown in Figure 15-8.**

Revenue Recognition · Give feedback · ✕

Product/service

#1 36 Month Contract

Schedule

Service interval · Service duration

Months · 36

Recognition date	Liability account	Amount Recognized	Income account
08/31/2023	$35,000.00	$1,000.00	$1,000.00
09/30/2023	$34,000.00	$1,000.00	$2,000.00
10/31/2023	$33,000.00	$1,000.00	$3,000.00
11/30/2023	$32,000.00	$1,000.00	$4,000.00
12/31/2023	$31,000.00	$1,000.00	$5,000.00
01/31/2024	$30,000.00	$1,000.00	$6,000.00
02/29/2024	$29,000.00	$1,000.00	$7,000.00
03/31/2024	$28,000.00	$1,000.00	$8,000.00

Cancel · Save

FIGURE 15-8: Revenue recognition schedule for a service item that has been invoiced.

7. **Click Cancel to close the Revenue Recognition task pane.**

8. **Send or close the invoice as per your usual steps.**

Running the Revenue Recognition report

The Revenue Recognition report is a record of revenue that has been recognized. QuickBooks automatically records revenue recognition entries at the end of each month, so if you enter an invoice that uses a revenue recognition–enabled service on August 1, the transaction doesn't appear on the Revenue Recognition report until September 1 because, until that date, there won't be anything to report. Here's how to run the Revenue Recognition report:

1. **Choose Reports (or Business Overview ⇨ Reports).**

   The Reports page appears.

2. **Type** Rev **in the Find a Report by Name field and then choose Revenue Recognition Report.**

   Although you cannot customize it, the Revenue Recognition report also appears in the Custom Report Builder section of the Reports page.

3. **Filter the report by date range if you want.**

   I discuss standard QuickBooks reports in Chapter 6 and the Custom Report Builder in Chapter 14.

The Revenue Recognition report is labeled as a beta feature, and for good reason. At the time of this writing, you can't export or even print the report. There are no buttons available for these actions. I hope this will be resolved by the time you're reading this, but if not, here's a workaround:

1. **Click the Add to Management Reports button.**

   The Add to Management Reports dialog box appears.

2. **Make a selection:**

   - Create a new management report and fill in the Name field.

   - Add to an existing management report and select the report from the list.

3. **Click Add.**

4. **Choose Reports ⇨ Management Reports (or Business Overview ⇨ Reports ⇨ Management Reports).**

5. **Click Preview and then print or save as a PDF.**

Management reports have a mandatory cover page you can't turn off. Alternatively, click the arrow in the Action column adjacent to the report and choose Export to DOCX, which enables you to save the report as a Microsoft Word document.

Automating depreciation

Accountants refer to depreciation as a non-cash expense, namely because you do not write a check to anyone, and you can't put depreciation on your credit card. Depreciation is a means of both matching expenses with revenue and recognizing the diminishing value of an asset over time. Let's say that you buy a $12,000 piece of equipment you plan to use for five years and then sell for $2,000. Generally accepted accounting principles (GAAP) require you to record the equipment on your balance sheet as an asset. You may be able to take a Section 179 deduction on your tax return to record the $12,000 expense in the year of purchase, but GAAP prevents you from recording a $12,000 expense all in one year. In this case, because you're expecting the asset in effect to lose $2,000 in value each year due to wear and tear, you'll need to record $2,000 in depreciation expense each year for five years. Of course, this is just for this one asset. You must perform similar calculations and entries for every depreciable asset your business purchases, which includes but is not limited to buildings, equipment, furniture, fixtures, vehicles, and so on.

REMEMBER

Land is not depreciable, so you must separate the value of any buildings from the value of the underlying land when computing depreciation.

As you can see from my brief example, fixed asset accounting can get tricky fast, which makes the Fixed Assets page a welcome addition for companies with Advanced subscriptions. Unlike Revenue Recognition, you don't have to enable a feature and can instead jump right into depreciating your assets:

1. **Choose Advanced Accounting ⇨ Fixed Assets from the sidebar menu.**

The Fixed Assets page appears.

2. **Click Add Asset.**

The Add Fixed Asset task pane appears.

3. **Enter the name of the asset.**

This can be anything that helps you identify a specific asset.

4. **Optional: Fill in the class, location, and/or description fields.**

5. **Enter an amount in the Purchase Price field.**

This is the amount that you paid for the asset.

You must still record the purchase of any assets directly in your books.

REMEMBER

6. **Optional: Enter an amount in the Salvage Value field that reflects your best estimate of what you can sell the asset for at the end of its useful life.**

The salvage value defaults to zero if you leave this field blank.

7. **Enter a number in the Useful Life field.**

The useful life of depreciable assets is usually recorded in years.

8. **Choose Straightline, Double Declining, or 150% Accelerated from the Depreciation Method list.**

Consult your accountant or a tax professional if you're not sure which one to choose.

9. **Enter the date that the asset first started depreciating in the Depreciation Start Date field.**

You can enter any date in this field. An Accumulated Depreciation Amount field appears if you enter a prior date.

10. **Click the Calculate button and the Accumulated Depreciation Amount field appears to compute the current accumulated depreciation amount.**

The Calculate button doesn't work until you fill in the Purchase Price, Depreciation Method, and Depreciation Start Date fields.

You cannot edit the accumulated depreciation amount, but you can record an adjusted entry to your books if the amount that QuickBooks computes differs from your current fixed asset accounting records.

11. **Fill in the Asset, Depreciation Expense, and Accumulated Depreciation Account fields.**

12. **Click Save to save the record.**

A depreciation schedule for the asset appears within the Add Fixed Asset task pane. Click any year to display the monthly depreciation for that year.

13. **Click Close to return to the Fixed Assets page.**

The asset appears on the Fixed Assets page.

The Actions column of the Fixed Assets page contains commands to View or Delete an asset. The View command displays a Fixed Assets Detail task pane that shows all of the inputs you provided, along with the depreciation schedule. At the time of writing, you are limited to viewing depreciation schedules online in QuickBooks because there is no provision for printing the schedules. QuickBooks does provide a Fixed Assets Detail report that provides an overview of your fixed asset accounting.

Click Add Multiple Assets to display a batch entry page that works in a similar fashion to the Batch Transactions feature I discussed in the "Batching Transactions" section earlier in this chapter.

Chapter **16**

Spreadsheet Sync

The Spreadsheet Sync feature serves as a conduit between QuickBooks Online companies and Microsoft Excel. As you'll see in this chapter, once you install an add-in, you can create refreshable reports in Excel that are directly connected to your QuickBooks companies. Most Spreadsheet Sync features require an Advanced subscription, but you can create consolidated reports that combine results from Simple Start, Essentials, Plus, and Advanced companies if the consolidated report includes at least one company that has an Advanced subscription. You can also use Spreadsheet Sync to add and edit list records and transactions as well as create or edit company-level budgets.

TIP

I discuss the QuickBooks App Store in Chapter 7, where you can find apps that allow you to import/export data into any subscription level, including Simple Start, Essentials, Plus, or Advanced companies. Another great tool to consider is Flash Reports for QuickBooks (www.finaticalsoftware.com).

Getting Started with Spreadsheet Sync

Spreadsheet Sync is a powerful feature that empowers you to make wholesale changes to lists and transactions. Access to the feature is limited in the following ways:

>> Except for multi-company reporting, all other Spreadsheet Sync features are available only with Advanced companies.

>> Anyone who wants to use Spreadsheet Sync must have admin privileges, which I discuss in Chapter 9. Accountant users have admin rights that enable access to Spreadsheet Sync as well.

>> Only one user at a time can be designated as the Spreadsheet Sync admin, although this access can be passed from one admin or accountant user to another.

The designated Spreadsheet Sync admin user can carry out any of the following actions:

>> **Create a report:** This includes standard and custom reports.

>> **Add and edit data:** This includes adding and editing list entries for most QuickBooks lists. This capability is why only one user can have access to Spreadsheet Sync at a time; otherwise, one user could overwrite the changes that another user is making at the same time.

>> **Run multi-company reports:** This involves creating combined Profit & Loss, Balance Sheet, and Trial Balance reports for up to 10 companies, including companies that have Simple Start, Essentials, or Plus subscriptions. All companies must use the same currency.

>> **Manage budgets:** Create and edit budgets in Excel that can be returned to QuickBooks.

Installing the Spreadsheet Sync Add-in

You must install a free Microsoft Excel add-in on any computer that you want to use Spreadsheet Sync with by carrying out these steps:

1. **In QuickBooks choose Settings ⇨ Spreadsheet Sync.**

   The instructions page shown in Figure 16-1 appears.

2. **Click Let's Go to begin the installation process, and then, if prompted, choose Open Excel.**

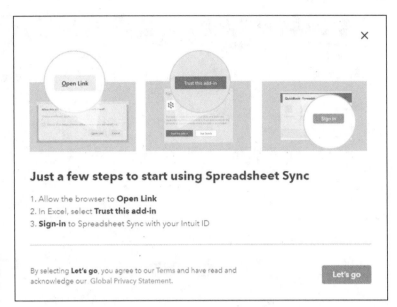

Just a few steps to start using Spreadsheet Sync

1. Allow the browser to **Open Link**
2. In Excel, select **Trust this add-in**
3. **Sign-in** to Spreadsheet Sync with your Intuit ID

By selecting **Let's go**, you agree to our Terms and have read and acknowledge our Global Privacy Statement.

Let's go

FIGURE 16-1:
Spreadsheet Sync
installation
instructions.

Your browser may ask you for permission to open Excel. Alternatively, a Spreadsheet Sync.xlsx workbook may simply appear in your Downloads folder. In that case, choose File⇨Open in Excel to open the workbook manually.

REMEMBER

At this point, Excel for macOS users may encounter a warning that the file format and the extension for the filename Spreadsheet Sync.htm do not match and that the file might be corrupted or unstable. You can safely disregard this warning and click Yes to continue.

3. **Click Accept and Continue, as shown in Figure 16-2.**

Excel add-ins enhance the application with additional functionality.

4. **If necessary, click Got It on the prompt that shows you the Spreadsheet Sync command on the Home tab of Excel's ribbon.**

5. **Choose File⇨Close to close the Spreadsheet Sync workbook.**

Spreadsheet Sync is now part of your Excel application.

6. **Choose File⇨New or press Ctrl+N (Cmd+N for Mac) to create a blank workbook.**

7. **Choose Home⇨Spreadsheet Sync to display the task pane shown in Figure 16-3.**

All Spreadsheet Sync–related tasks are initiated by way of this task pane. Going forward, you can carry out tasks in the task pane or by way of the Spreadsheet Sync ribbon tab that appears within workbooks that have an established connection to QuickBooks.

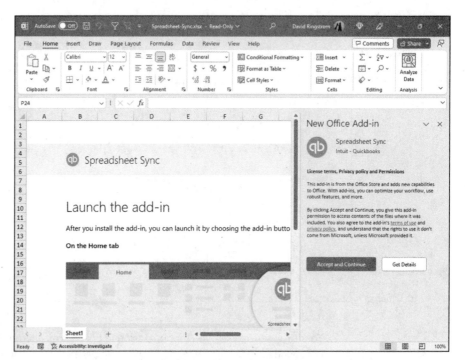

FIGURE 16-2:
Installing the
Spreadsheet
Sync add-in.

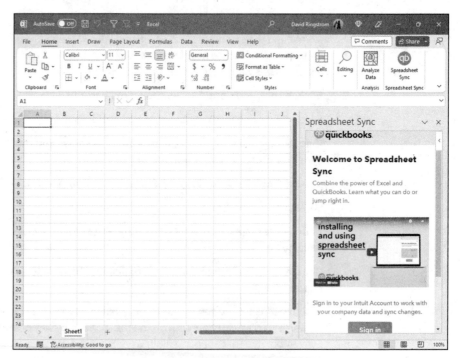

FIGURE 16-3:
Spreadsheet Sync
task pane.

Signing In to Spreadsheet Sync

Here's how to sign in to initiate a Spreadsheet Sync task or report with a new or existing Excel workbook:

1. **Activate the workbook and then the worksheet where you want to use Spreadsheet Sync.**

   Spreadsheet Sync erases the active worksheet without warning, so be sure to always start with a blank worksheet.

   WARNING

2. **Choose Home ⇨ Spreadsheet Sync if the Spreadsheet Sync task pane isn't currently displayed.**

   Links appear at the bottom of the sign-in page to show you how to set up a report, edit and post data to QuickBooks, and view Spreadsheet Sync FAQs.

3. **Click Sign In to display the login page, enter your QuickBooks Online credentials, and then click Sign In again.**

   Click Remember Me if you want Spreadsheet Sync to remember your email address or user ID. You need to enter your password each time you use Spreadsheet Sync during a new Excel session, but you remain logged into Spreadsheet Sync until you close Excel. Accountant users are prompted to choose their firm's name from a separate list.

   Only a single admin user can use Spreadsheet Sync, so if someone else previously accessed the feature, you're prompted to become the Spreadsheet Sync admin for your company. QuickBooks notifies the previous and current user by email any time this role has been reassigned.

   REMEMBER

4. **Select a QuickBooks company if prompted, and then click Next.**

   If you click No Thanks, you're returned to the initial sign-in screen.

   The Search for a Company or Firm list shows all active QuickBooks subscriptions you have access to, but you can't initiate reports for companies that have Simple Start, Essentials, or Plus subscriptions unless you're creating a multi-company report.

   REMEMBER

5. **If necessary, click Change Admin on the page shown in Figure 16-4.**

   This prompt appears if you weren't the last person to use Spreadsheet Sync.

   You return to the sign-in screen if you click No Thanks. At that point, you can't access Spreadsheet Sync.

   TIP

   You see the What Do You Want to Do? page shown in Figure 16-5. This is the starting point for initiating any new type of activity via Spreadsheet Sync.

FIGURE 16-4:
Only one admin or accountant user at a time can be designated as the Spreadsheet Sync admin.

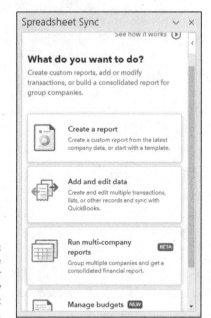

FIGURE 16-5:
This is the starting point for every new Spreadsheet Sync report or task.

REMEMBER

You're logged out of Spreadsheet Sync in the same fashion that you're logged out of QuickBooks Online after a period of inactivity. If this happens, click Sign In, enter your credentials as prompted, and then click Sign In again.

Utilizing the Spreadsheet Sync ribbon tab

Although you may not see it in Excel yet, a Spreadsheet Sync tab appears in Excel's menu structure, known as the ribbon, whenever you utilize a Spreadsheet Sync feature or activate a workbook that contains data provided by Spreadsheet Sync. As shown in Figure 16-6, the tab contains the following major commands:

>> **Company Settings:** Displays the Company Settings tab of the Spreadsheet Sync task pane and allows you to add a company to your existing report group, or to create a new group:

- Click Group Multiple companies if you have not yet created a report group.

- Click Add Company if you want to add a company to the report group.

REMEMBER

You must have the same user ID or email address with admin rights in every QuickBooks Books Online company that you want to include in a report group. An easy way to determine which companies you can include is to choose Settings ⇨ Switch Company.

>> **Get Started:** Displays the initial page of the Spreadsheet Sync task pane that allows you to choose an activity.

>> **Build Reports:** Displays the Create a Report page of the Spreadsheet Sync task pane, from which you can click Select a Report, or click Back to choose another company.

TIP

Click Cancel if the Select Report button is disabled, and then click Create a Report from the task pane.

>> **Refresh:** Contains options to refresh the current worksheet. *Current worksheet (Quick)* uses your existing filters, *Current Worksheet* displays a Filter dialog box, *All Sheets* refreshes all worksheets in the workbook that are tied to Spreadsheet Sync, and *Automatic Refresh* enables you to have Excel refresh your workbook when you open it, which enables you to have self-updating reporting.

>> **Manage Records:** Enables you to choose which report or table to retrieve data from.

Other commands relate to posting transactions, accessing help documentation, signing out of your QuickBooks company, and giving feedback on the feature to Intuit.

FIGURE 16-6:
The Spreadsheet
Sync ribbon tab
in Microsoft
Excel.

Uninstalling Spreadsheet Sync

You'll most likely find Spreadsheet Sync to be a highly useful tool, but you can uninstall the add-in at any time. Keep in mind that doing so means that you will no longer be able to update any of your reports until you reinstall the add-in again. Here's how to uninstall Spreadsheet Sync:

1. **Choose Insert ⇨ My Add-Ins in Microsoft Excel.**

   The Office Add-Ins dialog box appears.

2. **Hover your cursor over the Spreadsheet Sync add-in to display a three-dot menu, and then choose Remove.**

3. **Click Remove in the confirmation prompt.**

   Spreadsheet Sync no longer appears on the Home tab of the Excel ribbon.

Creating Refreshable Reports in Excel

As I discuss in Chapters 6 and 20, you can export most reports to Excel from QuickBooks, but each report is simply a snapshot in time. This means that you must manually export new versions of reports that you use in Excel on a repetitive basis. In Chapter 21, I discuss how you can partially automate this process with Power Query, but as you'll see here, Spreadsheet Sync creates direct connections between QuickBooks and Microsoft Excel.

REMEMBER

Although Spreadsheet Sync does not offer a real-time connection to your books, you can update or refresh your Excel-based reports with a couple of mouse clicks.

Initiating a report

Let's walk through the steps involved in creating an Excel-based report with Spreadsheet Sync:

1. **Activate a blank worksheet within an Excel workbook.**

WARNING

Spreadsheet Sync tasks erase the active worksheet, so be sure to initiate new reports or tasks within a blank worksheet. You can't undo the changes that Spreadsheet Sync makes to an Excel workbook.

2. **Click Run a Report from the Spreadsheet Sync task pane.**

   Carry out the steps in the "Signing Into Spreadsheet Sync" section earlier in this chapter, if needed.

3. **Select a company if you're prompted to do so.**

   QuickBooks allows you to choose a Simple Start, Essentials, or Plus subscription but later balks at generating the report, so only choose companies that have Advanced subscriptions.

4. **Click Run a Report.**

5. **Click Select Report.**

   Three tabs appear: Standard, Custom Reports, and Templates.

6. **Select a report from the task pane, as shown in Figure 16-7.**

   You can browse by category or search for a report by name.

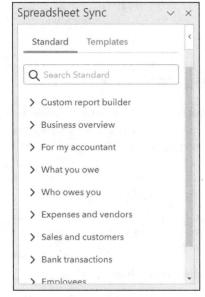

FIGURE 16-7:
You can generate and sync dozens of QuickBooks Online reports into Excel workbooks.

7. **Click Select Data to Get.**

8. **Make any desired adjustments to the report conditions, such as accounting basis, class, location, customer, vendor, item, and date range.**

   Options may vary by report.

9. **Optional: Click Save This Filter at the bottom of the Customize Report page to save the report conditions as a preset.**

   Going forward, a Load Preset list will appear on the Customize Report page so that you have the option to load the settings you saved.

10. **Click Run Report.**

    The report now appears in the active worksheet, along with a Spreadsheet Sync tab in Excel's ribbon, which I discuss in the "Utilizing the Spreadsheet Sync Ribbon Tab" section earlier in this chapter.

11. **Click Done to return to the main page of the Spreadsheet Sync task pane.**

    You can now add additional reports to the workbook as needed, but make sure to add and then activate a blank worksheet before starting the process of adding another report.

TIP

Spreadsheet Sync reports utilize the Table feature in Microsoft Excel, which tends to shade rows in blue and white. You can remove or alter this formatting by choosing Table Design ⇨ Table Styles (Quick Styles) ⇨ Clear or choose another style from the list. In Chapter 20, I discuss how you can use the Slicer feature to filter results within a table and how to create PivotTables, which you can tie to Spreadsheet Sync results.

Utilizing a template

As of this writing, Spreadsheet Sync offers a single Management Report template that you can use to create reports for two or more entities, including those that have Simple Start, Essentials, or Plus subscriptions. Here's how to use the Management Report Template:

1. **Activate a blank worksheet within an Excel workbook.**

    Spreadsheet Sync tasks erase the active worksheet, so be sure to initiate new reports or tasks within a blank worksheet. You can't undo the changes that Spreadsheet Sync makes to an Excel workbook.

2. **Click Run a Report from the Spreadsheet Sync task pane.**

    Carry out the steps in the "Signing In to Spreadsheet Sync" section earlier in this chapter, if needed.

3. **Select a company if you're prompted to do so.**

    QuickBooks allows you to choose a Simple Start, Essentials, or Plus subscription but later balks at generating the report, so only choose companies that have Advanced subscriptions.

4. **Click Run a Report.**

5. **Click Select Report.**

    Three tabs appear: Standard, Custom Reports, and Templates.

6. **Click the Templates tab.**

7. **Click Simple Management Report.**

Four new worksheets that don't yet contain dates are added to your workbook:

- *Notes and Controls:* This worksheet has parameters that control the output of your reports.

- *Trial Balance — Multiple Periods:* This worksheet initially displays an empty template for a multi-period trial balance report.

- *Balance Sheet — Multiple Periods:* This worksheet initially contains an empty multi-period balance sheet.

- *Profit and Loss — Multiple Periods:* You guessed it: A blank profit and loss template is hanging out here now.

8. **Set the parameters for your report by way of the Notes & Controls worksheet shown in Figure 16-8.**

WARNING

The Notes & Controls worksheet is tied to the Customize Report page of the Spreadsheet Task Pane. If you rename this worksheet, you must also update the Spreadsheet Sync settings. To do so, activate any worksheet that contains a Spreadsheet Sync report and then choose Spreadsheet Sync⇨Refresh⇨Current Sheet. Click the button adjacent to each of the Month, Year, and Period fields in the Conditions section to select the corresponding cell or to enter a formula. Then expand the Comparative Periods section and set the Period and Total Periods cells. Alternatively, you can rename the parameters worksheet back to Notes & Controls.

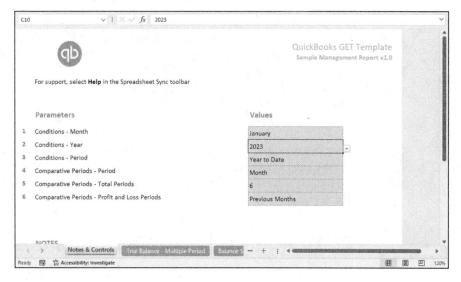

FIGURE 16-8: Set the parameters for your management report template by way of the Notes & Controls worksheet.

9. Click the Refresh button at the bottom of the task pane.

10. Select a company for each sheet from the drop-down lists shown in Figure 16-9.

REMEMBER

You must first create a report group that contains any Simple Start, Essentials, or Plus companies that you want to include before you can select them for use with this template. I show how to do this in the "Consolidating Multiple QuickBooks Companies" section later in this chapter.

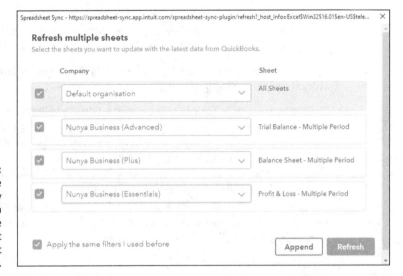

FIGURE 16-9:
You can choose which company to display on each Simple Management Report worksheet.

TIP

If you accidentally overwrite a worksheet in Excel for Windows, choose File ⇨ Info. Click any time stamp in the Manage Workbook section — if available — to open a backup copy of your workbook alongside the live copy of the file to restore any overwritten data. Alternatively, if you save your files to OneDrive, click the file-name at the top of the Excel workbook, choose Manage Versions, and choose an earlier version to open.

TIP

Most Spreadsheet Sync reports have predetermined formats, but you can add or delete columns as needed once a report appears within an Excel worksheet. There are no restrictions on adding or removing worksheets within workbooks that utilize Spreadsheet Sync.

Consolidating multiple companies

You can combine the profit and loss and balance sheet reports for two or more QuickBooks Online companies. At least one company must have an Advanced subscription, but the other companies can be a mix of Simple Start, Essentials, or Plus subscriptions. Here's how to create a Multi-Company Report:

1. **Choose Run Multi-Company Reports from the Spreadsheet Sync task pane.**

2. **Click the Select Group drop-down list or click Add New Group.**

   Here are the steps to add a new group:

   a. *Fill in the Group Name field.*

   b. *Choose a base currency for the reports.*

   Your spreadsheet is connected to a live foreign exchange (forex) feed if you choose one or more companies that have a different base currency.

   c. *Click the Add to Group checkbox for two or more companies.*

   You must have admin rights to each company that you want to consolidate, and your user ID/email address must be the same across all the companies.

   d. *Click Save.*

   e. *Click Build Multi-Company Reports.*

3. **Click Select Report.**

4. **Choose Balance Sheet – Multiple Periods or Profit and Loss – Multiple Periods.**

5. **Click Select Filters.**

6. **Complete the Conditions page.**

   You're prompted to choose between cash and accrual reporting basis. You're also asked to choose a date period or specify start and end dates. Click Comparative Periods if you want to create comparisons on a weekly, monthly, quarterly, or annual basis.

7. **Click Run Report.**

   You can insert a new worksheet and add a different report by carrying out steps 1 through 7 again.

   You can add additional worksheets and have reports for different time periods.

8. **Choose Refresh and then All Sheets from the Spreadsheet Sync task pane or ribbon tab.**

If the Spreadsheet Sync task pane starts reporting an error, saving, and closing your workbook, exiting Microsoft Excel and then opening your workbook again should clear up the issue. In the worst-case scenario, delete the affected worksheet(s) and create the reports again.

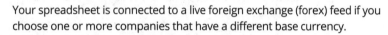

TIP

REMEMBER

TIP

Refreshing reports

Spreadsheet Sync does not offer a real-time connection to your books, so changes that you make to your accounting records don't appear in any Excel-based reports until you initiate a refresh. You can initiate a refresh by way of the Spreadsheet Sync task pane or the Spreadsheet Sync ribbon tab. The commands vary and have slightly different labels, so let's walk through both sets of options.

Use the following steps to initiate a refresh with the Spreadsheet Sync task pane:

1. **In Excel choose Home ⇨ Spreadsheet Sync to display the Spreadsheet Sync task pane.**

2. **Sign in to Spreadsheet Sync if necessary, choose a company and then click Next.**

3. **Activate an Excel worksheet that contains a Spreadsheet Sync report.**

4. **Click Run a Report in the Spreadsheet Sync task pane.**

5. **Click the Refresh button and then make a choice from the drop-down menu:**

   - **Quick Refresh (Current Sheet):** This refresh updates the active worksheet and utilizes the most recent set of filters.

   - **Advanced Refresh:** This command allows you to pick which worksheets you want to update and whether you want to edit the filters for any report.

     You may sometimes see an option to append new data to the bottom of an existing worksheet.

   - **Automatic Refresh:** This enables you to select one or more worksheets that should be updated on an unattended basis each time you sign into Spreadsheet Sync or open the workbook that contains the report(s) while you're signed into Spreadsheet Sync.

You can use the Spreadsheet Sync ribbon tab to gain a fourth option. The commands have slightly different labels, so I'll list all four here:

1. **In Excel, choose Home ⇨ Spreadsheet Sync to display the Spreadsheet Sync task pane.**

2. **Sign in to Spreadsheet Sync if necessary, choose a company, and then click Next.**

3. **Activate an Excel worksheet that contains a Spreadsheet Sync report.**

4. **Choose the Spreadsheet Sync ribbon tab⇨Refresh and then make a selection:**

- **Current Sheet (Quick):** This refresh updates the active worksheet and utilizes the most recent set of filters and is the equivalent of the Quick Refresh (Current Sheet) command in the task pane.

- **Current Sheet:** This command is not available in the task pane and allows you to update the filters in use for the current report before the refresh occurs.

- **All Sheets:** This command is the equivalent of the Advanced Refresh option in the task pane and allows you to pick which worksheets you want to update and whether you want to edit the filters for any report.

- **Automatic Refresh:** This command is identical to the Automatic Refresh option that is available in the task pane.

Managing List Records with Spreadsheet Sync

You can add or edit the following types of list records with Spreadsheet Sync:

» Vendors, Customers, and Projects

» Chart of Accounts

» Inventory Items

» Employees

» Classes & Departments

TIP

Spreadsheet Sync refers to the Locations list as Departments.

WARNING

You can't undo a sync within QuickBooks that adds to lists or edits existing records. However, you may be able to use the Undo command within Excel to undo changes to existing records that you've made, which you could then sync with QuickBooks.

REMEMBER

See Chapter 13 for instructions on creating a backup of your company that you can restore if you sync any data unintentionally.

You use the same initial steps whether you're crediting or editing records. An additional step is required to make the data from your lists appear in the worksheet:

1. **Choose Add and Edit Data from the Spreadsheet Sync task pane.**

2. **Make a selection, such as Vendors & Customers, from the Select Data to Add or Change list.**

   A blank template appears in your spreadsheet, as shown in Figure 16-10, along with a separate Notes & Controls worksheet that documents certain restrictions and procedures to use with Spreadsheet Sync.

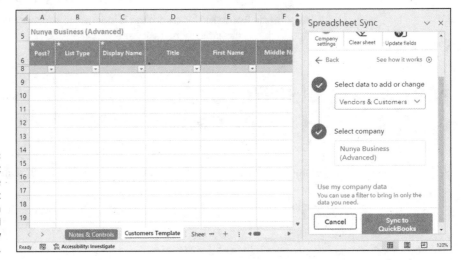

FIGURE 16-10: Your data doesn't appear within the Spreadsheet Sync transaction templates until you click Use My Company Data.

3. **Optional: Choose a company from the Company or Group section if you have more than one Advanced subscription.**

   This field isn't editable if you have just a single QuickBooks Online Advanced subscription.

4. **Optional: Click Use My Company Data.**

   Whether you retrieve your records or not, you can use the template to post new customers, vendors, and projects to QuickBooks. Choose Yes in Column A for any rows where you edit an existing customer or vendor record, or enter **Yes** in the rows where you add new records. Enter **Customer**, **Vendor**, or **Project** in Column B for new records, and at a minimum, enter a display name in Column C.

WARNING

You're prompted to choose a date range when you choose to use your company data. Spreadsheet Sync can become unresponsive if you choose too large of a span, particularly in companies that have been on QuickBooks Online for years or that have significant transaction volume.

5. **Optional: Add or change records as desired.**

   Drop-down lists appear in certain columns, such as the Yes/No/Archive in the Post column. If you don't see the drop-down lists, move down one more row. The gray row below the column headings isn't an editable row, so start with the next row beneath that.

6. **Choose Yes or Archive in the Post column for any changes that you want to sync to QuickBooks, as shown in Figure 16-11.**

   The Archive option marks the list item as inactive.

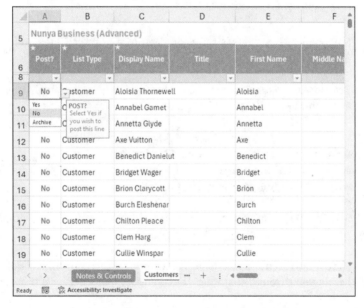

FIGURE 16-11:
Choose Yes, No, or Archive in the Post column when adding or updating records that you want to sync to QuickBooks.

7. **Click Sync to QuickBooks at the bottom of the Spreadsheet Sync task pane.**

8. **Click Yes to confirm that you want to sync the data.**

You can now close the Spreadsheet Sync task pane. You can display it when you need it by choosing Home ⇨ Spreadsheet Sync in Excel.

Reviewing, Editing, and Creating Transactions

You can review and edit the following types of transactions with Spreadsheet Sync:

>> Invoices

>> Bills

>> Invoice payments

>> Bill payments

>> Credit notes

>> Supplier credit notes

TIP Spreadsheet Sync refers to Credit Memos as Credit Notes and Vendor Credits as Supplier Credit Notes.

TIP Transaction lists typically have multiple required fields. Be sure to pay close attention to the onscreen instructions.

WARNING You can't undo a sync within QuickBooks that adds transactions, but you can do a second sync that voids unwanted transactions. You may be able to use the Undo command within Excel to undo changes to existing transactions that you've made, which you could then sync with QuickBooks.

REMEMBER See Chapter 13 for instructions on creating a backup of your company that you can restore if you sync any data unintentionally.

Here's how to use Spreadsheet Sync to edit or create transactions in QuickBooks. I walk you through customer- and vendor-related transactions specifically:

1. **Choose Add and Edit Data from the Spreadsheet Sync task pane.**

2. **Make a selection from the Select Data to Add or Change list, such as Invoices and Bills.**

   A blank template appears in your spreadsheet, as shown in Figure 16-12. Also appearing is a separate Notes & Controls worksheet that documents certain restrictions and procedures to use with Spreadsheet Sync and provides transaction counts and sometimes totals.

3. **Optional: Choose a company from the Company or Group section if you have more than one Advanced subscription.**

   This field isn't editable if you have just a single QuickBooks Online Advanced subscription.

4. **Optional: Click Use My Company Data.**

   Regardless of whether you retrieve your records, you can use the template to post new transactions that you sync to QuickBooks. Choose Yes in Column A for any rows where you edit an existing customer or vendor record, or enter **Yes** in the rows where you add new records. Enter **Invoice**, **Bill**, **Credit Note**, or **Supplier Credit Note** in Column F for new records, and at a minimum, enter a display name in Column C.

5. **A Conditions page appears, as shown on the left in Figure 16-12. It allows you to specify date ranges and other criteria, such as transaction type.**

TIP

   The Conditions page provides limited filtering criteria, but you can then use the filter buttons that appear in the row beneath each column heading to filter the records further.

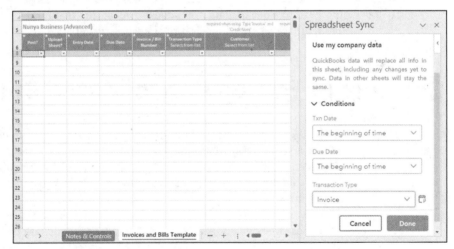

FIGURE 16-12:
A blank transaction template, along with the Conditions tab for specifying date ranges and other criteria such as transaction type.

6. **Optional: Add or change records as desired.**

   Drop-down lists appear in certain columns, such as Yes/No/Void in the Post column. If you don't see the drop-down lists, move down one more row. The gray row below the column headings isn't an editable row, so start with the next row beneath that.

You can use payment columns appearing to the right to record invoice payments and bill payments.

Templates that include an Upload Sheet column enable you to attach an Excel worksheet from the current workbook to the transaction in QuickBooks. Refer to the Notes & Controls worksheet for guidance. For instance, in the case of Invoices and Bills, the supporting worksheet name must be identical to the Invoice/Bill Number field in the template.

7. **Click Sync to QuickBooks at the bottom of the Spreadsheet Sync task pane.**

8. **Click Yes to confirm that you want to sync the data.**

Be mindful when editing transactions because you can easily solve one problem and create new ones, such as creating discrepancies between the payments posted against invoices or bills. Study the template carefully and read all notes and warnings. In Chapter 13, I discuss how you can back up and restore a QuickBooks Advanced company.

Some Spreadsheet Sync–related tasks insert template worksheets that have column headings but no data. This doesn't mean the feature is broken or malfunctioning; there's simply an additional necessary step.

Creating or Editing Consolidated Budgets

Companies with QuickBooks Plus subscriptions or that want to create subdivided budgets are limited to the budget-creating techniques I discuss in Chapter 12. Subdivided budgets are broken down by customer, location, or class, as opposed to consolidated budgets that are company-wide. Here's how to create consolidated budgets in Excel:

1. **Choose Manage Budgets from the Spreadsheet Sync task pane.**

2. **The next steps depend upon the choice that you make:**

   Use the following steps to create a new budget:

   a. *Select your company, if prompted.*

   b. *Fill in the Name Your Budget field.*

c. *Choose a period.*

Spreadsheet Sync enables you to create a budget for the previous year, current year, or any of the five subsequent years.

d. *Click Set Up Budget.*

To edit an existing budget, follow these steps:

a. *Select your company, if prompted.*

b. *Choose a budget from the Select Budget list.*

c. *Click Next.*

A Notes & Controls worksheet and a Consolidated Budget worksheet appear in your workbook.

The Notes & Controls worksheet shows your total budgeted revenue and expenses and includes data entry notes to keep in mind when budgeting.

3. **Update the Consolidated Budget worksheet, and then click Sync to QuickBooks in the Spreadsheet Sync task pane.**

TIP

You can only send the budget back to QuickBooks by way of the Spreadsheet Sync task pane, which you will likely close so that you can see more columns within the spreadsheet. In that case, choose Spreadsheet Sync ⇨ Company Settings to display the task pane again, and then click Back to return to the page where you can click Sync to QuickBooks.

5 QuickBooks Online Accountant Features

Chapter **17**

Client and Team Management

QuickBooks Online Accountant is a free practice management platform that enables accountants and their authorized team members to easily access their clients' QuickBooks companies on the fly with a single sign-on. Accounting practice owners receive a free QuickBooks Online Advanced subscription and a free Payroll Elite subscription for use in managing the accounting records for their firm. The platform also enables accountants to access subscription discounts that can be retained or shared with their clients, depending on who is paying for the subscription. You can manage any type of QuickBooks Online subscription in the Accountant version, including Self-Employed, Schedule C, and ProConnect Tax Online clients.

Getting Started with QuickBooks Online Accountant

The Accountant version of QuickBooks is free, and you're not required to provide any sort of proof that you're an accountant. Visit https://quickbooks.intuit.com/accountant and then click the Sign Up for Free button on the left side of the page to get started. Your home page will look like Figure 17-1 after you complete the registration process and sign in. Going forward, you'll sign in at https://qbo.intuit.com, just as your clients do.

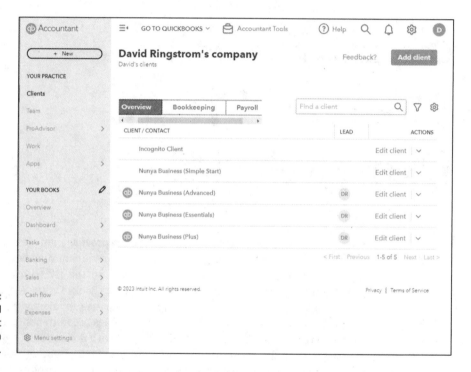

FIGURE 17-1:
A typical
Accountant
version
home page.

TIP

Intuit's free ProAdvisor program entitles you to Online, Advanced Online, and Payroll Certified ProAdvisor designations at no cost. QuickBooks Desktop certification is available to those who purchase the desktop bundle add-on through the ProAdvisor program. Free continuing professional education (CPE) is offered to certified public accountants (CPAs) for completing any of the certifications, as well as for attending webinars, virtual conferences, and in-person events led by QuickBooks Accountant University.

Adding companies to the client list

You can add to your client list in three ways:

» Establishing a new QuickBooks Online subscription for your client

» Adding a client or prospective client to the list without a subscription

» Accepting an accountant invitation from your client

Establishing new QuickBooks Online subscriptions

The Accountant version enables you to initiate Simple Start, Essentials, Plus, and Advanced subscriptions. Your clients need to initiate any other type of subscription, such as QuickBooks Self-Employed, and then invite you to be the accountant, as described in the section "Accepting client invitations" later in this chapter.

Follow these steps to start a QuickBooks subscription for a client:

1. **Choose Clients on the sidebar menu.**

2. **Click Add Client in the top-right corner.**

3. **Select Business or Person, depending on whether you're adding a business or a self-employed individual.**

4. **Provide a name and an email address for the company.**

5. **Optional: Click Add More Info to provide billing and shipping addresses, as well as the company phone number and website address.**

6. **Choose a billing option:**

   - **ProAdvisor Discount:** This option provides a permanent 30 percent discount on QuickBooks Online in exchange for Intuit billing you directly. You can pass along or retain the discount when you invoice your client.

   - **Direct Discount:** Intuit bills your client directly. The subscription starts with a 30-day free trial, followed by a 30 percent discount for 12 months. Your client must provide their billing information during the trial period.

   - **Revenue Share:** Intuit bills your client directly. The subscription starts with a free 30-day trial, followed by a 50 percent discount for three months. Intuit pays you 30 percent of the amounts billed to your client for 12 months, along with 15 percent of employee fees. You must opt into the free Revenue Share program to utilize this approach.

7. **Select a QuickBooks subscription level (Advanced, Plus, Essentials, or Simple Start).**

8. **Optional: Add Payroll, Contractor Payments, or Time subscriptions.**

9. **Optional: Click Make Me the Primary Admin.**

   You can transfer primary admin rights between you and your client at any time.

The Make Me the Primary Admin checkbox doesn't appear on the screen until you select a subscription level.

TIP

10. **Click Save.**

    The company is created and appears in the list of companies on your Clients page, although you may need to refresh the browser page or log out and back into the Accountant version.

REMEMBER

You have up to 180 days to import your client's data from QuickBooks Desktop when you initiate a subscription in the Accountant version. Conversely, clients who initiate their own subscription have only a 60-day window. Data can be imported as many times as needed during the respective windows. Each new import replaces any existing QuickBooks Online data.

Adding a client or prospective client without a subscription

Your client list can include customers who don't have a subscription or haven't yet sent you an accountant invitation. You can add such clients to your list in this manner:

1. **Choose Clients on the sidebar.**

2. **Click Add Client in the top-right corner.**

3. **Select Business or Person, depending on whether you're adding a business or a self-employed individual.**

4. **Provide a name and an email address for the company.**

5. **Choose No Subscription.**

6. **Click Save.**

You can add a subscription at any time by carrying out these steps:

1. **Click the Edit Client link for your client.**

2. **Scroll down to the Product section and choose Subscription.**

3. **From there, carry out Steps 6 through 10 in the previous section, "Establishing new QuickBooks subscriptions."**

Accepting client invitations

Clients who want to grant an accountant access to their company can carry out the following steps:

1. **Choose Settings⇨Manage Users.**

2. **Click the Accounting Firms tab.**

3. **Provide an email address and then click Invite.**

   The Accounting Firms tab of the Manage Users page reappears, showing the email address with a status of Invited. Your clients can click Resend Invite from this screen if needed.

In turn, you (the accountant) click the Accept Invitation button in the invitation email to open the Accountant version login page, choose an accounting firm, and then click Continue. The new client then appears on the client list. Email confirmations are sent to the client and accountant confirming that the invitation was accepted.

Customizing the Client List

You can customize the client list by using the list box above the table to filter the list to show all clients, for example, or only the QuickBooks Payroll clients in your list. You can determine which columns appear on the page, and you can hide or display inactive clients. Click Settings just above the list of clients and make choices from the Settings menu shown in Figure 17-2.

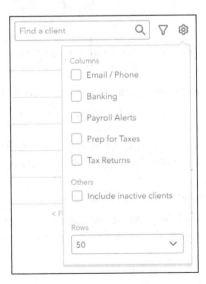

FIGURE 17-2:
Control the appearance of the client list with the Settings menu.

REMEMBER

The company settings button appears at the top-right corner of every page, whereas page settings buttons tend to appear lower on the screen. For instance, the Settings menu appears above the list of clients on the Clients page.

Removing Clients from Your Client List

You can choose to make a client inactive, or you can sever a relationship permanently by choosing to delete a client permanently. Let's first see how to keep one foot in the door with a client by marking them as inactive:

1. **Choose Clients from the sidebar.**

2. **Choose Make Inactive from the Action column drop-down list next to your former client's name.**

   A prompt asks whether you're sure you want to make the client inactive.

3. **Click Yes.**

It's likely that you'll no longer see this client on your list unless you choose to display inactive clients:

1. **Click the Settings button above the Action column on the Clients page.**

2. **Toggle the Include Inactive option on.**

   Alternatively, clear the Include Inactive checkbox if you want to hide such clients again.

At any point you can change a client's status back to Active with the following steps:

1. **Carry out the above steps to display inactive clients if you don't see the client on your list.**

2. **Choose Make Active in the Action column next to the client's name.**

   You can then hide inactive clients again if you choose.

As the saying goes, all good things must come to an end, so let's say that you know that the time has come for you and your client to part ways:

1. **Choose Clients from the sidebar.**

2. **Choose Delete Permanently from the Action column drop-down list next to your former client's name.**

   A prompt asks whether you're sure you want to delete the client permanently.

3. **Click Yes.**

   The client is removed from your client list, and you are removed from their list of accountants. The client remains listed as a customer in your firm's accounting records. You can mark such customer records as inactive, as I discuss in Chapter 2.

Your former client can invite you back to their books if they choose, just as you can decide whether to accept said invitation.

Accessing Clients' Books

The Accountant version provides single sign-on access to your clients' companies. This means that once you log in, you can access any client's books directly without re-entering credentials. You can access a client's QuickBooks company in three ways:

» Choose a company name from the Go to QuickBooks list at the top of Your Practice page.

» Click the QB icon to the left of any client's name on the Your Practice page.

» Click the client's name to display their page, and then click the QB icon adjacent to the company name.

TIP

Hover your mouse over any QB icon to display a caption that indicates either the client's current subscription plan or their cancellation status.

Once you navigate to a client's books, the Go to QuickBooks menu lists your client's company name but remains a drop-down list. At any point, you can choose another company name from the list or click Back to Practice to return to your client list. You can also sign out of the Accountant version entirely by clicking the button with your first initial in the upper-right corner and choosing Sign Out. This button signs you out of any QuickBooks company that you're accessing as well as the Accountant version.

REMEMBER

You and your clients have read-only access to canceled companies for one year from the subscription termination date. Terminated subscriptions can be reactivated at any time, even after the read-only period.

You can only resubscribe to or click Sign Out for companies that were terminated more than one year ago. You will then be required to sign back into the Quick-Books Online Accountant again.

Transferring Admin Rights

QuickBooks Online companies have a single primary admin user who is a super-user with absolute access. As I discuss in Chapter 9, one or more additional users can be designated as company admin users. Accountant users automatically have company admin rights to a company unless they are designated as the primary admin user.

The primary admin can relinquish their role, but primary admin rights can't be changed or altered by other users, including admin users.

Accepting primary admin rights from your client

Clients who prefer for their accountant to have primary admin rights can transfer access in the following fashion:

1. **Choose Setting⇨Manage Users.**

2. **Click the Accounting Firms tab.**

3. **Choose Make Primary Admin from the drop-down menu in the Action column.**

4. **The equivalent of an "Are you sure?" prompt appears, from which your client clicks Make Primary Admin.**

5. **A message confirms that you've been invited to be the primary admin.**

   QuickBooks doesn't offer any indication that you've been invited, so if your client is frazzled, they might forget whether they invited you.

At this point, you can expect an email with a subject line that has your client's company name and the phrase "Account Privileges Granted." Within the email are links to accept or decline this responsibility. If you accept, you're asked to log into and verify your Intuit account; once you've done so, a screen informs you that primary account administrator privileges have been successfully transferred to you, and the previous primary account administrator has been notified by email.

Transferring primary admin rights to your client

You can return primary admin rights to any billable user within your client's company that is designated as a company admin:

1. **Access your client's books via the Accountant version.**

2. **Choose Settings ⇨ Manage Users.**

3. **Choose Make Primary Admin from the drop-down menu in the Action column next to your client's name.**

4. **Choose Make Primary Admin from the Action column.**

   A message explains that only one user can serve as the primary admin, and transferring that role downgrades your access to admin.

5. **Click Make Primary Admin to confirm the transfer; otherwise, click Cancel.**

   An automatic email invites your client to become the primary admin. When they accept the invitation, they're prompted to log in to QuickBooks. A message explains that the primary admin role has been transferred successfully and that you, the former primary admin, have been notified.

Once your client accepts the invitation, the next time you log in to the client's QuickBooks company, you no longer appear in the Manage Users section of the Manage Users page. Your client is now the primary admin for the company, and you've become an admin user.

Setting Up Your Team

Whoever sets up the Accountant version for your firm becomes the primary administrator and can set up as many other team members as necessary. Each team member has their own login credentials and can selectively be assigned rights to clients' books, as well as the firm's books. All team members can utilize the Accountant tools described in Chapter 18 and certain workflow tools described in Chapter 19.

Accountant version users can be assigned one of three access levels:

» **Basic:** Users can access QuickBooks companies for designated clients.

» **Full:** Users can access QuickBooks companies for designated clients as well as the firm's books.

» **Custom:** This provides a middle ground between Basic and Full, meaning that users have at least one permission that has been customized.

Adding users

Either the primary administrator or any full-access users can set up and control user privileges in this fashion:

1. **Log in to the Accountant version as a primary admin or full-access user.**

2. **Choose Team from the left menu bar to display the Team page shown in Figure 17-3.**

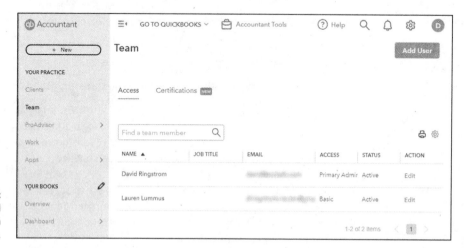

FIGURE 17-3:
View, edit, and add team members.

3. **Click the Add User button.**

   The three-step Add User wizard begins.

4. **On the first page of the Add User wizard, fill in the name, email address, and (optional) title of the team member you want to add.**

5. **Click Next.**

   The second page of the Add User wizard appears in Figure 17-4. On this page, you identify the privileges related to your firm that you want to provide to the team member. In this example, I set up a team member with custom access. This team member has access to the books of certain clients but doesn't have access to the firm's books or to firm-administration functions.

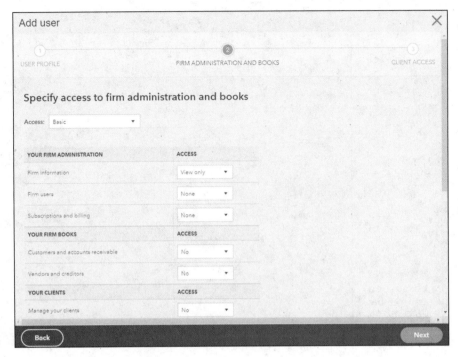

Add user   ✕

① ─────────────────────── ② ─────────────────────── ③
USER PROFILE   FIRM ADMINISTRATION AND BOOKS   CLIENT ACCESS

Specify access to firm administration and books

Access: Basic   ▼

YOUR FIRM ADMINISTRATION	ACCESS
Firm information	View only ▼
Firm users	None ▼
Subscriptions and billing	None ▼

YOUR FIRM BOOKS	ACCESS
Customers and accounts receivable	No ▼
Vendors and creditors	No ▼

YOUR CLIENTS	ACCESS
Manage your clients	No ▼

Back   Next

FIGURE 17-4: Specify the new user's access level to your firm's administration and books.

6. **Select the type of access you want to give to the team member.**

Assign Basic access to give access to client companies only, Full Access to give access to client companies and the firm's books, or Custom access to create a hybrid set of privileges.

7. **Click Next in the bottom-right corner of the page.**

The last page of the Add User wizard appears, as shown in Figure 17-5. On this page, you identify the clients for whom the team member should be able to perform work.

8. **Deselect clients if necessary, and then click Save.**

The new user is added to your team and assigned the status of Invited. In addition, the Status column of the Team page indicates that an email invitation was sent to the user. After the user accepts the invitation, their status changes to Active.

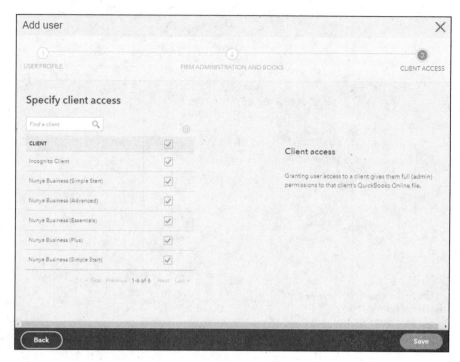

Team members who already have QuickBooks Online credentials can click Accept Invitation in the invitation email; otherwise, they need to click Create Account and log in immediately after completing the sign-up process. An error prompt appears when a team member attempts to access an area they don't have access to. Users with limited rights don't see the Team or Apps commands in the Your Practice area of the sidebar.

Assigning Lead Accountants

Lead accountants are the primary contact for your clients and typically have primary responsibility for overseeing the bookkeeping. Lead accountants can be but don't have to be the primary admin for a QuickBooks Online company. Users are designated as lead accountants when

» **A client invites an accountant.** Accepting the invitation grants the accounting firm access to the client's books and designates the invited accountant as the lead accountant.

» **A firm member creates a client company.** The team member within the firm that creates a client company within the Accountant version becomes the lead accountant.

Primary admin or full access users can reassign lead accountants by carrying out these steps:

1. **Choose Clients, click the Filter icon, and choose Edit Leads, as shown in Figure 17-6.**

2. **Choose a client for which you want to reassign the lead accountant.**

3. **Select a new lead accountant in the Lead column.**

4. **Choose Save.**

TIP

You can also assign a lead accountant by selecting the checkboxes for two or more clients, choosing a name from the Assign To drop-down list, and then clicking Save.

REMEMBER

You cannot inactivate a team member that is currently designated as a lead accountant for one or more clients. You must reassign the lead accountant role to another user if you want to deactivate the account of such departing team members.

Chapter **18**

Accountant Tools and Pages

The Accountant version of QuickBooks Online adds additional commands to the sidebar menu and the top of the screen within your client's companies. In this chapter, I walk you through the tools and pages that empower accountants to support their clients effectively and efficiently. I also show you how to open and exit any client's set of books, as well as your firm's books.

Understanding the Dual Sidebar Menus

The sidebar menu is light gray when you're accessing the Your Practice and Your Books area of QuickBooks Online, but it's dark gray when you're accessing a client's books. The New button at the top of the sidebar creates new transactions in your books when the sidebar is light gray and in the QuickBooks company that you're working within when the sidebar is dark gray.

The Your Practice section includes the following commands:

- **Clients:** This command displays your client list, which I discuss in detail in Chapter 17.

- **Team:** This command displays your list of team members, which I also discuss in Chapter 17.

- **ProAdvisor:** This command connects you to your free Silver membership in the Intuit ProAdvisor program. More details on the free benefits are available at `https://quickbooks.intuit.com/accountants/tools-proadvisor`.

- **Work:** This command displays practice management tools that I discuss in more detail in Chapter 19.

- **Apps:** Click here to launch the App Center. In Chapter 7, I discuss how you can search for enhancements that can fill in gaps in QuickBooks. The App Center also shows you which apps are installed in each company, if any.

The Your Books section appears immediately beneath the Your Practice commands and is how you use the free Advanced and Payroll Elite subscriptions that are provided for you to manage your firm's books.

Accessing your clients' books

Many of your clients are likely to have a single QuickBooks subscription, but those that have two or more subscriptions can switch between companies by choosing Settings ⇨ Switch Company and then choosing another company. This command is available to you as well, but it's not how you'll access your clients' companies. Instead, you'll use one of these two approaches:

- Click the QB logo to the left of any client's name in the Client/Contact column of the Clients page, as shown in Figure 18-1.

TIP

    The status of a client's subscription appears in a caption when you hover over the QB logo in the Client/Contact column. This enables you to see the subscription level and status, as well as whether a client has a payroll subscription.

- Click Go to QuickBooks at the top of any page in the Accountant version and choose the name of the company you want to open.

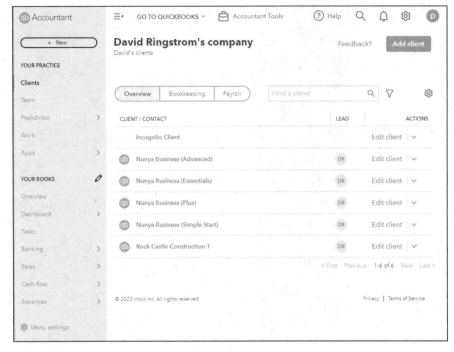

FIGURE 18-1:
Click the QB logo to the left of the client's name or use the Go to QuickBooks command to open a client's company.

As shown in Figure 18-2, the client's company appears onscreen, and the sidebar menu turns dark gray. You can carry out any task that your clients can, as well as perform additional tasks by way of the Accountant Tools that I discuss all through this chapter. Once you complete your work in a client's company, you can exit their books in three ways:

>> Click the client's company name immediately to the left of the Accountant Tools button. You can choose Back to Practice to return to the practice management area or choose another client's company name from the list.

>> The company name that you choose replaces the Go to QuickBooks button. Click the company name, and then choose Back to Practice to return to your Clients page, or choose another QuickBooks company. Clicking the QB Accountant logo at the top-left corner is an even faster way to return to your Clients page.

>> Click the button in the top right that has your first initial, and then choose Sign Out. Doing so logs you out of your client's company and the Accountant version at the same time.

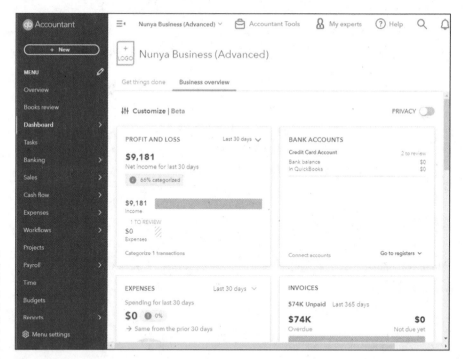

FIGURE 18-2:
A dark gray sidebar indicates that you're working within a client's books as opposed to your firm's books.

WORKING IN MULTIPLE WINDOWS

Hands down, the easiest way to have multiple windows is to use the QuickBooks Online Advanced Desktop app for Windows, which you can access by choosing Settings ⇨ Get the Desktop App. This free app allows you to access multiple QuickBooks companies at once. You can access your client's books no matter what subscription level they have. Any of your clients with Advanced subscriptions can download the Desktop App in the same fashion.

Conversely, in a web browser you can open two or more pages at the same time within a single QuickBooks Online company. To do so, click the Accountant Tools button, shown in Figure 18-2, and then choose New Window to duplicate the page you're viewing in another browser tab. Now you can use either tab to navigate to a different page within the company.

All the major browsers let you duplicate tabs, so the New Window command is simply a convenience. In most browsers, if you right-click any tab, the shortcut menu should include a command that contains the word *Duplicate*.

If you want to access two or more QuickBooks companies at the same time, you can't simply open another browser tab. Instead, you need to use a separate browser, such as Google Chrome, Mozilla Firefox, or Microsoft Edge. In Chapter 23, I show how you can use profiles in Chrome to access multiple QuickBooks companies simultaneously.

WARNING

Make sure that you sign out *before* closing the QuickBooks browser tab. In Google Chrome, anyone with access to your keyboard can click the three-dot menu at the top right, choose History, and then choose QuickBooks from the Recently Closed page to return to your practice or any client's books without providing credentials.

Touring the Client Overview Page

When you access a client's books by way of the Accountant version, an Overview command appears at the top of the sidebar menu. This Client Overview page differs from the Business Overview tab that appears when you choose Dashboard from the sidebar. Your clients can't see this page unless they have an Advanced subscription and use the Accountant Version sidebar rather than the Business Version sidebar. The Overview command also appears within the Your Books section of the sidebar when you're not working within a client's books. The Client Overview page includes the following sections:

>> **Company Setup:** As shown in Figure 18-3, this section shows your client's subscription level, payroll subscription status, and whether sales tax is enabled. It also has a listing of any enabled apps.

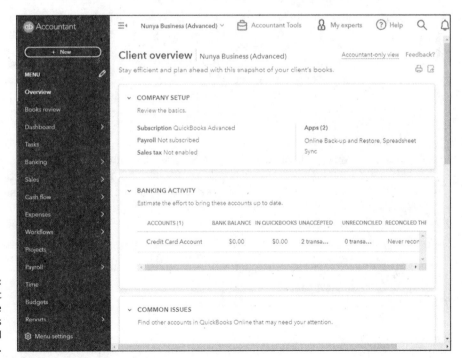

FIGURE 18-3:
The Client Overview page that accountants and Advanced users can view.

> » **Banking Activity:** Here you see a listing of the reconciliation status of any bank or credit card accounts, along with the bank balance and QuickBooks balance for each account. Click any account name or the number of unreconciled transactions to display the corresponding register.

TIP

Click your browser's Back button to return to the Client Overview page from a register page.

> » **Common Issues:** This listing alerts you to payments that haven't been deposited; uncategorized asset, income, and expense transactions; A/R and A/P aging amounts more than 90 days old; the opening balance equity amount; and any negative asset or liability accounts. It also includes a View Chart of Accounts link and a Reports button from which you can display the Balance Sheet or Profit and Loss report.

> » **Transaction Volume:** This section enables you to view the number of bank account transactions, sales receipts, invoices, invoice payments, bank deposits, journal entries, expenses, bills, and bill payments for any period that you choose.

Exploring the Books Review Page

A Books Review command that only you and your team can see appears on the sidebar when you're working within a client's books. This command doesn't appear within your firm's books. With the Books Review page open, you can choose Cleanup or Monthly from the drop-down menu to the right of the page title, as shown in Figure 18-4. Just below the page title, click the Edit icon to specify the date range that you're reviewing. Typically, the Books Review is set to the previous month. The Cleanup version and Monthly versions of Books Review are identical, except the Cleanup version has a Setup tab that's not available in the Monthly version.

REMEMBER

You can only choose from the months presented on the list. Perhaps you're setting up the books for a company as of June 1, but today's date is in the month of May. In that case, you can only select a month or months from January through April for the cleanup start dates. Once the calendar rolls around to June, you can then choose May.

TIP

You can record your progress through the Books Review process by choosing To Do, Waiting, and Done from the top-right corner of each section within the Books Review pages.

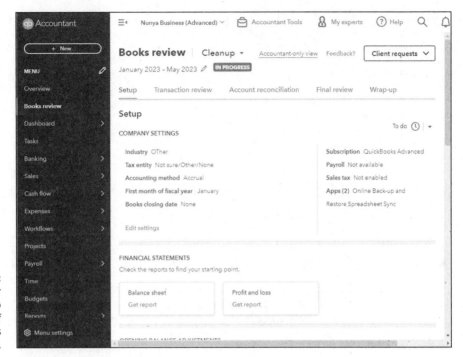

FIGURE 18-4:
The Setup tab for
the Cleanup
version of
the Books
Review page.

Starting out with the Setup tab

You typically only use the Cleanup version of Books Review when you're first bringing a new client onboard. You don't typically see the Setup tab on an ongoing basis. This tab includes the following sections:

TIP

>> **Company Settings:** This area repeats information that appears on the Client Overview page but offers an Edit Settings link that's an alternative to choosing Settings⇨Account and Settings.

Choose Cleanup from the list to the right of the Books Review page title at the top of the page if you don't see the Setup tab.

>> **Financial Statements:** Run a Balance Sheet or Profit and Loss report.

>> **Opening Balance Adjustments:** You can use this section to initiate adjusting journal entries and maintain documentation of said entries.

To create journal entries and maintain documentation, follow these steps:

1. Enter an adjustment amount in the Beginning Statement Balance column, shown in Figure 18-5.

   Enter either a positive or a negative amount, depending on your needs.

FIGURE 18-5:
The Opening Balance Adjustments section.

2. Select an account from the Adjusting Equity Account list that appears above the account listing.

   You can choose any equity account from the list.

3. Click Add Adjustment.

   The QuickBooks Journal Entry page appears.

4. Edit and then save the journal entry.

WARNING

The Opening Balance Adjustments section is a well-intentioned feature that's supposed to streamline creating adjusting entries. However, you may find that it creates more problems than it solves. For instance, the Adjusting Equity Account list may not show all equity accounts. The body of the adjustments screen may not display all the accounts that you want to adjust. Further, the resulting journal entry window may list your journal entry twice, leaving you to manually remove the duplication. This is a nice feature if it works as expected, but you'll probably be better served by going to the journal entry page directly and entering your entries there.

» **Potential Account Issues:** Lists any disconnected bank feeds as well as all accounts on the chart of accounts that haven't had activity recorded in the past 90 days.

» **Additional Items:** Typically includes recommendations to review the chart of accounts for industry- and entity-specific accounts, as well as duplicate accounts. As shown in Figure 18-6, the +Add button enables you to add new items to the list. You can also click any item name to display detailed notes, along with links to edit or delete the task.

FIGURE 18-6:
Click +Add to add new tasks to the Additional Items list.

Examining the Transaction Review page

The Cleanup and Monthly versions of the Books Review page has a Transaction Review page that displays the following:

» The number of unreviewed bank transactions.

» All uncategorized transactions for the specified period.

» All transactions without payees.

» All undeposited funds.

» All unapplied payments.

» Additional items that you want to check each month, such as personal transactions, loan payments, and recording cash transactions. You can add or delete items in this list in the same fashion as on the Setup page.

Evaluating the Account Reconciliation page

The next tab in both the Cleanup and the Monthly versions of Books review enables you to keep tabs on the reconciliation status of bank and balance sheet accounts. You can see the number of unreconciled transactions by account, as well as the last reconciled date. The Outstanding Transactions list shows uncleared transactions that are more than 90 days old. As with the other pages, you can add or remove tasks from the Additional Items section.

Use the Select Accounts button to choose which accounts appear on the list.

TIP

Flipping through the Final Review page

Contrary to its name, the Final Review isn't the final tab in the Books Review process. Instead, it's the next-to-last one in both the Cleanup and the Monthly versions of the Books Review page. This tab offers an Unusual or Unexpected Balance section that includes accounts payable and receivable transactions that are more than 90 days old. The Reports section includes links to review the Balance Sheet and Profit and Loss reports, and the +Add button allows you to add reports as needed.

Winding up with the Wrap-Up page

The Wrap-Up tab does indeed wrap up the Books Review process for both the Cleanup and the Monthly versions. On it are three summary tasks you can't alter, apart from changing their status:

>> Prepare Reports.

>> Send Report Package.

>> Close Company.

You can add as many tasks as needed to the Additional Items section by way of the +Add button.

Accessing Accountant Tools

As shown in Figure 18-7, the Accountant Tools button always appears at the top of the screen, no matter whether you're working in your practice or a client's books. As with the New button, the functionality of the Accountant Tools menu is partially predicated on context, meaning that certain tasks are carried out in your firm's books if the sidebar is gray or in your client's books if the sidebar is dark gray.

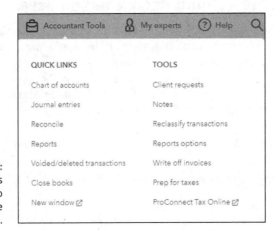

FIGURE 18-7: Accountant Tools is designed to streamline repetitive tasks.

Touring the tools list

The Accountant Tools menu includes the following commands:

>> **Chart of Accounts:** This alternative to choosing Settings⇨Chart of Accounts displays the Chart of Accounts page.

>> **Journal Entry:** This alternative to choosing +New⇨Journal Entry displays the Journal Entry transaction page. Click the clock icon at the top-left corner to display a list of recent journal entries.

>> **Reconcile:** This alternative to choosing Settings⇨Reconcile displays the Reconcile page. I discussed reconciling bank and credit card accounts in Chapter 5.

>> **Reports:** This alternative to choosing Business Overview⇨Reports (Reports) from the sidebar menu displays the Reports page. I discuss built-in reports in Chapter 6 and custom reports for Advanced subscriptions in Chapter 14. Later in this chapter, I discuss the Performance Center tab of the Reports page that only accountants can access.

>> **Voided/Deleted Transactions:** This command displays the Audit Log page filtered for deleted/voided transactions occurring in the current month.

TIP

The Export to CSV button enables you to create a comma-separated value file that contains any transactions displayed onscreen that you can then open in Microsoft Excel or Google Sheets.

>> **Close Books:** This command is an alternative to Settings⇨Advanced⇨Accounting. Click the words Close Books and then toggle on Close the Books if needed. Specify a Closing Date and indicate whether users should be required to enter a password before recording changes in a closed period.

>> **New Window:** This command is an alternative to using a command within your browser to duplicate the current window, which I discuss earlier in this chapter in the "Working in Multiple Windows" sidebar.

>> **Client Requests:** I discuss client requests in Chapter 19, but in short, this is a feature of the Accountant version that enables you to monitor requests that you've made of clients. Note that this command only appears on the Accountant Tools menu when you're actively working within a client's set of books.

>> **Notes:** This command displays a Notes page that you can use to record notes about a client's company. You can then specify whether the note should be visible to your team or only to you. This command is also only available within a client's books and isn't available when working in your practice or your firm's books.

TIP

You can notify a team member of a note by typing @ in the body of a new or existing note and then selecting from the list that appears. QuickBooks displays "No match found" if you are the only person on your team with access to a given client's books.

» **Reclassifying Transactions:** This command enables you to search for balance sheet or profit and loss transactions that you want to move to different accounts, classes, or locations. I discuss this feature in more detail in the "Reclassifying transactions" section of this chapter.

» **Reports Options:** This command displays a Report Tools button, viewable only to accountants, that allows you to specify the default date range and reporting basis for reports and displays the closing and reconciliation status of the books.

» **Write Off Invoices:** Your clients inexplicably don't have access to an easy way to write off invoices, but fortunately you do. I discuss this feature in more detail in the "Writing off invoices" section later in this chapter.

» **Prep for Taxes:** Think of this as an expanded version of the Books Review page that I cover earlier in this chapter. The page includes the following tabs:

- *Year-End Tasks:* A task list from which you can add or remove tasks as needed, as well as track the status of each task.

- *Documents:* A customizable document repository that is separate from any documents that your client may have uploaded to their company as attachments. Once you add a folder, you can use the drop-down menu to create a subfolder, add attachments or links, rename or delete the folder, and mark files for carrying forward to a new tax year.

- *Review and Adjust:* This page enables you to compare the prior and current year balance sheet and profit and loss reports.

- *Grouping & Statements:* Use this page to group related accounts to create alternate views of the financial statements.

- *Tax Mapping:* Here you can assign each account on your clients chart of accounts to the corresponding line on their tax return.

  In addition, a Tools button at the top-right allows you to download all the information to a ZIP file, carry forward the previous year's tax prep, or lock the current year tax prep.

TIP

The Prep for Taxes page allows you to transfer your client's accounting data to ProConnect Tax, Lacerte Tax, or ProSeries Tax after you select your professional software and your client's tax form from the Tax Mapping tab.

Reclassifying transactions

The Reclassify Transactions page shown in Figure 18-8 allows you to change the account for any transactions for any period, regardless of the closing date, so be careful! You can also change the class or location in Plus and Advanced companies. Follow these steps to reclassify transactions:

1. **Choose Accountant Tools⇨Reclassify Transactions.**

   The Reclassify Transactions page appears, as shown in Figure 18-8.

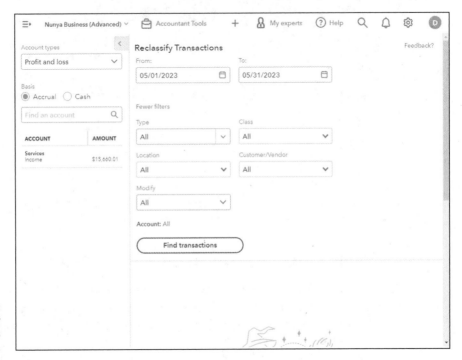

FIGURE 18-8:
The Reclassify
Transactions
page.

2. **Choose Profit and Loss or Balance Sheet from the Account Types list.**

3. **Choose Accrual or Cash.**

4. **Optional: Choose an account from the list to display all transactions for that account for the specified period.**

5. **Optional: Adjust the date range.**

6. **Optional: Make selections from the filter lists to isolate the transactions you want to reclassify.**

7. Click Find Transactions if you changed the date range or filters.

8. Choose one or more transactions from the resulting list, and then choose Reclassify.

9. As shown in Figure 18-9, optionally change the account, class, or location for the transactions, and then click Apply.

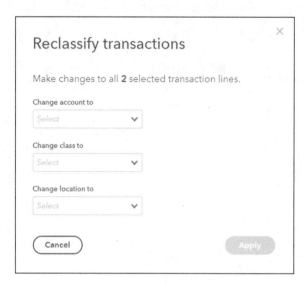

Reclassify transactions

Make changes to all **2** selected transaction lines.

Change account to

Select ▾

Change class to

Select ▾

Change location to

Select ▾

Cancel   Apply

FIGURE 18-9
The Reclassify Transactions dialog box.

Writing off invoices

Choose Accountant Tools ➪ Write Off to display the Write Off Invoices page shown in Figure 18-10, which enables you to view invoices and then write them off to an account of your choice. At the top of the page, you set filters to display the invoices you want to review. You can view invoices more than 180 days old, more than 120 days old, in the current accounting period, or in a custom date range that you set. You can also set a balance limit. Select any invoices that you want to write off, and then click the Write Off button. Select an account if needed from the confirmation prompt shown in Figure 18-11, and then click Apply to write off the invoices; otherwise, click Cancel.

WARNING

The Write Off feature doesn't make adjusting entries in the current period; instead, it adjusts the period in which the transaction was originally created, which can affect closed periods negatively. See the last section in Chapter 2 to see how to write off an invoice without affecting a prior period.

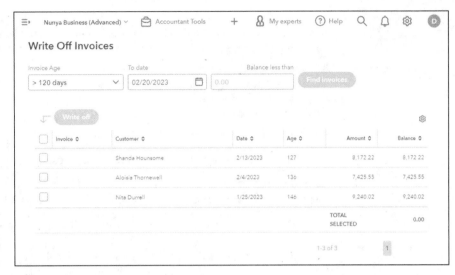

FIGURE 18-10:
The Write Off
Invoices page.

FIGURE 18-11:
Confirm that you
want to write off
the selected
invoices.

Undoing reconciliations

I feel like the Accountant Tools menu should include an Undo Reconciliations command, but it doesn't. Many of your clients would give their eye teeth for the ability to undo reconciliations, particularly those who previously had that ability in QuickBooks Desktop.

Even though it's not on the Account Tools menu, there's a way to undo the reconciliation of certain asset, liability, and equity accounts for your clients, which includes bank and credit card accounts. Follow these steps:

1. **Choose Accounting⇨Reconcile.**

    The Reconcile tab of the Accounting page appears.

Your clients see this page if they're using Accountant View, but Business View users need to choose Live Bookkeeping⇨Reconcile, which displays a Reconcile page that's almost identical.

2. **Choose History by Account.**

   The History by Account page appears.

3. **Choose an account from the list.**

   You can reconcile certain asset, liability, and equity accounts.

4. **Click the drop-down arrow in the Action column adjacent to the most recent reconciliation and choose Undo, as shown in Figure 18-12.**

5. **Click Yes after reviewing the warning prompt; otherwise, click Go Back.**

The Undo command doesn't appear on the Action column of the History by Account page for your clients. You can only undo reconciliations by way of the Accountant version.

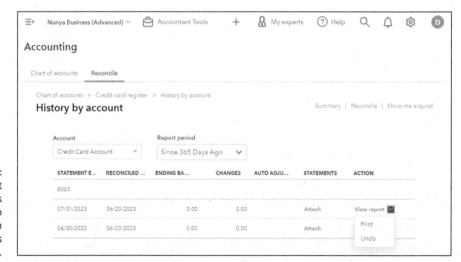

FIGURE 18-12: Accountant version users can undo reconciliations in any QuickBooks company.

Graphing Your Clients' Financial Data

QuickBooks Simple Start, Essentials, and Plus users have a limited array of charts available to them when they choose Dashboards⇨Business Overview. Advanced companies have access to the Performance Center tab, which is available across all subscription levels when accountants access a client's books through the Accountant version. You can share Performance Center charts with your clients by clicking Export and choosing one or more charts to be saved in a PDF file.

Perusing the Performance Center

The Performance Center enables you to generate prebuilt and custom charts for any of your clients by way of the following steps:

1. Choose Reports⇨Performance Center tab.

   The Performance Center tab appears on the Reports page.

   Your clients can't access this page if they have Simple Start, Essentials, or Plus subscriptions, but

REMEMBER

2. The Performance Center appears and displays 10 charts in most QuickBooks versions.

   Some charts, such as the A/R and A/P aging, are as of today, but other charts allow you to choose from a selection of date ranges. These charts appear by default on the Performance Center for all subscription levels:

   - Expenses Over Time

   - Revenue Over Time

   - Gross Profit Over Time

   - Net Profit Over Time

   - Accounts Receivable

   - Accounts Payable

   - COGS Over Time

   - NPM vs. Industry Benchmarks (Net Profit Margin)

   - GPM vs. Industry Benchmarks (Gross Profit Margin)

   Advanced companies include a Net Cash Flow chart. The Settings button enables you to specify the industry to use for charts that offer benchmarks.

   You can add up to 25 charts to any QuickBooks company.

TIP

3. You can modify the layout of the Performance Center in the following ways:

   - Click Customize Layout to rearrange the order of the charts and then click Done.

   - Click the three-dot menu between any chart to display a menu from which you can edit the chart by changing parameters, export the chart to a PDF file, or delete the chart from the Performance Center.

TIP

You can restore any built-in charts that you delete by selecting from the Quick Add Charts list. Any chart on the list can be added to the Performance Center tab multiple times if you want to adjust the settings to create different perspectives.

- Click Add a New Chart to create a customized chart.

Creating new charts

Accountants sometimes speak in shorthand, so this section relates to graphically presenting QuickBooks data, as opposed to maintaining a client's chart of accounts. (See Chapter 1 if you're looking for guidance on that.) You can add new charts based on any of the following categories:

>> Expenses

>> Revenue

>> Gross Profit

>> Net Profit

>> Accounts Receivable

>> Accounts Payable

>> COGS (Cost of Goods Sold)

>> Cash Flow

>> Current Ratio

>> Quick Ratio

Use the following steps to create a new chart, such as the one shown in Figure 18-13:

1. **Click Add a New Chart on the Performance Center tab of the Reports page.**

2. **Choose a category from the list, and then click Continue.**

3. **Specify the name for your chart.**

4. **Select the period for the chart.**

5. **Optional: Make a Group By selection, if available.**

   You can group charts by classes, locations, items, income, or customers.

6. **Optional: Apply filtering options, if available.**

   Some charts offer the ability to filter by classes, locations, items, customers, or income. These options are predicated by a company's subscription level.

7. **Optional: Choose to compare a chart against a time period, if available.**

   You can choose to compare it to the previous period or the previous year, same period.

8. **Optional: Choose between vertical bars and trend line, if available.**

   Vertical bars is another term for a column chart, and trend line is another way of referring to a line chart.

9. **Click Add to Dashboard to save your chart, or click the X in the upper-right corner to discard the chart.**

   You can also click Back to change your chart type.

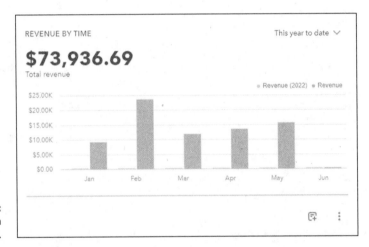

FIGURE 18-13:
An example of a revenue chart.

TIP

You can click the Note button below any chart to add up to 10,000 characters about the chart. The three-dot menu offers the following options:

» **Edit Chart:** Returns you to the Add New Chart page, where you can tweak your settings.

» **Export Chart:** Creates a PDF file containing the chart.

» **Delete Chart:** Removes the chart from the Performance Center dashboard.

REMEMBER

The Export button for the Performance Center gives you the option to export multiple charts to a PDF file and control the order that the charts appear in.

TIP

The Create Custom Charts link that appears to the left of the Add Quick Charts button in Advanced companies launches the Custom Report Builder feature. I discuss this feature in more detail in Chapter 14.

Chapter **19**

Practice Management

I n this chapter, I walk you through the practice management features that the Accountant version provides. The practice management tools are immediately available whenever you log in to the Accountant version. You can also return to them at any time by clicking on your client's company name at the top of the screen and then choosing Back to Practice.

Introducing the Work Page

The Work command appears within the Your Practice section of the sidebar in the Accountant version. Your clients can't see the Work page, and you decide which elements of the Work page each of your team members can see. As shown in Figure 19-1, the Work page tracks work to be completed for both your clients and your members of your firm by way of

» Automated notifications from your clients' QuickBooks companies

» Projects and tasks that you create

» Requests that you send to your clients

The Work page in Figure 19-1 is mostly blank because I've only set up one project thus far.

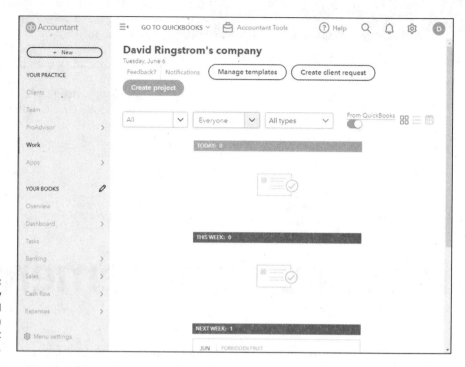

FIGURE 19-1:
A mostly unpopulated Work page within the Accountant version.

TIP

I discuss adding team members in Chapter 17.

REMEMBER

The word *projects* has two different connotations in QuickBooks. Plus and Advanced users can use projects to track related transactions as a means of monitoring the profitability of certain endeavors. Conversely, in the Accountant version, projects are containers for one or more tasks to be completed.

The Work page offers three different views — Grid, List, and Calendar — that you can filter by using three buttons and a toggle:

TIP

>> **All:** The first filter defaults to giving you a bird's-eye view of your practice. From this list, you can choose Clients Only to see only tasks related to your clients, or Firm Only to view only internal tasks. You can also choose a specific client.

 You must create a project or task for a client before they show up on this list.

>> **Everyone:** The second filter shows you tasks assigned to everyone in the firm. You can choose Me to see your personal to-do list or choose a specific team member to see that person's tasks.

>> **All types:** The third filter controls which types of items appear on screen. You can choose Projects, Tasks, or Requests from this list.

>> **From QuickBooks:** This toggle controls whether automated notifications generated by each client's QuickBooks company appear on your Work page.

You can use all three filters in conjunction with one another so that you see as much or as little detail as you need in each moment.

The Work page also has three buttons in the top-right corner:

>> **Manage Templates:** This button displays the Templates page that allows you to create project templates, which are basically preconfigured to-do lists for work to be done on an ongoing basis. As shown in Figure 19-2, the Templates page includes four Quick Start templates that are prepopulated with related tasks. You can't modify the built-in templates, but you can duplicate them as starting points for your own templates.

>> **Create Client Requests:** This button displays the Create a Request task pane, shown in Figure 19-3, that you can use to document a request you're making of a client. You can optionally notify your client of the request, which saves you from having to log the request and then separately email it.

>> **Create Project:** This button displays the Create Project task pane, shown in Figure 19-4 when there is work to be completed that doesn't fit within a template you've created.

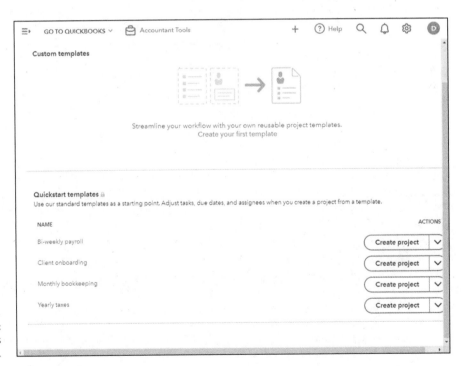

FIGURE 19-2: The Templates page.

FIGURE 19-3:
The Create
a Request
task pane.

FIGURE 19-4:
The Create
Project task pane.

You can view the tasks and requests you create in three different ways on the Work page, but the next section covers how to create templates.

Creating templates

The repetitive nature of accounting-related tasks means it's easy for items to fall off your radar or blur into the woodwork. You can counter this by creating project templates that are composed of tasks or steps to be completed. Here's how to create a template:

1. **Choose Work on the sidebar and then click Manage Templates.**

   The Templates page shown in Figure 19-2 appears.

2. **Click Create Template to display the task pane shown in Figure 19-5.**

3. **Type a name for the template, such as Month-End Tasks, in the Project Name box.**

4. **Optional: Enable the Repeat toggle to display the Due Date options shown in Figure 19-5.**

   You can set projects to recur on a weekly, biweekly, monthly, quarterly, or yearly basis on specific days of your choice. The scheduling options presented vary, based on the frequency you select.

5. **Optional: Use the Details field (see Figure 19-6) to add narrative information about the project.**

6. **Click Add a Task to display the fields shown in the Tasks Pane in Figure 19-6.**

7. **Assign a name to the task, such as** Bank Reconciliation.

8. **The Due Date field for the task lets you choose between Set Later or Offset.**

   Set Later means you need to set the due date when you create a new project based on this template. Conversely, Offset enables you to schedule the task a specified number of days prior to the project due date.

9. **Add additional tasks as needed, and then click Save Template.**

10. **Create additional templates as needed, and then click the Work link at the top-left side of the page or choose Work from the sidebar menu.**

TIP

The Save Template button is disabled if you haven't filled in a required field in the task pane.

FIGURE 19-5:
Establishing a
recurring project.

FIGURE 19-6:
Adding a task to a
project.

Creating client requests from the Work page

A client request can be anything related to a client's QuickBooks company or your business relationship with them. Here's how to create a client request:

1. **Choose Work on the sidebar menu and then click Create Client Request.**

   The task pane shown in Figure 19-3 appears.

2. **Choose a client name from the list.**

3. **Enter a title for the request, such as Engagement Letter.**

   This is similar to crafting a subject line for an email.

4. **Specify a due date for the request.**

   The due date is a required field.

5. **Enter the details of the request, much like the body of an email.**

6. **Optional: Click Documents to upload one or more documents related to the request.**

   This is similar to adding an attachment to a QuickBooks transaction.

   The Documents button doesn't appear within the Create a Request task pane until after you choose a client from the list.

TIP

7. **The Notify Client option defaults to enabled, but you can turn it off if you don't want to notify your client of the request.**

8. **Click Share to save the request.**

   The Share button retains its label even if you toggle off the Notify Client option.

9. **The request appears on your Work page, as shown in Figure 19-7.**

   A Sent indicator appears at the bottom of the task if you notified your client of the request. This takes the form of a gray shaded area beneath the task along with an envelope icon and the word Sent.

If you choose to notify your client, they receive an email message notifying them of the request, and then the request appears within their QuickBooks company.

Creating client requests from the Accountant Tools menu

You can also initiate client requests while you're working within a client's set of books:

1. **Choose Accountant Tools ⇨ Client Requests.**

   A Client Requests task pane appears.

2. **Click +Add Request.**

3. **Enter a title for the request, such as Engagement Letter.**

   This is similar to crafting a subject line for an email.

4. **Specify a due date for the request.**

   The due date is a required field.

5. **Enter the details of the request, much like the body of an email.**

6. **Optional: Click Documents to upload one or more documents related to the request.**

   This is similar to adding an attachment to a QuickBooks transaction.

7. **The Notify Client option in the Share with Client section is enabled by default, but you can toggle it off if you don't want to notify your client in this fashion.**

8. **Click Share to save the request.**

   The Share button retains its label even if you toggle the Notify Client option off.

9. **The request appears in the Client Requests task pane and is also on the Work page when you return to the Your Practice section of the Accountant version.**

Viewing requests within your clients' companies

Here's how your clients can view requests that you make of them:

1. **Choose My Accountant from the sidebar menu.**

   The My Accountant page shown in Figure 19-7 appears. Your clients can choose Due Date or Recently Updated from the Sort By list.

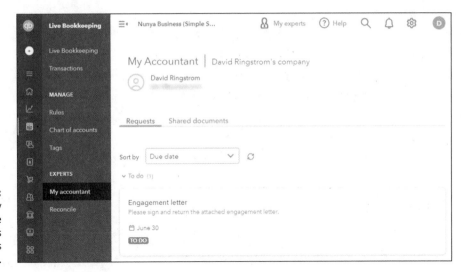

FIGURE 19-7:
The My
Accountant page
within a client's
QuickBooks
company.

TIP

You can view the My Accountant page in the same fashion that your clients see it by activating their company within the Accountant version and then choosing My Accountant from the sidebar menu.

2. **Click any task to display the task pane shown in Figure 19-8.**

3. **Optional: Your client can expand the Documents section to view documents you've shared or upload new documents.**

4. **Optional: Your client can expand the Comments section to view any comments that you have made, but the only way that they can respond is by uploading a document.**

TIP

It's a bit baffling to me that your clients cannot respond to comments, as this was a feature in the past. I suspect, and definitely hope, that this is an unexpected side effect caused by other recent improvements and that the ability for clients to respond to requests you make of them will be restored.

WARNING

You can't edit or delete comments added to a request.

Your clients can't delete requests, but you can. Click on any request on the Work page to display the task pane for the request, and then Click the Delete Request icon at the top right. QuickBooks asks you to confirm the deletion and reminds you that any documents attached will remain in the Documents tab. You can also change the status of a request to In Progress or Completed. Your clients cannot change the status.

Engagement letter

📅 Due June 30

TO DO

Please sign and return the attached
engagement letter.

📄 Documents   1 >

💬 Comments   0 >

FIGURE 19-8:
The To Do task
pane within a
client's
QuickBooks
company.

Managing projects and tasks

Projects typically are a collection of tasks to be completed by a specified date. Each project is assigned to a client or to your firm, and each task within a project has a due date and is assigned to a team member. Here's how to create a task-tracking project:

1. **Choose Work from the sidebar menu, and then click Create Project.**

   The panel shown in Figure 19-4 appears.

2. **Optional: Choose a template from the Project Template drop-down list.**

3. **Enter a name for the project, such as Annual Budget.**

4. **Choose between My Firm or a client name from the Firm or Client drop-down list.**

   Use My Firm to track internal projects that aren't related to a specific client.

5. **Set a project due date.**

   You must schedule the due dates for any tasks associated with this project on or before the project due date.

6. **Assign the project to a team member by using the Assigned To field.**

   Assign the project to the team member responsible for the overall project. You can assign tasks to other individuals.

TIP

   Click the Repeat slider to set up the time frame to use for recurring projects, such as monthly bank statement reconciliation or quarterly payroll tax filings.

7. **Enter narrative information about the project in the Details field.**

8. **Optional: Click Add a Task to add one or more tasks to the project.**

9. **Click Save to save the project.**

TIP

Projects scheduled for more than 30 days in the future don't appear on the Grid View of the Work page but do appear in List View, as I discuss in the next section.

You can edit any project or task that you add, but you can't edit the automatic tasks that a QuickBooks company posts. Click on any project or task on the Work page to display a task pane like what you used to create the project. You can edit the project details as well as add, remove, or update tasks. Buttons along the bottom of the task pane enable you to delete the project, convert it to a template, or duplicate it.

TIP

You can't convert a project into a task or a task into a project.

As you make progress on a task, you can update its status directly from Grid View on the Work page. Click the arrow on a task card to change its status, as shown in Figure 19-9.

FIGURE 19-9:
Use the arrow on a task or project card to display the list of available statuses.

Tasks can have a status of To Do, In Progress, Blocked, or Done. You use Blocked status when something is stopping you from completing a task.

Looking at Work page views

As I discussed previously, the Work page allows you to filter your to-do list as granularly as you want. The Work page also offers three different views:

» **Grid:** This default view uses cards that allow you to monitor requests, projects, and tasks due within the next 30 days, as shown earlier in Figure 19-1.

» **List:** The List button appears at the top-right corner of the Grid and displays all requests, projects, and tasks in list form, as shown in Figure 19-10.

» **Calendar:** The Calendar button also appears at the top-right corner of the grid and shows you the number of requests, tasks, or projects that are due on a given day, as shown in Figure 19-11.

FIGURE 19-10:
The List View.

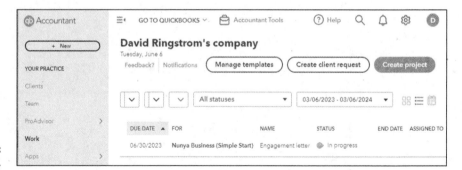

REMEMBER

Filters that you apply affect all three views.

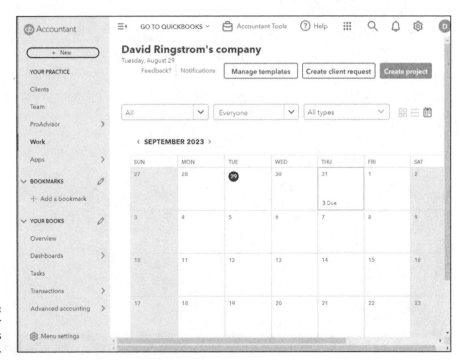

FIGURE 19-11:
The Calendar
View with 3 tasks
due on August 31.

Communicating with Team Members about Work

At the risk of stating the obvious, communication is paramount when you're working in a team environment. You can provide notifications by email for a variety of actions associated with the projects and tasks on the Work page. If you want to turn notifications on or off, click the Notifications link at the top of the Work page shown in Figures 19-10 and 19-11. Doing so displays the Notifications tab of the Company Settings task pane shown in Figure 19-12.

Click the Edit icon in the top-right corner of the Email section to turn email notifications on and off for various actions that take place on the Work page. Click Save when you finish, and then click Done.

TIP

By default, each team member is notified of new assignments and due dates, but team members configure their notification settings within the Accountant version.

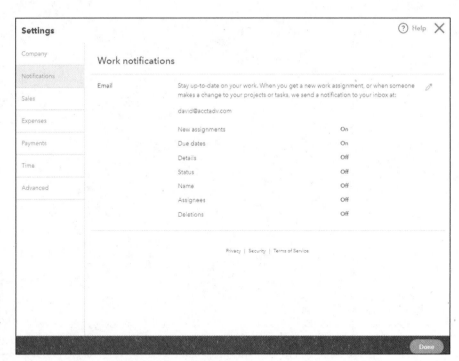

FIGURE 19-12:
Set up email notifications for team members regarding work.

Using Your Free QuickBooks Online Advanced Subscription

The Accountant version offers one free QuickBooks Online Advanced subscription for use with an accounting firm's books, along with a free Payroll Elite subscription, which is accessed by way of the Your Books section of the sidebar menu. Accountant version users have up to 1,060 days to migrate their accounting records from QuickBooks Desktop into their firm's free Advanced company. You can import your desktop data multiple times during this window if needed; each import overwrites any existing data in the firm's Advanced company.

REMEMBER

The Your Books subscription integrates with the Accountant version and is intended to house your accounting firm's data, not a client's data or a subsidiary of your accounting firm. Every client in your Client List is automatically established as a customer in the Your Books company, but team members aren't set up as employees.

6
Microsoft Excel Analysis

Chapter **20**

Analyzing QuickBooks Data in Excel

D ata within accounting programs is often trapped under glass, and not just in QuickBooks. Most users have constraints regarding how much they can customize reports. (See Chapter 6 for more information about customizing reports.) In Chapter 14 I discuss the Custom Report Builder that Advanced subscribers can use, but in this chapter I show you ways that you can unlock your accounting data with Excel.

If you don't have much experience in Excel, the book *Microsoft Excel For Dummies*, by Greg Harvey, can help you get up to speed. If you haven't set up your QuickBooks company yet, you can follow along with this chapter by using the sample company available at `https://qbo.intuit.com/redir/testdrive`.

I used the Microsoft 365 version of Excel when writing this chapter. You can carry out everything I discuss in this chapter in Excel 2013 and later. You can accomplish most techniques within Google Sheets as well.

Disabling Protected View in Microsoft Excel

Microsoft Excel treats any reports downloaded from the internet, such as any report you export from QuickBooks, as a threat and opens them in Protected View. This is a sandbox mode within Excel that enables you to safely view a report so that you can determine whether it truly is a threat.

Spoiler alert: Any reports exported from QuickBooks Online are perfectly safe, but the fact remains that Protected View can slow your work down, especially if you frequently export reports from QuickBooks to Excel. Allow me to demonstrate what I mean by exporting the Accounts Receivable Aging Summary report to Excel:

1. **Choose Reports on the sidebar menu.**

   The Reports page appears.

2. **Choose Accounts Receivable Aging Summary in the Favorites or Who Owes You sections.**

3. **Optional: Create more on-screen space for your report by clicking the Collapse button to hide the sidebar menu.**

   Reports can appear in multiple sections, so choose whichever section is easiest for you to access or click the star next to a report to add it to the Favorites section.

4. **Click Export⇨ Export to Excel.**

   See Chapter 6 for more information about running reports in QuickBooks.

5. **Open the report in Excel by double-clicking the report name in your Downloads folder; alternatively, you can choose File⇨Open⇨Browse in Excel and then open the workbook.**

6. **Click Enable Editing on the message bar shown in Figure 20-1 to access your report.**

You can't edit workbooks in Protected View until you click Enable Editing, but you can navigate to any visible cell or worksheet in the workbook. Figure 20-2 shows that the actual amounts appear onscreen in your report once you click Enable Editing.

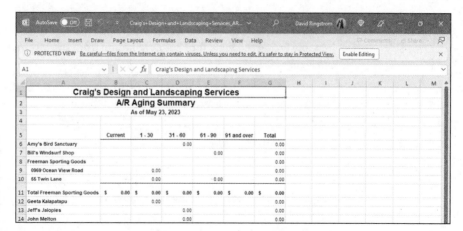

FIGURE 20-1:
Protected View can cause numbers in your reports to be temporarily hidden.

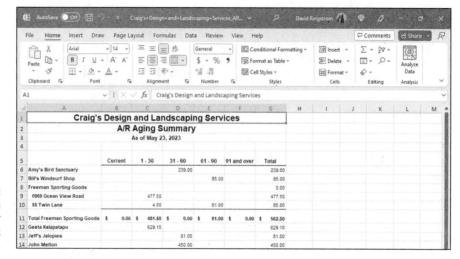

FIGURE 20-2:
Any hidden amounts appear when you click Enable Editing.

Protected View is well-intentioned, but you can disable the feature if you wish:

1. **Choose File ⇨ Options in Excel for Windows.**

   The Options dialog box opens.

   Excel for macOS doesn't offer the Protected View feature.

2. **Choose Trust Center ⇨ Trust Center Settings.**

   The Trust Center dialog box opens.

3. **Click Protected View in the left column and clear the checkbox titled Enable Protected View for Files Originating from the Internet, as shown in Figure 20-3.**

   You can clear the checkbox titled Enable Protected View for Outlook Attachments as well, if you wish.

WARNING

   Always leave Enable Protected View for Files Located in Potentially Unsafe Locations checkbox turned on.

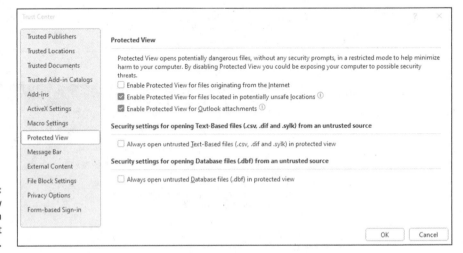

FIGURE 20-3:
Protected View
settings within
Excel's Trust
Center.

4. **Click OK twice to close the Trust Center and Options dialog boxes.**

   Now you no longer must click Enable Editing whenever you open a QuickBooks report in Excel.

TIP

   You can use Protected View situationally in Excel for Windows should you encounter a spreadsheet of unknown provenance. To do so, choose File⇨ Open⇨Browse and click once on the workbook name. Click the arrow next to the Open button and choose Open in Protected View.

Filtering Data

The Filter feature in Excel is one of my favorites because it enables me to get a bird's-eye view of data within a report by clicking the Filter button at the top of any column or take things a step further by collapsing a report to show specific data.

Maybe you want to isolate just the overdue amounts on your accounts receivable aging schedule. The Filter feature is one way that you can accomplish this. Here's how to do so:

1. **Click any cell in the body of your report and then choose Data ⇨ Filter (or Home ⇨ Sort & Filter ⇨ Filter).**

   You can also press Ctrl+Shift+L (Cmd+Shift+L for Mac users).

2. **Click the Filter button at the top of any column, such as cell E5 in Figure 20-4.**

3. **Clear the checkboxes for data that you don't want to see in this context, such as $0.00 and (Blanks), and then click OK.**

4. **As shown in Figure 20-4, only rows that contain an amount in the 61–90 column are displayed.**

   You can filter on as many columns as you want.

FIGURE 20-4:
A filtered accounts receivable aging report.

5. **Choose Data ⇨ Clear to remove the filter settings and see the entire report again.**

   Alternatively, choose Data ⇨ Filter to turn the Filter feature off, which, in turn, displays the entire report again. The Clear command keeps the filter buttons in place while clicking Filter toggles the buttons off.

REMEMBER

The Filter feature protects hidden rows, meaning that if you color-code, delete, or otherwise alter anything in any of the visible rows, nothing in the hidden rows is affected. However, deleting an entire column does remove any data that's within hidden rows, but only in the column that you deleted.

Now let's take the filter feature a step further by creating the ability to filter for all overdue amounts:

1. **Type the word** Overdue **in cell H5.**

2. **Enter** =SUM(D6:F6)>0 **in cell H6 and then copy the formula down the column.**

   An easy way to do so is to click on cell H6 and then double-click the notch (known as the *fill handle*) in the lower-right corner of the active cell, in this case cell H6 (see Figure 20-5). This formula returns TRUE if the sum of columns D through F is greater than zero; otherwise, it returns FALSE.

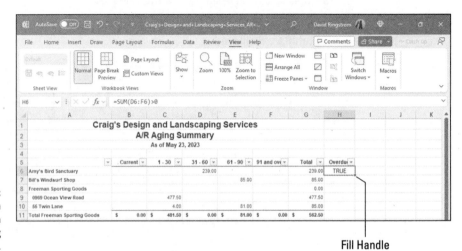

FIGURE 20-5:
Adding an
Overdue column
to the aging
report.

Fill Handle

3. **Choose Data ⇨ Filter to turn the filter feature off.**

4. **Make sure your cursor is somewhere within the aging schedule and then choose Data ⇨ Filter.**

   You cannot filter data in column H unless you turn the Filter feature off and then on again so that it recognizes the new column by placing a filter button in cell H5.

5. **Click the Filter button in cell H5, clear the checkbox for** FALSE, **and then click OK.**

Sometimes the filter feature is sufficient to help you get at what you want to see within an accounting report. In other cases, you may need to perform some data cleanup before you can achieve the desired results.

Preparing QuickBooks Reports for Analysis

In Chapter 6, I discuss the differences between customizing classic reports and enhanced reports. The differences carry over to Excel as well because you may need to clean up different issues on classic reports versus enhanced reports. Both report formats usually violate one or more of the following ground rules for analysis-ready data:

>> All columns are contiguous, meaning the data set has no blank columns.

>> All rows are contiguous, meaning the data set has no blank rows.

>> The data set has no subtotal or total rows, which avoids double counting.

>> The data has no groupings, such as segregating invoices by customer and bills by vendor.

>> All dates should be numeric values, yet QuickBooks reports store dates as text instead.

>> All amounts need to be numeric values, yet enhanced reports store dollar amounts as text. Classic reports do store dollar amounts as numbers.

TIP

You can ensure that dates and amounts on enhanced reports will be formatted properly by choosing Export to CSV when exporting, although opening such files in Excel automatically removes leading zeros, such as from inventory item IDs or certain ZIP codes. In Chapter 21, I show how to use Power Query to open CSV files while preserving leading zeros. You can't export classic reports to the comma-separated value file format.

>> Blank cells within amount columns should be completely blank, but enhanced reports sometimes fill such cells with two dashes. This causes Excel formulas that reference such cells to return an error such as #VALUE!, while PivotTable reports treat the entire column as being composed of text instead of numbers, which means the amounts are counted instead of summed.

>> You can't display more than 20 columns on an enhanced report, whereas you can display every available column on classic reports. For instance, the classic version of the Transaction List by Date report allows you to display and export up to 32 columns of data, but the enhanced version of this report limits you to exporting up to 20 columns.

>> Enhanced reports exported to Excel don't include the header and footer rows that appear by default on classic reports. However, you can turn the headers and footers off on classic reports and save them as customizations.

I'll export the Transaction List by Date report to Excel as both enhanced and classic reports so that you can see the differences and steps that are necessary to overcome some of the nuances.

Exporting enhanced reports

You can identify enhanced reports by way of the "New Enhanced Experience" caption on the Reports page in QuickBooks. You can still export every enhanced report to Excel as a classic report. I'll export the enhanced Transaction List by Date report to Excel so that you can see how to transform any problematic columns:

1. **In QuickBooks, choose Reports from the sidebar menu.**

   The Reports page appears.

2. **Type** by date **in the Find a Report field and then press Enter.**

   Alternatively, choose Transaction List by Date in the For My Accountant section.

3. **Choose This Year from the time period drop-down list.**

   Alternatively, choose any period you want or choose Custom from the list to set a specific date range.

4. **Click Export ⇨ Export to Excel.**

   You may need to manually open the workbook from the downloads bar or folder unless you carried out the automation steps earlier in this chapter.

5. **Select column A, which contains transaction dates stored as text.**

   You can leave dates stored as text, but you'll have the best experience if you convert the dates to numeric values.

TIP

   Dates and numbers that are left-aligned in Excel are often, but not always, stored as text. You can use the ISNUMBER worksheet function in Excel to test the contents of any cell.

6. **Choose Data ⇨ Text to Columns.**

   The Convert Text to Columns wizard appears as shown in Figure 20-6. Ostensibly, this feature allows you to take text in one column and split it into two or more columns, but you can also use it to transform text-based dates or amounts into numeric values.

REMEMBER

   You can transform only one column at a time with the Convert Text to Columns wizard, so if you have multiple date columns, you need to clean up each one individually.

7. **Click Finish.**

Alternatively, you can click Next twice and then click Finish if you want to see the options available within the Convert Text to Columns wizard.

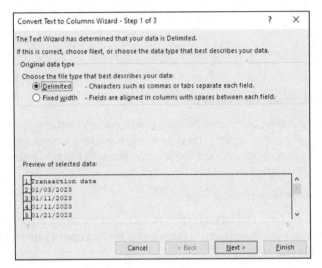

FIGURE 20-6:
Excel's Convert
Text to Columns
wizard.

8. **Select column J, which contains transaction amounts stored as text.**

9. **Choose Data ⇨ Text to Columns ⇨ Finish.**

The transaction amounts are now stored as numbers instead of text.

10. **Choose Home ⇨ Find and Select ⇨ Replace.**

Make sure that column J is still selected before you choose the Replace command; otherwise, you replace text across the entire worksheet instead of within a single column.

11. **Enter two dashes in the Find What field.**

12. **Enter a zero in the Replace With field or leave the field blank, as shown in Figure 20-7.**

In older versions of Excel, blank cells in columns otherwise filled with numbers caused PivotTables to treat the entire column as text, so it's generally best in this context to fill the empty cells with zeros.

13. **Click Replace All ⇨ OK ⇨ Close.**

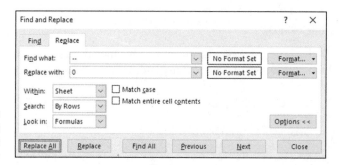

FIGURE 20-7:
Replacing
two dashes
with zeros.

14. **Choose any cell in your data.**

Spreadsheet users often think they must select all within a data set before carrying out an action in Excel. Selecting everything is necessary for applying formatting (such as colors, fonts, and number formats), but isn't necessary for performing data actions.

15. **Choose Insert ⇨ Table ⇨ OK.**

The My Table Has Headers checkbox should be selected automatically in the Create Table dialog box, confirming that the first row of your list contains column titles.

16. **Optional: Choose Table Design ⇨ Total Row.**

This command adds a total row to the bottom of your list. The last column is automatically summed or counted, depending on whether that column contains numbers or other content (such as dates or text). Click any other cell in the total row to display a button that displays a menu from which you can choose a mathematical function, such as Sum, Average, or Count. When you make a choice from the list, Excel adds the corresponding formula to the total row for that column. If you then filter or slice the table, the total row only tallies the visible rows.

17. **Choose File ⇨ Save to save the transformed report.**

Saving the workbook at this point gives you the option to close without saving and reopen if you make a mistake during any of the upcoming analysis techniques.

The report is now in an analysis-ready format. Now you'll see the steps required for classic reports.

TIP

In Chapter 21, I discuss how to use Excel's Power Query feature to automate the manual and repetitive steps that you just carried out.

Exporting classic reports

Most reports in QuickBooks utilize the classic format. Here's how to export and prepare such reports to Microsoft Excel:

1. In QuickBooks choose Reports from the sidebar menu.

The Reports page appears.

2. Type "by date" **in the Find a Report field and then press Enter.**

Alternatively, choose Transaction List by Date in the For My Accountant section.

3. Click the Switch to Classic View button.

Classic reports do not have a Switch to Enhanced View button. Your only option is to choose the report again from the Reports page if you want to return to the Enhanced View.

4. Choose This Year from the Report Period list.

5. Click the Customize button.

6. Expand the Header/Footer section, clear all five checkboxes, and then click Run Report.

Removing headers and footers from classic reports is optional but can help you avoid frustration. The headers and footers reside within merged cells, which in turn means you can unwittingly trigger error prompts like We can't do that to a merged cell.

In Chapter 6, I discuss how you can save such customizations so that you don't have to repeat them every time you run a report.

7. Click the Export button above the top corner of the report and then choose Export to Excel.

8. Right-click on column A and press Delete.

It's best to eliminate unnecessary blank columns from Excel worksheets, partly to avoid having to navigate through them.

9. Select column A if necessary, which now contains transaction dates stored in a text-based format.

You can leave dates stored as text, but you will have the best experience if you convert the dates to numeric values. For instance, PivotTables and the Filter drop-down menus group numeric dates by month, whereas text-based dates are shown individually.

10. **Choose Data ⇨ Text to Columns.**

The Text to Columns wizard appears. Ostensibly, this feature allows you to take text in one column and split it into two or more columns, but you can also use it to transform text-based dates or amounts into numeric values.

11. **Click Finish.**

Alternatively, you can click Next twice and then click Finish if you want to see the options available within the Text to Columns wizard.

12. **Choose any cell in your data.**

Sometimes users think that they must select all the cells in a report before carrying out an action in Excel. Selecting everything is necessary for applying formatting (such as colors, fonts, and number formats), but it's not necessary for performing data actions.

WARNING

At this point, only a single cell should be selected within your report. If you leave column J selected, you will create a one-column table instead of converting the entire report into a table.

13. **Choose Insert ⇨ Table or press Ctrl+T (Cmd+T in macOS), and then click OK in the Table dialog box that appears.**

The My Table Has Headers checkbox should be selected automatically, confirming that the first row of your list contains column titles.

14. **Optional: Choose Table Design ⇨ Total Row (or press Ctrl+Shift+T in Windows or Cmd+Shift+T in macOS).**

This command adds a total row to the bottom of your list. The last column is automatically summed or counted, depending on whether that column contains numbers or other content (such as dates or text).

15. **Click any other cell in the total row to display a button that shows a menu from which you can choose a mathematical function such as Sum, Average, and Count, as shown in Figure 20-8.**

When you make a choice from the list, Excel adds the corresponding formula to the total row for that column. If you then filter or slice the table, the total row tallies only the visible rows.

16. **Choose File ⇨ Save to save the transformed report.**

Saving the workbook at this point gives you the option to close without saving and reopen if you make a mistake during any of the upcoming analysis techniques.

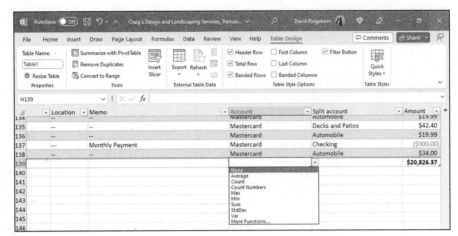

FIGURE 20-8:
Adding
mathematical
function to the
total row
of a table.

Slicing data

The Slicer feature streamlines filtering tasks in Excel by enabling you to filter lists with a single mouse click. You can create slicers for as many columns as you want within your data, but unlike the filter feature, your data does have to be formatted as a table, which I described how to do in the previous section. It's time now to add one or more slicers to your report:

1. **Click any cell in your table, and then choose Table Design⇨Insert Slicer to display the Insert Slicers dialog box shown in Figure 20-9.**

   You can use slicers to filter PivotTables as well. I show you how to create a PivotTable in the section "Summarizing Data with PivotTables," later in this chapter.

WARNING

   Make sure to select a cell near the top of your table when inserting slicers. If you select a cell near the bottom of the table, your slicers may vanish off the screen when you make a selection. If this happens, choose Data⇨Clear to redisplay all hidden rows.

2. **Choose one or more fields, such as Transaction Type and Account, and then click OK.**

   A slicer appears for each field that you choose. You can add as many slicers as you want, but keep in mind that it usually doesn't make sense to slice on columns that contain dates or numbers. Slicing works best for text-based cell contents.

FIGURE 20-9:
Insert Slicers
dialog box.

3. **Click any item in the Transaction Type slicer, such as Bill Payment (Check).**

Your list is filtered with one click, as shown in Figure 20-10. The Total Row now reflects statistics for the visible rows only.

TIP

Hold down Ctrl (Cmd in macOS) to select two or more items within a slicer.

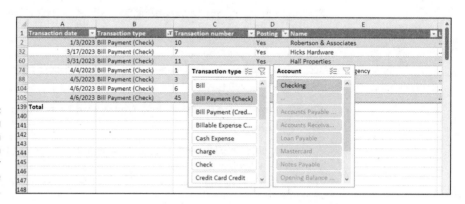

FIGURE 20-10:
Slicers allow you
to filter data
formatted as a
table or
PivotTable
with a single click.

If you use two or more slicers, the second and later slicers reflect any matches based on choices made in the first slicer. In Figure 20-10, Bill Payment (Check) is selected, which means that the only account that has activity is the Checking account. All other accounts are disabled, with no activity in them.

Click the Clear command to reset a slicer, which removes the filter.

You can make choices from as many slicers as you want. As shown in Figure 20-10, any items on the slicer that are displayed in the list are shaded. Items that don't have shading indicate available choices that haven't been selected. Disabled items represent choices that are inapplicable based on other slicing choices you've made. Slicing filters your data but gives you visual cues that aren't available when filtering unless you click the Filter button for a given column.

I'd love to tell you much more about the many automation opportunities that the table feature offers, but this book is about QuickBooks, so I'll close this discussion with a couple of tips:

>> Expand the Quick Styles section of the Table Design menu and then click the first icon at the top left to remove the shading from the table or choose Clear at the bottom of the gallery. Alternatively, you can choose from the prebuilt styles or create a new style.

>> You can right-click a slicer and choose Remove from the shortcut menu if you want to turn off a given slicer.

>> Choose Table Design ⇨ Convert to Range ⇨ Yes if you no longer want the data to be in a table. This command removes any slicers you have in place.

Sorting data

Sorting enables you to rearrange data sequentially, such as from A to Z or highest to lowest. Sort commands appear when you click a Filter button. Sort commands also appear on the Home and Data menus. In Excel, you can sort up to 64 columns by following these steps:

1. **Choose any cell within a list that you want to sort.**

Excel is always tracking what's referred to as the *current region,* the contiguous block of cells surrounding your cursor. For this reason, you don't need to select all your data in advance.

2. **Choose Data⇨Sort A-Z, Data⇨Sort Z-A, or Home⇨Sort & Filter⇨Sort A to Z or Sort Z to A.**

The names of these commands are Sort A to Z or Sort Z to A if your cursor is in a column of text, and Sort Smallest to Largest or Sort Largest to Smallest if your cursor is in a column of numbers.

3. **Optional: Click the Sort button to display the Sort task pane if you want to sort based on two or more columns.**

You can also use the Sort task pane to sort based on color or conditional formatting. If you dig deep enough, you can sort on custom lists or even sort lists sideways, meaning sorting columns from left to right or right to left versus sorting rows up and down the spreadsheet.

Summarizing Data with PivotTables

The PivotTable feature in Excel enables you to transform lists of data into meaningful summary reports simply by clicking or dragging fields within the PivotTable Fields task pane. Even better, nothing you do in a PivotTable affects the original data. Although it can seem intimidating, I want to assure you that this feature is one of Excel's easiest features to master.

Understanding PivotTable requirements

Be sure that your data conforms to all the data analysis ground rules that I listed in the "Preparing QuickBooks Reports for Analysis" section earlier in this chapter, and then convert your dataset into a table. The table feature enables a PivotTable to "see" any data that you append to the bottom of your current report, such as if you were to copy and paste data for a new month; otherwise, the new data you add to your list might be left off your PivotTable report.

Follow these steps to create a PivotTable:

1. **Select any cell in your list.**
2. **If necessary, choose Insert⇨Table⇨OK.**
3. **Choose Table Design⇨Summarize with PivotTable (or Insert⇨PivotTable).**

The Create PivotTable task pane appears.

4. **Accept the default settings by clicking OK.**

A blank PivotTable canvas appears on a new worksheet in your workbook, along with a PivotTable Fields task pane. You also see two new tabs in the Excel ribbon: PivotTable Analyze and Design.

REMEMBER

The PivotTable Analyze and Design tabs, as well as the PivotTable Fields task pane, are context sensitive. If you move your cursor to any cell outside the Pivot-Table canvas, the menus and task pane disappear; they reappear when you click inside the PivotTable canvas again. This behavior can be a bit disconcerting if you're new to the feature.

Adding fields

At this point, you're ready to add fields to your PivotTable:

1. **In Excel for Windows, click the checkbox for Account from the PivotTable Fields task pane. In Excel for macOS, drag the Account field into the Rows quadrant.**

When you click the checkbox for a given field, Excel for Windows places text or date-based fields in the Rows quadrant. Excel for macOS places all fields in the Values quadrant when you click a field's checkbox.

TIP

You can drag fields into other quadrants at any time. You can only place fields in the Filters or Columns quadrant by dragging the field name or right-clicking the field name and choosing a quadrant.

2. **Drag the Transaction Date field into the Columns quadrant.**

If your transaction dates are numeric values, Excel 2019 and later automatically group the transactions by month and then day. Otherwise, you will see a column for each date.

3. **Click the checkbox for the Amount field to position it in the Values quadrant.**

I didn't apply any number formatting to the numbers within the PivotTable in Figure 20-11 so that you can see the raw format that first appears. You can change the formatting in a PivotTable in the same fashion as any other cells in Excel.

TIP

Double-clicking any number within a PivotTable drills down into the underlying transactions, like drilling down into a QuickBooks report. A new worksheet displays that shows you the data that the number you double-clicked is based upon.

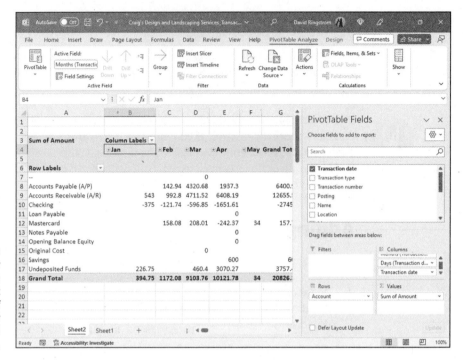

FIGURE 20-11:
PivotTables allow
you to create
instant
summaries of
your data by
dragging and
dropping fields.

Refreshing and resizing PivotTables

PivotTables display a snapshot in time of your data. This is different from formu‐
las, which recalculate automatically. You can refresh a PivotTable in three ways:

REMEMBER

» Right-click on the PivotTable and choose Refresh.

» Choose PivotTable Analyze⇨Refresh.

  The PivotTable Analyze tab is present only when your cursor is inside a PivotTable.

» Choose Data⇨Refresh All.

The Refresh command refreshes only a single PivotTable, whereas Refresh All
refreshes all PivotTables within a given workbook. Keep in mind that refreshing
only includes data that the PivotTable can "see." If your PivotTable is based on a
table, then your PivotTable automatically considers any new data when you
refresh. If your PivotTable is based on a normal range of cells, you must carry out
the following steps any time you add additional data to the original source data:

1. **Select any cell in your PivotTable.**

2. **Choose PivotTable Analyze⇨Change Data Source.**

   The Change PivotTable Data Source dialog box appears.

3. **Update the Table/Range field to reflect the expanded cell coordinates of your data set.**

4. **Click OK.**

Excel automatically refreshes your PivotTable after you click OK in the Change PivotTable Data Source dialog box. You may notice that the name of the dialog box changes to Move PivotTable after you select a new range of data. This is an odd but benign Excel quirk.

Removing fields

You can remove fields in one of four different ways:

>> Clear the checkbox for a field in the main area of the PivotTable Fields task pane.

>> Drag any field out of a quadrant and off the PivotTable Fields task pane and release your left mouse button.

>> Click the arrow on the right side of any field in a quadrant and choose Remove Field from the drop-down menu.

>> Right-click the field within the PivotTable and choose Remove from the shortcut menu.

TIP

I could go on and on about PivotTables, but I'll limit myself to a couple of closing tips:

>> Plus and minus buttons appear within PivotTables when you have two or more fields in the Rows or Columns quadrants. For instance, drag Name into the Rows quadrant to view activity by account and then name. Use these buttons to expand or collapse individual segments of reports or choose PivotTable Analyze⇨Collapse Field to collapse all segments, or PivotTable Analyze⇨Expand Field to expand all segments. Your cursor must be within the contents of a row field to use these commands.

>> Choose PivotTable Analyze⇨Insert Timeline to select a date-based field and then click OK. As shown in Figure 20-12, timelines are like slicers but are used to filter PivotTables for specific date ranges.

>> See *Microsoft Data Analysis for Dummies* by Paul McFedries if you want to delve more deeply into PivotTables.

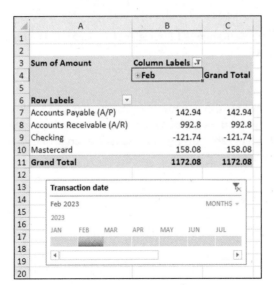

FIGURE 20-12:
Timelines allow
you to control the
contents of a
PivotTable based
on date ranges.

The figure shows a spreadsheet with the following content:

	A	B	C
3	**Sum of Amount**	Column Labels	
4		Feb	**Grand Total**
5			
6	**Row Labels**		
7	Accounts Payable (A/P)	142.94	142.94
8	Accounts Receivable (A/R)	992.8	992.8
9	Checking	-121.74	-121.74
10	Mastercard	158.08	158.08
11	**Grand Total**	**1172.08**	**1172.08**

Transaction date

Feb 2023   MONTHS

2023

JAN   FEB   MAR   APR   MAY   JUN   JUL

» Understanding the differences between enhanced and classic reports

» Manipulating Power Query results

» Keeping Power Query reports fresh

Chapter **21**

Automating QuickBooks Analysis with Power Query

I n Chapter 20, I explain how you can export QuickBooks reports for analysis in Microsoft Excel. I also explain how you can manually create a PivotTable report from your data. In this chapter, I show you how to automate the steps by using Power Query to create set-and-forget connections to reports. You still need to export reports to Excel from QuickBooks, but if you save over an exported report that's linked to Power Query, the rest of the linking and transformation process is mostly automated. If you read to the end of the chapter, you can find out how to make the process completely automated.

You can use Power Query to automate all sorts of report clean-up steps, such as *unpivoting* data, or transposing reports from columns into rows. This makes wide reports much easier to work with and unlocks capabilities such as PivotTables and filtering that are difficult or impossible in the native format of certain reports.

Introducing Power Query

As you may surmise by the name, Power Query enables you to connect to data sources, such as reports that you export from QuickBooks. The connections are refreshable, so you can save new copies over your previous exports to have a set-and-forget approach to reporting. You can instruct Excel to refresh the data connections automatically, as well as refresh any PivotTables or PivotCharts that are tied to the data when you open the workbook. In short, it's a means of automating repetitive tasks without writing programming code.

For this chapter, I used the sample company for QuickBooks Online, which you can access at `https://qbo.intuit.com/redir/testdrive`. I chose this company to provide an easy way for you to generate reports that have actual data in them. You can also follow along with your own data.

Let's export the Chart of Accounts Report from QuickBooks to a CSV file so that you can get an initial lay of the land with Power Query:

1. **In QuickBooks choose Settings ⇨ Chart of Accounts.**

   The Chart of Accounts list appears.

2. **Click Run Report.**

   The Account List report appears.

3. **Click Export ⇨ Export as CSV.**

   The Save As dialog box appears.

4. **Save the comma-separated value (CSV) file in a location of your choice.**

5. **Launch Microsoft Excel, and press Ctrl+N (or Cmd+N in macOS) if a blank workbook doesn't appear on the screen.**

6. **Choose Data ⇨ Get Data ⇨ From File ⇨ From Text/CSV.**

   If you're using Excel 2016, choose Data ⇨ New Query.

7. **Select the CSV file that you saved in step 4 and then click Import.**

   A dialog box appears and displays a preview of the CSV file.

8. **Click Transform Data to launch the Power Query Editor.**

   Alternatively, you could click Load, which bypasses the Power Query Editor and imports data directly into a new worksheet.

At this point the Power Query Editor appears on your screen.

Touring the Power Query Editor

The Power Query Editor enables you to transform data that you have imported into your workbook. As you'll see in the "Transforming Enhanced reports" and "Importing Classic reports" sections later in this chapter, Power Query can make it easy to transform QuickBooks reports into analysis-ready data formats. Let's look at some of the major features of the Power Query Editor:

>> **Ribbon interface:** Power Query has a tabbed interface much like Excel's.

>> **Queries pane:** This pane along the left side lists all available queries in each workbook. In this case the name of the CSV file that you imported into the Power Query Editor appears here.

>> **Current view:** A worksheet-like grid offers a live preview of your data, in this case you're seeing the contents of the CSV file that you imported.

>> **Query settings:** A task pane on the right side of the screen enables you to rename a query and shows as a list of transformation steps that have been applied to your data. In this case only two steps should appear:

- **Source:** This step links Power Query to the data source you specified — in this case a CSV file. In this example, you could click the Settings button to display a dialog box from which you can click Browse, select a different CSV file with the same layout, and then click OK. Doing so replaces the current data that appears in the Power Query Window, and is then returned to Excel.

  Every Power Query connection has a Source step, which means you can swap a newer version of your data into your workbook at any time rather than repeating the Power Query steps again.

- **Changed Type:** This step signifies that Power Query has automatically changed the data type for one or more columns. You can manually change the data type for a given column in the Current View by clicking the icon at the left-hand side of the column heading.

>> **Status bar:** A row of information appears along the bottom of the screen to give you various information about your query.

You can't work in Excel and Power Query at the same time. This means that if you're working in the Power Query Editor, the only way you can access your spreadsheet is to choose Close and Load on the Home tab of Power Query's ribbon or close Power Query and discard any changes.

Let's now carry out a couple of transformation steps:

1. **Choose Home ⇨ Use First Row as Headers.**

   This moves the data from the first row of the Current View grid up into the frame, thereby replacing the generic headers, meaning Column1, Column2, and so on.

2. **Choose Home ⇨ Choose Columns.**

   The Choose Columns dialog box appears.

3. **Deselect the Account Subtype, Description, and Total Balance fields, and then click OK.**

   The Current View grid should now only have two columns.

4. **Click the Filter button in the Account Type column heading, clear Select All, select Income and Expense, and then click OK.**

   The Current View grid should now only display Income and Expense accounts.

5. **Choose Close & Load.**

   The Power Query Editor closes, and the data you saw in the Current View grid now appears in a new Excel worksheet.

The preceding steps may feel rather pedestrian, meaning you're probably thinking, "Well, I could have just done the same thing in Excel." That's true, but the difference with Power Query is that you can save a new version of the CSV file over the original, and then right-click the Account List in the Excel worksheet and choose Refresh to import the new data without redoing the transformation steps. You can even automate the refresh process, which I discuss in the "Keeping Power Query Results Current" section later in this chapter.

Automating QuickBooks Report Analysis

In Chapter 20, I discuss how to export Enhanced and Classic reports from QuickBooks. Reports that are exported to Excel from QuickBooks tend to store dates and sometimes amounts as text, which can result in repetitive clean-up work. You may also find yourself copying and pasting data from QuickBooks exports into other workbooks. Power Query eliminates the copying and pasting and also provides a set-and-forget approach for cleaning up QuickBooks reports automatically.

Transforming Enhanced reports

The Transaction List by Date report is one of a handful of reports that use what Intuit sometimes refers to as Modern View, or an Enhanced report. Such reports are much more analysis ready than Classic reports, but all Enhanced reports have a couple of potential snags:

>> Date columns are formatted as text, which means certain Excel features don't recognize the data as being date-based.

>> Amount columns are formatted as text, which means certain Excel features don't recognize the data as being numeric values.

One way to eliminate these first two issues is to choose Export to CSV instead of Export to Excel after you click the Export button.

TIP

>> Zero amounts and blank fields are represented by two dashes instead of a zero or blank cells. Formulas that refer to such cells often return #VALUE!.

Connecting to an Enhanced report

You can use Power Query to manually clean reports once and then have the transformation applied automatically again if you save over the original QuickBooks export:

1. **In QuickBooks choose Reports (or Business Overview ⇨ Reports).**

The Reports page appears.

2. **Start typing** Transaction List by Date **in the Search field, and then choose that report title in the search results.**

The Search field makes it easy to locate reports without scrolling through the entire list.

3. **Select a date range, such as This Year, and then click Run Report.**

Many QuickBooks reports default to the current month, but you can designate any period.

4. **Click the Export button and then choose Export to Excel (or Export to CSV) on the resulting menu that appears.**

See Chapter 6 for more information about running reports in QuickBooks.

5. **Open and save the report in a location that's memorable for the next time you want it.**

By default, reports that you export from QuickBooks land in your Downloads folder. In this case, you want a more permanent location for this report because you'll be saving over this file again in the future.

You may need to choose the Text Files filter instead of the default Excel workbook filter in the Open page or dialog box in Excel if you want to open a CSV file.

6. **Close the Excel workbook or CSV file.**

7. **Press Ctrl+N (Cmd+N in macOS) or choose File ⇨ New ⇨ Blank Workbook in Excel to create a blank workbook or select any worksheet in an existing workbook.**

8. **Choose Data ⇨ Get Data ⇨ From File ⇨ From Workbook (or From Text/CSV).**

    If you're using Excel 2016, choose Data ⇨ New Query ⇨ From File ⇨ From Workbook (or From Text/CSV)

9. **Browse for and select the file that you saved in Step 5, and then click the Import button in Excel for Windows (or Transform Data in Excel for macOS).**

    A Navigator dialog box appears, as shown in Figure 21-1.

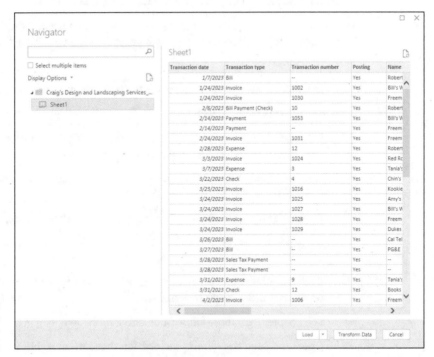

FIGURE 21-1: The Power Query Navigator window.

10. The next step depends on the type of file that you exported:

- *Excel workbook:* Choose the worksheet that contains the data you want to access, typically Sheet1 for an Enhanced report, and then click Transform Data.

In Chapter 20, I discuss how Protected View in Excel for Windows sometimes prevents data from appearing onscreen, meaning reports show all zeroes instead of amounts. Protected View can affect Power Query as well. If you see only zeros instead of amounts in the data preview, click Cancel in the Navigator window. Open your QuickBooks report in Excel, click Enable Content if needed, and then save the QuickBooks report with a new filename and close it. You should then be able to carry out Steps 1 through 10 again without issue.

- *CSV file:* Click Transform Data. There's nothing to select because a comma-separated value file is a single document as opposed to a workbook that could contain multiple worksheets.

Transforming an Enhanced report

The Applied Steps list in Figure 21-2 shows that the Applied Steps window has four steps:

- **» Source:** This step ties Power Query to your data source — whatever it may be. You can click the settings button and select a different data source that has the same layout. This means you don't necessarily have to save over the previous report; you can always change the source to point to a newer version of your file instead.

- **» Navigation:** This step causes Power Query to populate the Current View with your data.

- **» Promoted headers:** This step moves the data from the first row of your file into the column headings of the Active View. If your actual headings are further down on the report, you can remove this step by clicking Promoted Headers and then clicking the X that appears.

Be careful when removing items from the Applied Steps list. In this case, if you remove Promoted Headers, the Changed Type step triggers an error because it's no longer able to reference the Date column by name. I show you a safe way to remove both steps at once in the "Transforming a Classic reports" section later in this chapter.

- **» Changed Type:** This step means that the data type has been changed for one or more columns. In this case, the Date column had dates stored as text, but Power Query automatically added a step to change the text into dates.

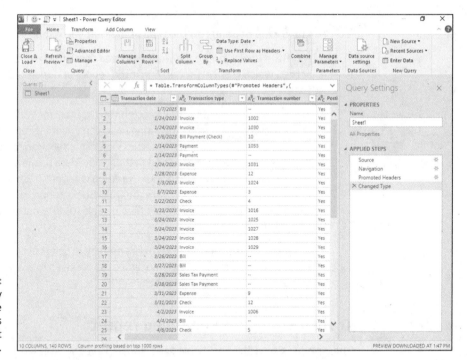

FIGURE 21-2:
The Power Query
Editor shows the
QuickBooks
report you just
imported.

These automatic steps free us up to transform the Amount column shown in Figure 21-3 into numeric values. The first step is to replace the double dashes in the column with zeros:

1. **Click on the Amount column heading to select the entire column, as shown in Figure 21-3.**

2. **Choose Home ⇨ Replace Values.**

   The Replace Values dialog box shown in Figure 21-4 appears.

3. **Type two dashes (--) in the Value to Find field.**

4. **Type a zero (0) in the Replace With field, and then click OK.**

   A Replaced Value step appears on the Applied Steps list.

TIP

   Notice how the Changed Type command (refer to Figure 21-3) doesn't offer a settings button. This means you can't tell which column types were changed, although you may be able to figure it out by clicking the Promoted Header step, which shows you what the data looked like *before* the Changed Type command was added. Power Query offers the unique ability to walk around like this within a data transformation.

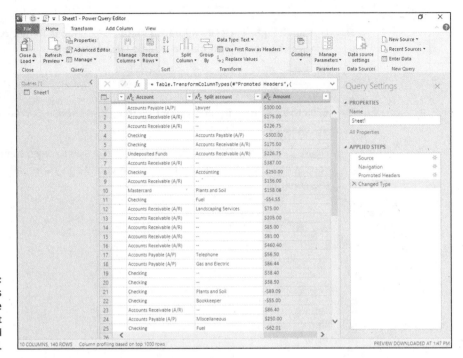

FIGURE 21-3:
Amounts
sometimes are
stored as text
within Excel
workbooks.

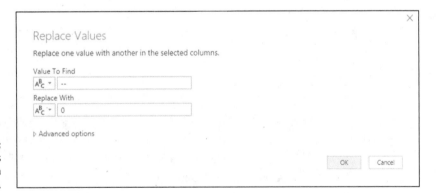

FIGURE 21-4:
Replace Values
dialog box in
Power Query.

REMEMBER

Always click on the last step on the list before carrying out another transformation step. In some cases, you can insert a step within the series, but it's generally best to work from the top down to avoid unexpected errors that can force you to discard your work and start over. You can't undo steps in Power Query as you can in Excel. Your ability to undo is limited to removing steps from the Applied Steps list.

5. **Optional: Right-click the Replaced Value step, choose Rename, and change the name to Replaced Double Dashes with 0.**

Renaming steps in Power Query makes it much easier to understand what a transformation is doing.

6. **Click the ABC icon in the Amount heading and choose Currency, as shown in Figure 21-5.**

Figure 21-5 shows the data types that you can assign to any column within your query. The Using Locale option allows you to apply international settings to a column.

FIGURE 21-5:
Data type options
in Power Query.

TIP

Some rows in the Amount column would have reported Error if we hadn't replaced the dashes with zeros. It's important to remove text like this from a column *before* changing the data type, as described in these steps.

7. **Choose Home ⇨ Choose Columns.**

The Choose Columns dialog box opens, as shown in Figure 21-6.

TIP

The Choose Columns dialog box provides an easy way to remove unwanted columns from a report.

8. **Clear the Transaction Number, Posting, and Split Account checkboxes and then click OK.**

The fields are presented in the order in which they appear in the report, but you can click the AZ button to alphabetize them or use the Search field to shorten the list.

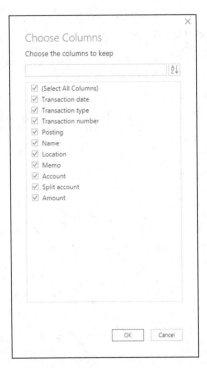

FIGURE 21-6:
The Choose
Columns
dialog box.

9. **Click the settings button next to the Removed Other Columns step in the Applied Steps pane, as shown in Figure 21-7.**

   You can revise a step that you've added to a Power Query transformation if a settings icon appears.

FIGURE 21-7:
You can revise
any Power Query
step that has a
Settings button
in the Applied
steps list.

10. **You can now remove any other columns you missed the first time, such as the Location and Memo fields, and click OK.**

    At this point, the report should have five columns, as shown in Figure 21-8.

11. Choose Home ⇨ Close and Load.

At this point, you've cleaned up the anomalies that QuickBooks injects into the reports, so you can return the data to Excel, as shown in Figure 21-8.

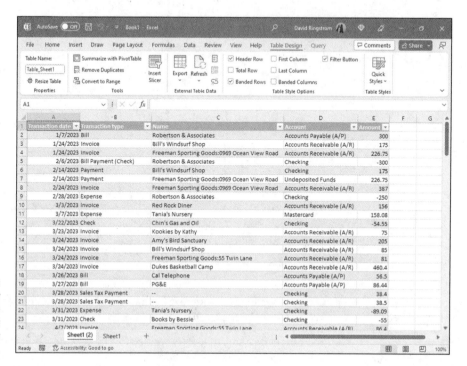

FIGURE 21-8: Power Query results are returned to a new worksheet by default.

Importing Classic reports

Most reports that you export from QuickBooks utilize the Classic report format. This means that the reports most likely have unnecessary heading rows, blank columns, and other challenges, such as nonprintable characters. In this section I'll show you an additional benefit of Power Query, which is to unpivot reports that have many columns, such as the Profit and Loss by Customer report. As you'll see, unpivoting a report transforms it into a concise columnar format that makes it much easier to filter or base a PivotTable on.

Connecting to a Classic report

Use the following steps to export the Profit and Loss by Customer report to Excel:

1. In QuickBooks, choose Reports (or Business Overview ⇨ Reports).

The Reports page appears.

2. **Start typing** Profit and Loss by Customer **in the Search field and then choose that report title in the search results.**

   The report defaults to This Year-to-Date, but you can choose a different time frame and then click Run Report.

3. **Click the Export button and then choose Export to Excel on the resulting menu.**

   You can only export classic reports to Excel or PDF formats.

4. **Open and save the workbook in a memorable location.**

   By default, reports that you export from QuickBooks land in your Downloads folder. In this case, you want a more permanent location for this report because you'll save over this file again in the future.

5. **Close the Excel workbook.**

6. **Press Ctrl+N (Cmd+N in macOS) to create a blank workbook.**

   Alternatively, you can choose File ⇨ New ⇨ Blank Worksheet in Excel or select any worksheet in an existing workbook.

7. **Choose Data ⇨ Get Data ⇨ From File ⇨ From Workbook.**

   If you're using Excel 2016, choose Data ⇨ New Query.

8. **Browse for and select the file that you saved in Step 5, and then click the Import button.**

   A Navigator dialog box appears.

9. **Choose the worksheet that contains your data — in this case Profit and Loss by Customer — and then click Transform Data.**

TIP

   See the Warning in the "Importing Enhanced Reports" section to find out how to recover when you see all zeros in the Active View instead of the actual numbers from QuickBooks.

Transforming a Classic report

The same four Applied Steps items I discuss in the "Connecting to an Enhanced report" section appear for this report as well. The issue is that the column headings for the body of the report appear in row 5 on Classic reports versus row 1 for Enhanced reports. This means you need to remove the third and fourth steps from the list and then promote the headers again once you've eliminated the extraneous rows at the top of the report. Here's how to get started:

1. **Right-click the third step in the Applied Steps pane on the right side of the screen and choose Delete Until End from the shortcut menu.**

   The Promoted Headers and Changed Type steps that Power Query tends to add automatically are helpful with Enhanced reports but can create problems with Classic reports.

2. **Click Delete when prompted.**

TIP

You can also hover your mouse over a step in the Applied Steps pane and then click the X to the left of its name to remove it from the list instead of performing Steps 1 and 2.

WARNING

Be careful not to delete the Navigation step because doing so means you can no longer see your data. If this happens, the path of least resistance to seeing your data again is to choose File ⇨ Discard and Close and then restart your import.

3. **Choose Home ⇨ Remove Rows ⇨ Remove Top Rows.**

The Remove Top Rows dialog box appears, as shown in Figure 21-9.

The Remove Rows command allows you to remove rows from the top or the bottom of a report. You can also remove duplicates, alternate rows, and rows that contain errors.

4. **Enter** 4 **in the Number of Rows field and then click OK.**

The goal is to move the headings in Row 5 up to the first row of the Current View grid.

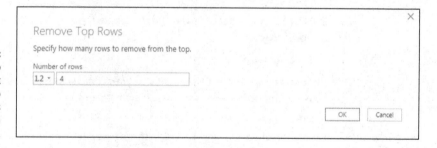

FIGURE 21-9:
The Remove Top Rows dialog box allows you to remove rows from the top of a report.

5. **Click Use First Row as Headers on the Home tab.**

This moves titles from the first row of the grid up into the column headings.

6. **Double-click the Column1 heading, type** Account, **and then press Enter.**

TIP

You can also rename columns by right-clicking the heading and choosing Rename or by pressing the F2 key.

7. **Click on the Account column heading to select the entire column.**

At this point your screen should look like Figure 21-10.

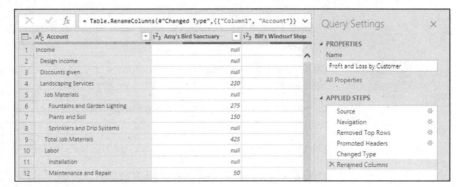

FIGURE 21-10:
The Profit and Loss by Customer report just before being unpivoted.

Unpivoting Power Query results

Horizontally oriented reports, such as the Profit and Loss by Customer report, can be difficult to work with in Excel because you can end up frittering away your day by scrolling from side to side. In this case, unpivoting the report collapses it from spanning 30 columns down to 3, so you can sift through the data by filtering or slicing, as well as summarizing the data with a PivotTable. Here's how to unpivot the report:

1. **Choose Transform ⇨ Unpivot Columns ⇨ Unpivot Other Columns.**

    The report should now look like Figure 21-11.

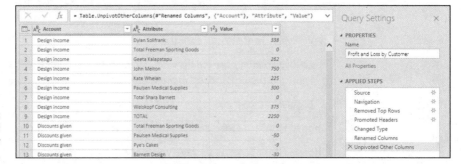

FIGURE 21-11:
The unpivoted Profit and Loss by Customer report.

2. **Click the Filter button in the Attribute heading and then choose Text Filters ⇨ Does Not Begin With.**

3. **Enter the word** Total **in the first Enter or Select a Value field.**

REMEMBER

    Unlike Excel, Power Query inputs are case sensitive, so typing **total** in the field means that any rows that begin with *Total* remain in place.

4. **Enter the word** TOTAL **in the second Enter or Select a Value field, and then click OK.**

TIP

Click Settings to the right of a Filtered Rows step in the Applied Steps list if you need to revise your filter criteria.

5. **Click the first column, which should be labeled Account, and then choose Transform ⇨ Format ⇨ Clean.**

    The Clean command removes nonprintable characters from within your data.

6. **With the first column still selected, choose Transform ⇨ Format ⇨ Trim.**

    The Trim command removes extraneous spaces from worksheet cells.

TECHNICAL STUFF

The Clean and Trim steps are required only when you're running into anomalies in your data. In my case, I couldn't perform the upcoming steps of filtering out the rows that begin with the word *Total* without applying the Clean and Trim steps. You must always use the steps in this order to achieve the expected outcome.

7. **Click the Filter button in the first column and then carry out these steps to remove the totals and subtotals from the data:**

    a. *Choose Advanced in the Filter Rows dialog box.*

    b. *Choose Account from the first Column field, set Operator to Does Not Begin With, and then enter* **Net** *in the Value field.*

    c. *Choose Account from the second Column field, set Operator to Does Not Begin With, and then enter* **Gross** *in the Value field.*

    d. *Click Add Clause to add a third row.*

    e. *Choose Account from the third Column field, set Operator to Does Not Begin With, and then enter* **Total** *in the Value field.*

    f. *Click OK.*

8. **Choose Home ⇨ Close and Load to return the data to Microsoft Excel.**

9. **Choose File ⇨ Save As to save your workbook if you want to convert newer versions of the report that you connected to, such as the Profit and Loss by Customer report.**

    In the next section, I show you how to add an automated total row to the report, filter with the Slicer feature, and bring a newer version of your QuickBooks report into your Excel workbook.

Analyzing and Adjusting Power Query Results

Most Excel worksheets comprise normal worksheet cells, or what Microsoft terms a "normal range of cells." Conversely, Power Query results are returned to cells formatted as tables, which enable some special characteristics. Tables can typically, but not always, be identified by alternating bands of color. A sure-fire way to identify whether a portion of a worksheet is formatted as a table is by way of the Table Design tab that appears in Excel's ribbon when you click on any cell within the table.

TIP

You can convert any list of data in an Excel worksheet into a table by clicking any cell within a list and then choosing Insert ⇨ Table ⇨ OK.

Analyzing Power Query results

Now that the data is in Excel, you can take your analysis further in a couple of ways:

>> **Total Row:** Choose Table Design ⇨ Total Row to add a total row to any existing table. The last column is automatically counted or summed, depending on the type of data in the column. Click any cell within the total row to display a drop-down menu from which you can choose a mathematical function, or None if you prefer to not have a calculation appear in the total row of a given column.

TIP

The Table Design tab appears in the Excel ribbon (menu) only when your cursor is within a table. If you click any cell outside of a table, the ribbon tab vanishes, but it reappears when you click within a table again.

>> **Slicer:** Choose Table Design ⇨ Insert Slicer, select one or more fields, and then click OK. You can now filter the list by choosing any item from the slicer. Hold down the Ctrl key (Cmd in macOS) to select multiple items from the slicer. Click the Clear Filter button at the top-right corner of the slicer to view all items again.

>> **PivotTable:** Choose Table Design ⇨ Summarize with Pivot Table and then click OK to create a blank PivotTable report. I discuss PivotTables in more detail in Chapter 20.

TIP

If you're not familiar with PivotTables, click any cell within the Power Query results and then choose Insert ⇨ Recommended PivotTables to display some suggested reports. If you're using Microsoft 365, choose Home ⇨ Analyze Data to generate reports and charts by using plain-English terms.

Editing Power Query results

You may invariably discover that you missed some details in transforming your report or that you filtered data or hid a column that you want to see. You can return to the Power Query Editor at any point by using any of these methods:

» Click any cell within a list generated by Power Query and then choose Query ⇨ Edit.

» Right-click any cell within a list generated by Power Query and then choose Table ⇨ Edit Query.

» Right-click any connection in the Queries & Connections task pane and choose Edit.

TIP

The Queries & Connections task pane appears automatically whenever you return results to Excel from Power Query. You can display the task pane at any time by choosing Data ⇨ Queries & Connections.

Click Close and Load within the Power Query Editor to save your changes and return to Microsoft Excel.

Keeping Power Query Results Current

Data that you return to Excel from Power Query is a snapshot in time rather than a real-time feed. A major benefit of Power Query is that you have to perform the transformation steps only once. Going forward, you can save new versions of your QuickBooks reports and other data sources over the original files that you connected to Power Query and then refresh the results manually. You can also instruct Excel to refresh results from Power Query automatically when you open the workbook that contains the Power Query results that you returned to Excel.

Updating Power Query results manually

When you want to transform a newer version of a report, such as the Transaction List by Date or Profit and Loss by Customer reports, use the following steps:

1. **Follow the usual steps in QuickBooks to export the report to Excel.**

2. **Open the report in Excel, and then choose File ⇨ Save As and save the report over the original file that you selected with Power Query.**

3. **Open the workbook where you created the Power Query transformation, and then choose Data ⇨ Refresh All.**

Although Power Query establishes a connection to data sources, such as reports that you export from QuickBooks, it doesn't create a live feed. The latest version of your data appears in your workbooks only after you refresh the data.

Refreshing Power Query results automatically

You can instruct Power Query to refresh automatically when you open a workbook that contains one or more queries:

1. **Click any cell within a list of data generated by Power Query.**

   The Query menu appears in the Excel ribbon only when you click a cell within data that has been brought into Excel from Power Query.

2. **Choose Query ⇨ Properties or choose Data ⇨ Properties to open the External Data Range Properties dialog box, and then click the Query Properties button to the right of the Name field.**

3. **Clear the Enable Background Refresh checkbox, select the Refresh Data When Opening the File checkbox, and (if available) select the Enable Fast Data Load checkbox, as shown in Figure 21-12.**

   Enable Background Refresh enables you to keep working in your spreadsheet while data from an external source is being refreshed. However, it tends to create confusion because the refresh happens more slowly — to the point that you may think nothing is happening.

   The Refresh Data When Opening the File option instructs Excel to reach out to the external workbook automatically and grab the latest version of the data, thereby creating a self-updating reporting tool.

   Fast Data Load speeds the refresh process by directing all of Excel's resources to the refresh process, which in turn means you can't carry out any work in Excel while the refresh occurs. However, the refreshing happens faster, so it's a minor trade-off.

   You can change these options at any time. For example, you might turn off Refresh Data When Opening the File if you want to archive a snapshot of a data set for a particular point in time.

4. **Click OK to close the Query Properties dialog box.**

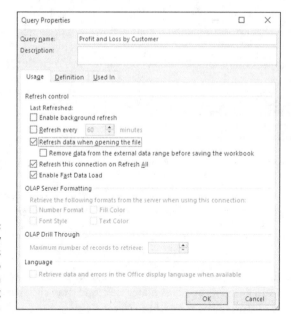

FIGURE 21-12:
Adjusting query
properties
enables you to
have a
self-updating
report.

REMEMBER

Query properties that you set are unique to each Power Query connection, so you must carry out the preceding steps every time you establish a new data connection via Power Query.

Now that you've set the query properties for your Power Query connection, you need to eliminate one other speed bump to streamline the update process. Follow these steps to disable the Enable Content security prompt that otherwise appears every time you open your workbook:

1. **Save and close your workbook that contains a Power Query connection.**

2. **Reopen your workbook.**

   Resist the urge to click the Enable Content prompt so that you can suppress it permanently for this workbook. If you did click Enable Content, close your workbook, reopen it, and proceed to Step 3.

3. **Choose File ⇨ Info ⇨ Enable Content ⇨ Enable Content to suppress the security prompt.**

   As shown in Figure 21-13, the Enable Content option makes the document a trusted document. When you mark a document as such, Excel no longer requires you to choose Enable Content before you refresh the workbook.

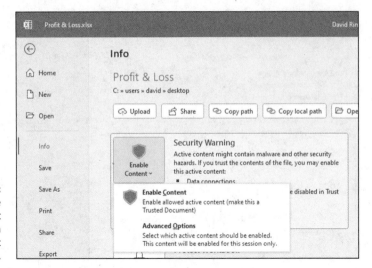

FIGURE 21-13:
Suppressing the
Enable Content
prompt for a
specific
workbook.

If you're presenting the data in the form of a Table, you're all set. But if you're using the PivotTable feature, which I discuss in Chapter 20, you need to change one more setting to ensure that your report is completely self-updating. Follow these steps:

1. **Select any cell within a PivotTable, and choose the PivotTable Analyze menu.**

   The PivotTable menus are context-sensitive, so the PivotTable Analyze and Design menus vanish when your cursor isn't within a PivotTable.

2. **Choose PivotTable Analyze ⇨ Options.**

   The PivotTable Options dialog box appears, as shown in Figure 21-14.

3. **Click the Data tab, select the Refresh Data When Opening the File checkbox, and then click OK.**

   This option instructs Excel to refresh your PivotTable when you open the workbook.

WARNING

Make sure that you set both your Power Query connection and any PivotTables based on Power Query data to refresh automatically when you open the file; otherwise, you might find yourself reviewing stale information. Choose Data ⇨ Refresh All in Excel to be certain that everything in your workbook is updated.

TIP

If you want to learn more about Power Query, please see *Excel Power Pivot & Power Query For Dummies* by Michael Alexander.

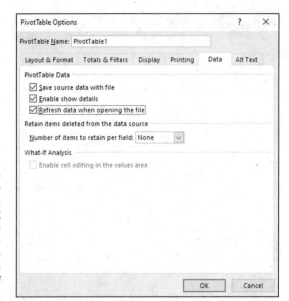

FIGURE 21-14:
You must also click Refresh Data When Opening the File to enable a PivotTable that's tied to Power Query to update itself automatically.

7

The Part of Tens

Understand ten common journal entries.

Practice using ten Chrome shortcuts.

Chapter **22**

Ten Common Journal Entries

QuickBooks goes to great lengths to shield users from as much accounting as possible, but in this chapter you roll up your sleeves and do some old-school accounting in the form of journal entries. The good news is that journal entries are typically a tiny percentage of the transactions you enter into QuickBooks — if you even have to do it at all. I start by showing you how to get to the journal entry screen and record a journal entry in general terms. Then you work through ten common journal entries.

TIP

You may be surprised to learn that behind the scenes *every* transaction you input into QuickBooks is transformed into a journal entry. Look for the More button at the bottom of most transaction pages and then choose Transaction Journal to view the underlying journal entry for any transaction you have entered. Remember, the More button doesn't appear until you have saved the transaction at least once.

Understanding Debits and Credits

Regardless of whether you see it, every accounting transaction is composed of debits and credits. The sum of the total debits must always match the sum of the total credits. A transaction can have any number of debits and credits as long as the sum of each matches. The Balance Sheet report in QuickBooks Online offers a great way to understand debits and credits because certain accounts have natural debit balances, whereas others have natural credit balances. At a high level, your balance sheet is broken down into three categories:

>> **Assets:** This section reflects what your business owns or is owed. Asset accounts typically have a debit balance but may sometimes have a credit balance, such as if you overdraw a bank account.

>> **Liabilities:** This section reflects records monies that your business owes to others and typically has a credit balance. You might encounter liability accounts that have a debit balance when you pay more payroll taxes than are due, for instance.

>> **Equity:** This section reflects the net worth of the business, meaning assets minus liabilities. Equity accounts typically have a credit balance, but they can have a debit balance. This might happen, for example, if an owner is taking more money out of the business than they should.

It's time to move the high-level discussion of debits and credits to the Profit and Loss statement. This statement can have several categories, but I collapse it down to two:

>> **Revenues:** This section reflects income that your business has earned. Behind-the-scenes revenue or income accounts typically have credit balances.

>> **Expenses:** This section reflects costs that your business has incurred, which means that expense accounts typically have debit balances.

With that explanation in hand, allow me to explain why your bank is making it difficult for you to comprehend the concept of journal entries. Perhaps you run a transaction journal for a $1,000 Sales Receipt transaction that looks something like this.

Account	Debits	Credits	Description
Cash	$1,000.00		Revenue from sales receipt
Revenue		$1,000.00	Revenue from sales receipt

In this scenario, you're increasing both cash and revenue, and the journal entry is in balance. Where things get confusing is when your bank reports activity on your account from *their* perspective. You see, they're holding onto your money for you and must return it to you upon demand. To *them*, your money is a *liability*, whereas to *you*, it's an *asset*. You just increased your asset by $1,000 with the previous journal entry. Here's what the bank's journal entry looks like.

Account	Debits	Credits	Description
Cash	$1,000.00		Record customer deposit
Liabilities		$1,000.00	Record customer deposit

Both of these are also increases. Their asset, cash, is increased by $1,000, but because they're just holding the money for you, their liabilities also increase. Conversely, you earned $1,000, so your asset, cash, is increased, and your revenue is increased. Maybe that amount makes up your only earnings for the year, and you had no expenses. At the end of the fiscal year, QuickBooks automatically records a journal entry that debits income by $1,000 and credits retained earnings by $1,000, like this.

Account	Debits	Credits	Description
Revenue	$1,000.00		Close fiscal year
Retained earnings		$1,000.00	Close fiscal year

In this case, revenue is decreased by $1,000, so your revenue starts over at zero for the new year. Retained earnings is increased by $1,000 and represents money that has been earned but has not yet distributed to the company's owners. This is a grossly oversimplified example because a normal closing entry zeroes out all income and expense accounts by debiting or crediting as needed to bring the account balances to zero, with the net remaining amount being offset to retained earnings.

Creating Journal Entries

Most transactions are easily entered through the corresponding transaction pages in QuickBooks, but certain adjustments can be made only by way of a journal entry or are most easily recorded in that fashion. Here's how to create a journal entry:

1. **Choose +New ⇨ Journal Entry.**

   The journal entry page appears, as shown in Figure 22-1.

FIGURE 22-1:
The Journal
Entry page.

2. Input a date into the Journal Date field.

Enter the date that you want the transaction to affect your books. Many journal entries are known as adjusting entries, such as those that record depreciation or recognize prepaid expense, and are typically recorded on the last day of a month. There's no hard and fast rule, though.

REMEMBER

Journal entries that affect a bank or credit card account should always reflect the actual transaction date so that the activity shows up properly when you go to reconcile your account.

3. Optional: Change the Journal Number.

QuickBooks increments this number automatically, but you can enter up to 21 characters in this field.

4. Choose an account from the first row of the journal entry in the Accounts column.

On most other transaction pages, QuickBooks refers to accounts as categories. In this case, you're choosing an account from your chart of accounts.

I discuss reviewing and customizing your chart of accounts in Chapter 1.

TIP

REMEMBER

You don't *have* to enter debits and credits in any particular order on a journal entry, so the first line of the entry can contain a debit or a credit. With that said, if your journal entry references *both* balance sheet and income statement accounts, try to reference a balance sheet account in the first line of the journal entry, no matter whether the amount you're entering is a debit or a credit. This isn't a hard-and-fast rule, but following it helps you avoid anomalies when viewing certain reports.

5. **Enter a debit or credit amount as a positive amount.**

   You can't enter a debit and a credit on the same line. If you enter a debit amount and a credit amount in the same row, the second amount you enter is kept, and the first amount is erased.

WARNING

   You can, but you shouldn't, enter negative amounts in the Debits and Credits fields. For one, it's difficult to ensure that your journal entry balances. For another, the minus sign instructs QuickBooks to record the negative credit that you entered as a debit and a negative debit as a credit, so your entry posts in the opposite fashion than you're expecting.

6. **Enter a description for the journal entry row.**

   I provide some descriptions in the journal entries that I discuss later in this chapter.

7. **Optional: Choose a name from the list, meaning a customer or vendor.**

   Be particularly careful about choosing names on journal entries because doing so can circumvent the checks and balances that the transaction pages in QuickBooks put in place for you. For instance, if you incorrectly tag a customer on a journal entry, you can end up in a situation where the ending balance on your aged accounts receivable report no longer matches the accounts receivable balance on your balance sheet.

8. **Repeat Steps 2 through 4 on the second row of the journal entry.**

   You can enter as many rows as you like and leave unneeded rows blank.

TIP

   It's always best to consult an accountant if you have uncertainties about recording a journal entry.

9. **Click Save to save your transaction.**

   A Make Recurring button appears once you save the transaction. I discuss recurring transactions in Chapter 7.

10. **Run a balance sheet or profit and loss report in QuickBooks to ensure that your journal entry had the desired effect.**

    It's easy to enter debits and credits in the wrong places, so check to see if the account balances changed as you expected. If you entered the amounts incorrectly, use the Search command at the top of the screen to access your journal entry, move the debit and credit amounts into the proper columns, and then save your journal entry again.

Correcting a Bank Balance

Maybe you're reconciling your bank account, which I discuss in Chapter 5, and find that your account balance is off by a minor amount, say 40 cents. You might choose to scour your books to find the transaction that was incorrectly entered, or you might decide to just adjust your bank balance.

If your bank balance is 40 cents higher than the bank thinks it should be, you can enter a journal entry along these lines.

Account	Debits	Credits	Description
Miscellaneous expense	$0.40		Adjust bank balance to actual
Cash		$0.40	Adjust bank balance to actual

Conversely, if the bank thinks you have more money than you believe you have and you want to go with their number, your journal entry might look something like this.

Account	Debits	Credits	Description
Cash	$0.40		Adjust bank balance to actual
Miscellaneous income		$0.40	Adjust bank balance to actual

Adjusting Asset or Liability Accounts

I cover one example of adjusting an asset account in the "Correcting a Bank Balance" section earlier in this chapter. The tricky part about adjusting asset and liability accounts is making sure you post the journal entries correctly because otherwise, you end up doubling the original difference. Here's a quick refresher:

>> You typically use a debit to increase an asset account and a credit to reduce it.

>> You typically use a credit to increase a liability account and a debit to reduce it.

The liability accounts that you'll likely end up adjusting most often are payroll liabilities, such as payroll taxes. Many payroll taxes are assessed on a percentage basis, which over time can result in some rounding differences accumulating in your accounts. Let's say that you know you need to remit $1,500 in payroll taxes for December. The sum of your payroll tax accounts should be $1,500, but it could be $1,500.10, with the extra 10 cents reflecting rounding. Here's how to enter a journal entry to correct the balance.

Account	Debits	Credits	Description
Payroll Taxes Payable	$0.10		Adjust balance to actual
Payroll Tax Expense		$0.10	Adjust balance to actual

Assuming that you haven't paid the payroll tax amount yet, your balance sheet should reflect a balance of $1,500.00. If it reflects $1,500.20, you recorded the entry backward. Use the Search button to retrieve your journal entry, flip the debits and credits between columns, and then save your journal entry again.

Recording a Recurring Fee

Let's say that your bank charges an ongoing fee of $15 per month. A journal entry to record such a fee looks like this.

Account	Debits	Credits	Description
Bank charges	$15.00		Record monthly bank charge
Cash		$15.00	Record monthly bank charge

Once you enter the journal entry, you can click Make Recurring and then carry out the following steps:

1. **Assign a template name, such as** Monthly bank fee.

2. **Leave the type set to Scheduled, which is the default.**

3. **Enter** 0 (zero) **in the Create Days in Advance field.**

4. **Leave the interval set to Monthly on Day. Choose the day of the month that the fee typically is assessed, such as the 15th, and leave Every Months set to 1 (one).**

5. **Choose a starting date for the journal entry from the Start Date field.**

6. **Leave the End Date field set to None if you expect the fee to continue in perpetuity, or set an end date for the transaction.**

   I cover more of the ins-and-outs of recurring transactions in Chapter 7.

Entering Petty Cash Expenditures

Petty cash is a small amount of physical currency that you might keep in a drawer to fund coffee runs, tips for the DoorDash driver, a quick run to the office supply store, and other sorts of small expenditures. To fund the petty cash drawer, you can write a check in QuickBooks to Cash that you take to the bank to convert to cash, or you can use an ATM card and enter the transaction as an expense, but rather than choosing an expense account, you choose Petty Cash as the category (account). The purpose of a journal entry is to record the expenditures from the petty cash fund so that your books reflect the amount of cash you physically have on hand.

Here's the behind-the-scenes journal entry to fund the petty cash account.

Account	Debits	Credits	Description
Petty Cash	$100.00		Fund petty cash
Checking		$100.00	Fund petty cash

This entry reduces your checking account by $100 and increases petty cash, another asset account, by $100. Here, then, is what an expenditure journal entry might look like.

Account	Debits	Credits	Description
Meals/Entertainment	$23.48		Starbucks run for Client Z
Office Supplies	$3.74		Emergency purchase of paper clips
Postage	$8.89		Certified mail postage
Petty Cash		$36.11	Record petty cash expenditures

At this point, you hopefully still have $63.89 in your drawer to put toward future petty cash expenditures. If there's a difference, you can adjust the petty cash account in the same fashion as you do a bank account.

Recording a Prepaid Expense

Prepaid expenses apply a similar matching principal to depreciation but typically over a shorter time span. For instance, let's say that you purchase a business owner's insurance policy on January 1, 2024. Your behind-the-scenes journal entry might look like this.

Account	Debits	Credits	Description
Insurance Expense	$1,200.00		Annual insurance premium
Cash		$1,200.00	Annual insurance premium

There's nothing particularly wrong with recognizing all the insurance expense in one month, but it can skew budgeting, and it doesn't match the expense with the associated income from the other 11 months of the year. You might record the entry like this instead.

Account	Debits	Credits	Description
Prepaid Expenses	$1,200.00		Annual insurance premium
Cash		$1,200.00	Annual insurance premium

This entry has no impact on your profit and loss statement, and although it reduces your cash account by $1,200, it also increases an asset account by $1,200. This doesn't mean you need to record such expenses with a journal entry. You can instead use a Check or Expense transaction and then choose Prepaid Expenses instead of Insurance Expense for the category or account. From there, you need to set up a recurring entry to amortize the prepaid expense.

Amortizing a Prepaid Expense

If you've been reading through the other journal entries in this chapter, you probably have a sense of what this entry looks like.

Account	Debits	Credits	Description
Insurance Expense	$100.00		Recognize prepaid insurance
Prepaid Expenses		$100.00	Recognize prepaid insurance

You can set this up as a recurring journal entry in the same way I described the recurring bank fee earlier in this chapter. You do, however, set an end date for such a journal entry so that you start recognizing an expense as an asset that has been fully amortized. Doing so results in a negative asset on your balance sheet and might overstate your monthly expenses.

Maintaining an Allowance for Doubtful Accounts

An allowance for doubtful accounts is an accounting construct by which a business recognizes that some percentage of customers will renege or refuse to pay their invoices due, also known as accounts receivable. Recording an allowance for doubtful accounts can reflect a business reality, but it can also have income tax benefits because the journal entry results in a Bad Debt expense that reduces taxable income. As with accumulated depreciation, the allowance isn't recorded directly against the asset account — in this case, accounts receivable — but rather against a contra account (an offset to another account), such as Allowance for Doubtful Accounts.

The business has $100,000 in accounts receivable, and based on past experience, 5% of these unpaid invoices are expected to be written off. A journal entry recognizing this eventual expense looks like this.

Account	Debits	Credits	Description
Bad Debt Expense	$5,000.00		Bad debt allowance
Allowance for Doubtful Accounts		$5,000.00	Bad debt allowance

Just as Accumulated Depreciation is a contra account to any fixed asset accounts you may have, Allowance for Doubtful Accounts is a contra account to Accounts Receivable. If later in the year you decide that conditions have improved and that a 3 percent allowance is sufficient, you can reflect that change with the following journal entry.

Account	Debits	Credits	Description
Allowance for Doubtful Accounts	$2,000.00		Adjust bad debt allowance
Bad Debt Expense		$2,000.00	Adjust bad debt allowance

In this case, the journal entry reduces Allowance for Doubtful Accounts by $2,000, to a new balance of $3,000. Bad Debt Expense is reduced in the same fashion.

Writing Off Bad Debt

Maybe you have a customer who goes out of business before paying your $500 invoice. You can record the following journal entry.

Account	Debits	Credits	Description	Name
Bad Debt Expense	$500.00		Write off invoice	
Accounts Receivable		$500.00	Write off invoice	Defunct Co.

The end result of this entry is that a $500 credit is applied to the customer's account because you can't associate a journal entry with a specific invoice. Thus, this journal entry falls into the arena of "not that you would, but you could." See Chapter 2 for a forms-based approach to writing off bad debt that applies the credit against the invoice that will never be collected.

Posting Depreciation

Depreciation is an accounting concept designed to spread the cost of an asset (such as the cost of a warehouse) over its usual life rather than recognizing it all in one period. Maybe the asset costs $480,000 and has a 40-year useful life. A number of different generally accepted accounting principles (often referred to as GAAP) are available for computing depreciation, but in this case, I'm keeping it simple with straight-line depreciation, with which you divide the cost of the asset by its useful life, less any salvage value, which for this example is assumed to be zero. $480,000 divided by 40 years is $12,000 of depreciation per year, or $1,000 of depreciation per month.

The behind-the-scenes journal entry to purchase the building might look like this.

Account	Debits	Credits	Description
Buildings	$480,000.00		Warehouse purchase
Cash		$480,000.00	Warehouse purchase

If you purchased the building on January 1, 2024, you need to record $12,000 of depreciation in calendar 2024. A typical monthly depreciation entry might look something like this.

Account	Debits	Credits	Description
Depreciation Expense	$1,000.00		Record monthly depreciation
Accumulated Depreciation		$1,000.00	Record monthly depreciation

Notice that the offset to the depreciation is an account called Accumulated Depreciation. Because Accumulated Depreciation has a credit balance, on the balance sheet it offsets the Building account. The net difference is known as the book value of the asset.

REMEMBER

Book value is an accounting construct that reflects the unamortized value of the asset. Conversely, market value is what you can get if you sell the warehouse to someone else. Your books don't typically reflect the market value of assets you hold. This is a great conversation to have with your accountant if you have questions because numerous theories and strategies can be applied to valuing assets.

TIP

In Chapter 15, I describe how to automate depreciation journal entries in Advanced companies by way of the Fixed Assets feature.

Chapter **23**

Ten Cool Chrome Shortcuts

Keyboard shortcuts can help you fight back against the repetitive and transactional nature of accounting work. In this chapter, I get you started with ten Google Chrome keyboard shortcuts. Chances are pretty good that these shortcuts work in other browsers as well.

If you're looking for QuickBooks Online keyboard shortcuts, I have you covered at www.dummies.com. Search for *QuickBooks Online For Dummies* to find this book's Cheat Sheet.

Throughout this chapter, I mention supplemental shortcuts that complement the ten primary shortcuts I've chosen. You can access a complete list of keyboard shortcuts for Chrome at https://support.google.com/chrome/answer/157179

Speeding Up Surfing

Working on the Internet, and QuickBooks Online specifically, can result in a number of repetitive tasks. Even small tweaks in your browsing habits can have a cumulative effect that results in reclaiming some of your day and minimizing wear and tear on your wrists. In this section, I show you how to save a few key-strokes when typing in web page addresses, and how to see more of your screen when you get to your destination.

Navigating to websites faster

Type a site name, such as **intuit**, in the address bar and then press Ctrl+Enter to automatically add www. and .com to the beginning and end, respectively, and navigate to that site.

REMEMBER

This technique works only for primary domains, like www.intuit.com. You can't navigate to https://qbo.intuit.com in this manner because the site's address is qbo.intuit.com versus www.qbo.intuit.com.

Toggling full-screen mode

Chrome's full-screen mode means two different things depending on which operating system you're using:

>> **Windows:** Press F11 to toggle the tabs, address bar, and bookmarks bar on or off.

>> **Mac:** Press Ctrl+Cmd+F to expand or contract the size of a Chrome window. This action does not affect tabs, the address bar, or bookmarks bar.

Accessing Downloads and History

Historically, Chrome had a Downloads bar at the bottom of the screen to provide easy access to downloads. That feature has been retired in favor of a Recent Downloads button at the top of the screen that displays your downloads in a card that stays on screen for a brief period. In this section, you find out how to easily access your downloads and your history as well.

Displaying the Downloads page

Press Ctrl+J (or Cmd+Shift+J in macOS) to display the Downloads page in a new tab. This provides easy access to reports that you've recently exported to Micro-soft Excel from QuickBooks Online.

TIP

Press the Tab key twice to navigate to the first download. You can then use the Down Arrow key to navigate through the Downloads list. Press Enter in Windows to open a download or use your mouse to click Show in Folder. On a Mac, press Enter to download the file again, or else click Show in Finder with your mouse to open the corresponding folder.

Displaying the History page

Press Ctrl+H (or Cmd+Y in macOS) to display the History page. Press the Tab key four times to navigate to the first link in the list. You can use the Down Arrow key to move through the list. When you get to the page you want to open, press Enter to open the link in the current tab, which replaces the History page.

Working with Tabs

Every bit of information you consume on the Internet appears in tabs within your browser. In this section, I show you several ways to maximize your use of tabs.

Opening and activating a new tab

Press Ctrl+T (or Cmd+T in macOS) Mac to create and activate a new browser tab. Your cursor is placed in the address bar, ready for you to type a web address, often referred to as a URL (uniform resource locator).

REMEMBER

Press Ctrl+N (or Cmd+N in macOS) to create a new tab in a separate window. You can press Ctrl+Shift+Tab (or Cmd+Option+Left Arrow in macOS) to activate another tab in the current window, but you need to press Ctrl+Tab (or Cmd+` in macOS) to switch between windows. That backward apostrophe is known as the grave symbol and shares space with the ~ key just below the Esc key on your keyboard.

Closing the current tab

Press Ctrl+W (or Cmd+W in macOS) to close the current tab. If you have only a single tab open, your Chrome window closes as well. When you have multiple tabs open in the window, only the active tab closes. Use Ctrl+Shift+W (or Cmd+Shift+W in macOS) to close the current window.

TIP

Press Alt+F4 (or Cmd+O in macOS) to close a Chrome window, which includes all open tabs.

Saving open tabs as a bookmark group

Press Ctrl+Shift+D (or Cmd+Shift+D in macOS) to create a new folder with bookmarks to your current set of open tabs. This is a great way to remember your place when carrying out a research project that involves multiple web pages. You can also press Ctrl+D (or Cmd+D in macOS) to create a bookmark for the currently open tab.

Opening your home page in the current tab

Press Alt+Home (or Cmd+Shift+H in macOS) to open your home page in the current tab. If this doesn't work when you first try it, you may need to enable the Home Page feature by using these steps:

1. Click the three-dot button in the upper-right corner of Google Chrome and then choose Settings.

2. Type the word Home in the Search Settings field.

3. Toggle the Show Home Button on and then specify a home page, such as `https://qbo.intuit.com`, to display the login page for QuickBooks Online.

Activating a specific tab

Press Ctrl+1 (or Cmd+1 in macOS) to activate the first tab in your Chrome window. You can use 1 through 8 to access the first eight tabs. Ctrl+9 (or Cmd+9 in macOS) activates the last open tab, so if you have ten open tabs, you can't jump directly to the ninth tab.

REMEMBER

You can press Alt+Left Arrow (or Cmd+Option+Left Arrow in macOS) to navigate one tab to the left or use Alt+Right Arrow (or Cmd+Option+Right Arrow in macOS) to move one tab to the right.

Creating a tab in a new profile

Press Ctrl+Shift+M (or Cmd+Shift+M in macOS) to choose a different profile and create a new Chrome window, which in turn enables you to log into an additional QuickBooks Online company at the same time.

Press Alt+Tab (or Ctrl+Left Arrow/Ctrl+Right Arrow in macOS) to switch between windows. Speaking of Windows, Ctrl+Tab allows you to switch between open windows within applications like Microsoft Excel. On a Mac Ctrl+Tab switches you between open applications.

QuickBooks Online Advanced and Accountant users can download and install the QuickBooks Online desktop app, which also enables you to log into multiple companies at once if all are associated with the same Intuit account. See Chapter 13 for more details.

If you bump yourself out of QuickBooks by closing the wrong browser tab, simply display the History page and then choose the first QuickBooks page on the list to pick up immediately where you left off rather than logging in again.

Index

About the Author

David Ringstrom, CPA, is the president of Accounting Advisors, Inc., an Atlanta-based spreadsheet consulting and training firm he started in 1991. David helps his clients streamline repetitive business processes with more effective use of software such as QuickBooks and automated tools that he creates in Microsoft Excel.

David spends much of his time teaching webinars on Microsoft Excel and occasionally QuickBooks. He also owns StudentsExcel, an online service that helps accounting professors teach Excel more effectively. Since 1995, David has written freelance articles about spreadsheets and accounting software, some of which have been published internationally. He has served as the technical editor for more than three dozen books, including *QuickBooks Desktop For Dummies*, *Quicken For Dummies*, and *Peachtree For Dummies*, and he's the author or coauthor of six books, including *Idiot's Guide to Introductory Accounting* and *Exploring Microsoft Excel's Hidden Treasures*.

He resides in a historic neighborhood in Atlanta, Georgia, with his children, Rachel and Lucas, and his dogs, Ginger and Eddie.

Author's Acknowledgments

Actions we take today can and sometimes do shape our lives many years down the road. The time I spent in the 1990s answering questions that other spreadsheet users had in the Lotus 1-2-3 forum on CompuServe, back before the internet became public, helped me connect the dots and set my eventual speaking and writing career in motion. Therefore, I want to acknowledge you, dear reader, and the goals you're pursuing. Keep your eyes on the prize. As the text on your car's side mirror says, "Objects may be closer than they appear."

Thank you to Gail Perry and Lisa Bucki for their support as my coauthors on my first book opportunity, *Idiot's Guide to Introductory Accounting*. That experience was enjoyable and opened many doors for me. Nancy Garfield and Cora Andrews provided feedback that helped improve this version of the book.

As always, I want to give a shout-out to everyone on the Wiley team who helped bring this book to life. Special thanks to Dan DeLong, technical editor extraordinaire, whose suggestions have made all four editions of *QuickBooks Online For Dummies* better. Thanks also to Charlotte Kughen, who returned as my project editor for this edition, and to Karen Davis for copy editing.

Publisher's Acknowledgments

Executive Editor: Lindsay Berg

Project Editor: Charlotte Kughen

Copy Editor: Karen Davis

Technical Editor: Dan DeLong

Production Editor: Tamilmani Varadharaj

Cover Image: © AsiaVision/Getty Images

Leverage the power

Dummies is the global leader in the reference category and one of the most trusted and highly regarded brands in the world. No longer just focused on books, customers now have access to the dummies content they need in the format they want. Together we'll craft a solution that engages your customers, stands out from the competition, and helps you meet your goals.

Advertising & Sponsorships

Connect with an engaged audience on a powerful multimedia site, and position your message alongside expert how-to content. Dummies.com is a one-stop shop for free, online information and know-how curated by a team of experts.

- Targeted ads
- Video
- Email Marketing
- Microsites
- Sweepstakes sponsorship

20 MILLION PAGE VIEWS EVERY SINGLE MONTH

15 MILLION UNIQUE VISITORS PER MONTH

43% OF ALL VISITORS ACCESS THE SITE VIA THEIR MOBILE DEVICES

700,000 NEWSLETTER SUBSCRIPTIONS TO THE INBOXES OF *300,000* UNIQUE INDIVIDUALS EVERY WEEK

# of dummies

Custom Publishing

Reach a global audience in any language by creating a solution that will differentiate you from competitors, amplify your message, and encourage customers to make a buying decision.

- Apps
- Books
- eBooks
- Video
- Audio
- Webinars

Brand Licensing & Content

Leverage the strength of the world's most popular reference brand to reach new audiences and channels of distribution.

For more information, visit **dummies.com/biz**

PERSONAL ENRICHMENT

9781119187790	9781119179030	9781119293354	9781119293347	9781119310068	9781119235606
USA $26.00	USA $21.99	USA $24.99	USA $22.99	USA $22.99	USA $24.99
CAN $31.99	CAN $25.99	CAN $29.99	CAN $27.99	CAN $27.99	CAN $29.99
UK £19.99	UK £16.99	UK £17.99	UK £16.99	UK £16.99	UK £17.99

9781119251163	9781119235491	9781119279952	9781119283133	9781119287117	9781119130246
USA $24.99	USA $26.99	USA $24.99	USA $24.99	USA $24.99	USA $22.99
CAN $29.99	CAN $31.99	CAN $29.99	CAN $29.99	CAN $29.99	CAN $27.99
UK £17.99	UK £19.99	UK £17.99	UK £17.99	UK £16.99	UK £16.99

PROFESSIONAL DEVELOPMENT

9781119311041	9781119255796	9781119293439	9781119281467	9781119280651	9781119251132	9781119310563
USA $24.99	USA $39.99	USA $26.99	USA $26.99	USA $29.99	USA $24.99	USA $34.00
CAN $29.99	CAN $47.99	CAN $31.99	CAN $31.99	CAN $35.99	CAN $29.99	CAN $41.99
UK £17.99	UK £27.99	UK £19.99	UK £19.99	UK £21.99	UK £17.99	UK £24.99

9781119181705	9781119263593	9781119257769	9781119293477	9781119265313	9781119239314	9781119293323
USA $29.99	USA $26.99	USA $29.99	USA $26.99	USA $24.99	USA $29.99	USA $29.99
CAN $35.99	CAN $31.99	CAN $35.99	CAN $31.99	CAN $29.99	CAN $35.99	CAN $35.99
UK £21.99	UK £19.99	UK £21.99	UK £19.99	UK £17.99	UK £21.99	UK £21.99